THEORY AND INTERPRETATION OF NARRATIVE

James Phelan, Peter J. Rabinowitz, and Robyn Warhol, Series Editors

Literary Identification

from Charlotte Brontë to Tsitsi Dangarembga

Laura Green

The Ohio State University Press

Columbus

Library of Congress Cataloging-in-Publication Data
Green, Laura Morgan.
Literary identification from Charlotte Brontë to Tsitsi Dangarembga / Laura Green.
p. cm. — (Theory and interpretation of narrative)
Includes bibliographical references and index.
ISBN 978-0-8142-1199-1 (cloth : alk. paper) — ISBN 0-8142-1199-2 (cloth : alk. paper) — ISBN 978-0-8142-9300-3 (cd)
1. Fiction—Women authors—History and criticism. 2. Bildungsromans—History and criticism. 3. Identification (Psychology) in literature. 4. Brontë, Charlotte, 1816–1855—Criticism and interpretation. 5. Eliot, George, 1819–1880—Criticism and interpretation. 6. Beauvoir, Simone de, 1908–1986—Criticism and interpretation. 7. Dangarembga, Tsitsi—Criticism and interpretation. 8. Kincaid, Jamaica—Criticism and interpretation. 9. Woolf, Virginia, 1882–1941—Criticism and interpretation. 10. Hall, Radclyffe—Criticism and interpretation. 11. Winterson, Jeanette, 1959–Criticism and interpretation. I. Title. II. Series: Theory and interpretation of narrative series.
PN3401.G74 2012
809.3'93522—dc23

2012008364

Paper (ISBN: 978-0-8142-5639-8)
Cover design by Melissa Ryan
Type set in Adobe Sabon and Nueva Std
Text design by Juliet Williams

CONTENTS

ACKNOWLEDGMENTS

The path from a readerly question—What do we mean when we talk about identifying with literary characters?—to critical conclusions has been a winding one, and I'm grateful for the help I've received along the way: to Catherine Gallagher for early comments and to Margaret Homans for encouragement throughout; to Dr. Nancy Olson and Dr. Victoria Morrow for their thought-provoking seminar, "Non Lacan! Psychoanalysis for Scholars," at the Western New England Psychoanalytic Society; to the entire Northeastern University English department, so many of whose members have offered support and camaraderie—Elizabeth Britt, Elizabeth Dillon, Chris Gallagher, Carla Kaplan, Kathleen Kelly, Patrick Mullen, Stuart Peterfreund, and particularly Marina Leslie and Guy Rotella. Completing the book while serving as department chair would have been much more daunting without the administrative support of Linda Collins, Melissa Daigle, Cheryl Delaney, and Jean Duddy. I received institutional support from the Provost's Office in the forms of a Research and Scholarship Development Fund grant in 2003–2004 and sabbatical leave in 2008.

Beyond Northeastern, the Boston area is a pleasurable place to be a Victorianist. The members of the works-in-progress group Boston Reading are inspiring interlocutors; I thank particularly, for their comments on the Introduction and Chapter One, Mary Wilson Carpenter, Debra Gettelman, Anna Henchman, Maia McAleavy, John Plotz, and Martha Vicinus. I am triply grateful to Martha for extending her friendship, for convening Boston Reading, and, with Nancy Simonds, for livening up the neighborhood. I thank Elaine Lang for her insight and for recommending the work of Lynne Layton. My personal "Best of Boston" is the companionship, of mind and heart, of Mary Loeffelholz. I am also indebted to the other member of our household, Sasha, for her companionable purring.

I have been writing for and with Elizabeth Young and William Cohen for almost twenty-five years; I cannot imagine completing this or any book without them. I am lucky, too, in the friendship of Julie Croston, Jane Garrity, Karen Jacobs, Kelly Hager, Caroline Mailhot, Debra Minkoff, Silke Aisenbrey, Grace Moreno, Steven Shareshian, Jacqueline Stevens, and Kerry Walk. I have had welcome occasions during the writing of this book to leave my desk and celebrate milestones with my parents, Philip and Dorothy Green; my brother, Robert, and Jill, Violet and Zed; and the Loeffelholz family.

At The Ohio State University Press, I am grateful to Sandy Crooms, to two anonymous readers, and to the editors of the Theory and Interpretation of Narrative series: James Phelan, Peter Rabinowitz, and Robyn Warhol.

For opportunities to present parts of this work in talk form, I thank the Northeastern English Department's Barrs Lecture Series; Heather Love, former co-chair of the Gender and Sexuality Studies seminar at the Mahindra Humanities Center at Harvard, and James Buzard, John Picker, and John Plotz of the Victorian Literature and Culture Seminar there; panel organizers at meetings of the International Society for the Study of Narrative, particularly Rachel Ablow and Ellen McCallum; and the Simone de Beauvoir and Virginia Woolf Societies. A version of part of Chapter Two appeared in *Tulsa Studies in Women's Literature;* a version of part of Chapter Three appeared in *Victorians' Institute Journal;* and a version of part of Chapter Four appeared in *Twentieth-Century Literature;* I thank the journals for permission to reproduce these materials.

INTRODUCTION

THIS BOOK seeks to account for the persistence of a particular genre of realist fiction, the novel of formation, from nineteenth-century English through contemporary Anglophone literature. Through readings of novels by nineteenth-, twentieth-, and twenty-first-century women writers, as well as of memoirs, essays, and interviews that record reading experiences, I argue that this genre reproduces itself through the elaboration of bonds between and among readers, characters, and authors that I call, collectively, "literary identification." These connections begin but do not end with a reader's recognition of aspects of her- or himself in a fictional character. Forms of literary identification may also extend beyond the boundaries of the text to create relationships between readers and authors. Particular literary identifications may be limited by historical and cultural change or difference, but themes and rhetorical structures that foster literary identification continue to undergird the novel of formation in new and evolving contexts.

I have preferred "novel of formation" to the still common though contested term "Bildungsroman." With its origin in late-eighteenth-century German literary culture and Romantic criticism, the term Bildungsroman trails a history of debates, distinctions, and categories, many of which never applied comfortably to nineteenth-century English fiction and which are even less appropriate to Anglophone fiction of the twentieth and twenty-first centuries.[1] The nineteenth-century English authors I discuss, Charlotte Brontë and George Eliot, may have been influenced by the

Enlightenment and Romantic German models to which the term initially refers, but the twentieth- and twenty-first-century authors draw on other literary influences (including, but not limited to, those English forebears) in extending the tradition in different social and national contexts. "Novel of formation" is the alternative phrase used by, among others, Marianne Hirsch, who proposed it some years ago as "a neutral term, free of prior critical associations" (295). I have also preferred it to the phrase "novel of development" because, as the readings below will show, while the protagonists of these novels are always depicted at *formative*—self-constructing or self-defining—moments, their continued psychological *development* is sometimes withheld, incomplete, or cast into question.

To the extent that the term Bildungsroman, even when used outside its original Romantic context, associates the genre with Enlightenment culture, with European literary traditions, and with a normatively male authorship (beginning with Goethe), it also fails to reflect the prevalence, in the English and Anglophone literary tradition, of female-authored and female-centered fictions of individual formation whose trajectories differ from the masculine model of *Bildung* or apprenticeship while nevertheless continuing a recognizably related project of narrating the formation of a self in relation to a world of others. The past several decades have seen the consolidation of a critical and pedagogical canon of novels of female formation. More recently, queer and postcolonial novels of formation have begun to recast the conventions and concerns of both the initial European tradition and the revisionary female canon.[2] While critics often signal these developments by the addition of modifiers such as "female," "postcolonial," or "counter" to the term Bildungsroman, at this point, even such compound phrases seem to concede unnecessary defining authority to superseded historical conditions and literary conventions. As the European history of the form has not been discarded but rather sublated and transformed in contemporary iterations, so the "novel of formation" includes and expands beyond the genre of the Bildungsroman and its critical history.

I conceive of the novel of formation, in other words, as a capacious genre, potentially including any novel whose focus is the mental and moral growth of a character, within a specific social situation, who is positioned as the novel's central consciousness. Novels of formation, as my examples illustrate, have since the early nineteenth century been a dominant English, and later Anglophone, genre, which has continued to adapt and transform itself in postmodern and postcolonial contexts. The narrative's larger arc may move from early childhood to the brink of maturity (as in George

Eliot's *The Mill on the Floss* and Jeanette Winterson's *Oranges Are Not the Only Fruit*), or it may be restricted to the events of a year or two in adolescence (as in Tsitsi Dangarembga's *Nervous Conditions*). The protagonist may dominate both plot and point of view (as in Charlotte Brontë's *Villette*) or share the stage with characters who approach her in importance (as in *Nervous Conditions*). Novels of formation may be narrated in the first or the third person, ignore or incorporate events in the public sphere, and end in marriage, death, the discovery of vocation, or inconclusion. The mood of a novel of formation may be one of rebellion (as in Radclyffe Hall's *The Well of Loneliness*), confusion (as in Virginia Woolf's *The Voyage Out*), disaffection (as in Jamaica Kincaid's *Lucy*) or despair (as in Dangarembga's *The Book of Not*). Often implicitly or explicitly building on authorial experience (as do all of these examples), the novel of formation shares many narrative characteristics with more directly autobiographical genres.

Within these broad boundaries, novels of formation share some defining characteristics. A genre emerging within nineteenth-century fictional realism, the novel of formation assumes both the singularity and coherence of the self and the facticity and totality of the social world. The social world, in turn, includes other singular and coherent selves as well as events that are causally and consequentially related in space and time. The selfhood of a protagonist may, in the course of a narrative, be assailed and fractured (mental breakdown and illness are frequent hazards), and the significance of other people or events may appear chaotic or obscure. But the aimed-at, even if not fully achieved, coherence of the subject and the essentially causal relations between people and events give the novel of formation its characteristic structure. Because these relations are most visible retrospectively, the novel of formation is not only a representation but perhaps more important a history of the effects of persons and events, private and public, on the subject whose formation it narrates.

The broad generic range that I ascribe to the novel of formation is narrowed in this study by a focus on novels of formation written by and about women. Novels of formation are and have been written and read by men and women, and the gender of readers and the trajectory of their identifications are not predicted or exhausted by the gender of a novel's author or protagonists. Men may identify with female protagonists in novels written by men or women, and vice versa. Nevertheless, to point to identification and the formation of the self in the context of both literature and psychoanalytic theory—the discipline on which I draw in using the term "identification"—is to invoke processes to which gender identity has been and remains central. In the novel of formation, as in the classic psychoanalytic narrative, the self always forms as a *gendered* self, although the protagonist's experience of gender may be neither simple nor satisfactory.

To a significant though not exclusive degree, the exemplary self of the novel of formation is gendered female. As Nancy Armstrong has influentially argued, the rise of English domestic fiction not only disseminated the gender ideology that emphasized separate spheres for women's experience (subjective, private, organized around sexual and social reproduction) and men's (active, public, organized around the accumulation of financial or political power) but also established the psychology of the female subject as the bourgeois norm: "The modern individual was first and foremost a woman" (8), particularly, perhaps, as a subject of discursive representation. As the Germanic Bildungsroman tradition, initially indicatively male, encountered and was partly incorporated by nineteenth-century English domestic fiction, a genre developed whose exemplary protagonists, along with its readers and its writers, increasingly were women.[3]

Since the normative cultural narrative of female formation, throughout the eighteenth and most of the nineteenth century, culminated in marriage, plots of courtship and marriage dominated novelistic representations of women's experience from the eighteenth century (e.g., Richardson, Burney, and Austen) onward. Novels of courtship center on a moment at which the protagonist's romantic career commences, generally cover at most a year or two of her life, and minimize the importance of childhood experience or formation. While they may represent their period of focus as one of transformation for the protagonist, courtship novels ultimately emphasize a change in her circumstances rather than in her mental or moral interior. In Samuel Richardson's novel *Pamela,* for example, the heroine's virtue, never in question, finally triumphs over Mr. B's assumption of *droit de seigneur;* in Jane Austen's *Pride and Prejudice,* Elizabeth Bennett's superior merits similarly enable her triumph over the vulgarity of both her mother's low relations and her husband's lofty ones. Although Elizabeth renounces a mistaken attitude—"Vanity, not love, has been my folly. . . . Till this moment, I never knew myself" (137)—this self-recognition takes the form of a single, plot-driven *éclaircissement* (the letter from Darcy revealing her misunderstanding of his and Wickham's relationship) rather than of a prolonged internal evolution. By the time Darcy proposes, Elizabeth has retreated from this initial vehemence of self-blame, insisting only that "the conduct of neither, if strictly examined, will be irreproachable; but since then, we have both, I hope, improved in civility" (240). By what will come to be the conventions of the novel of formation, such an "improve[ment]," at the level of "civility" rather than morals, hardly registers as change or growth.[4] Courtship plots in novels of courtship are less about the formation of selves than about, to borrow the final words of *Pride and Prejudice,* "uniting them" (298)—the heroine and her appropriate mate—in ways that largely reinforce other unities, such as those of class, and that produce a sense of resolution.

Over the course of the nineteenth century, however, plots of formation begin to reshape, though not to eliminate, the courtship plot. The novel of formation absorbs the courtship-and-marriage plot as just one, often contested, element of its protagonist's ethical and intersubjective challenges. In a novel of formation, events emphasize change over time, rather than sudden revelation, and the working-out of the courtship plot exceeds or even opposes a social "truth, universally acknowledged" about the necessity of marriage as its end. Novels of formation expand the narrative lens so that the concentrated moment of romantic or marital choice is not the sole crisis for the female protagonist; while that crisis may remain important to the resolution of her narrative, it occurs in the context of a larger web of self/other relations and other conflicts. As Susan Fraiman observes, novels of female formation "insist that personal destiny evolves in dialectical relation to historical events, social structures, and other people" (10).

Jane Eyre, appearing at the beginning of the Victorian period, is a generic as well as a chronological boundary case: Like predecessor narratives by Richardson or by Austen, it features a prominent and triumphantly resolved plot of courtship and marriage, and a heroine whose virtue is rewarded. The courtship plot, however, is interwoven with extensive, independent attention to the protagonist's childhood and to adult relationships other than those with Rochester; and Jane's retention of her chastity is represented not as a sign of her impregnable virtue but rather as the outcome of an emotionally costly psychological struggle.

More radically, courtship plots in novels of formation may fail to resolve themselves in marriage or any other form of unity. Writing about the Victorian "failed-marriage plot," Kelly Hager makes this point about courtship plots more generally: "All English novels of the eighteenth and nineteenth century do not, in fact, end with the marriage of hero and heroine, and the domestic novel does not always establish closure and ask its readers to believe that society has thus been stabilized" (12). In nineteenth-century and early twentieth-century novels, such a failure often comes about as the result of a natural tragedy (the flood of *The Mill on the Floss,* the shipwreck in *Villette,* the fever of *The Voyage Out*) that gives symbolic form to the protagonist's irresolvable conflict with social norms (particularly gender norms) or her ambivalence about marriage itself. In narratives of female formation from the twentieth century and after, it is possible to imagine alternatives to marriage other than death: the narrative may suspend questions of courtship by attenuating its temporal moment, focusing, as in *Nervous Conditions,* on a preadolescent moment; deemphasize courtship in relation to other aspects of self-formation (intellectual in Simone de Beauvoir's *Memoirs of a Dutiful Daughter;* political in *The Book of Not;* vocational in *Lucy*); or focus on non-normative (e.g., queer) forms of courtship not resolvable in marriage (as in *The Well of Loneliness* and *Oranges Are Not the Only Fruit*).

This is not to deny, however, that nineteenth-century (and many Modernist) novels of formation are shaped by a powerful and widely disseminated ideology of sexual difference and complementarity. As Armstrong has claimed, "the gendering of human identity provided the metaphysical girders of modern culture—its reigning mythology" (14). One of the most profound results of this "mythology" for women and the novel of formation is that, as Fraiman points out, "The female protagonist's progress, at least until the twentieth century, is generally contingent on avoiding the abyss of extramarital sexuality, on successfully preventing 'things' from happening to her. Her paradoxical task is to see the world while avoiding violation by the world's gaze" (7). This is the "abyss" that Jane Eyre so dramatically avoids. But, as that novel suggests, the taboos on direct representation of women's sexuality or desire, as well as the ideological confinement of women within domestic space, could produce as well as circumscribe narrative. Jane's efforts to repress and avoid her desire for Rochester, for example, lead her to elaborate moments of self-assertion and provide an opportunity for the elaboration of other kinds of intimacies, such as her various relationships to the Riverses.

Nineteenth-century novelists themselves frequently reflected on the aptness of such psychologized female protagonists as subjects for modern narratives of formation. In *The Mill on the Floss,* Eliot's narrator invokes such a distinction between female interiority and male activity:

> While Maggie's life-struggles had lain almost entirely within her own soul, one shadowy army fighting another, and the slain shadows forever rising again, Tom was engaged in a dustier, noisier warfare, grappling with more substantial obstacles, and gaining more definite conquests. So it has been since the days of Hecuba, and of Hector, Tamer of horses; inside the gates, the women with streaming hair and uplifted hands offering prayers, watching the world's combat from afar, filling their

> long, empty days with memories and fears; outside, the men, in fierce struggle with things divine and human, quenching memory in the stronger light of purpose, losing the sense of dread and even of wounds in the hurrying ardor of action. (308–9)

The feminine action "inside the gates" moves inside the soul in Eliot's novel, which can evoke the "shadowy army" of Maggie's psychomachia with more detail than it musters for Tom's "substantial obstacles." By the time Henry James explicates his similar choice to center *The Portrait of a Lady* (1881) on something so apparently insubstantial as "a young woman affronting her destiny," in order to "show what an 'exciting' inward life may do for the person leading it even while it remains perfectly normal" (10, 17), his labored defense is already belated. Not only Eliot, but also before her Richardson, Austen, Brontë, and Gaskell, and after her Hardy—to round up only some obvious suspects—had by the 1880s demonstrated thoroughly "how absolutely, how inordinately, the Isabel Archers, and even much smaller female fry, insist on mattering." They not only embody an affective world of struggle and choice but also adumbrate its further evolution. In Hardy's *Tess of the D'Urbervilles* (1887), it is Tess, the female protagonist, who experiences "feelings which might almost have been called those of the age—the ache of modernism" (124).[5]

While gender norms may be more varied, less explicitly invoked, or more explicitly resisted in twentieth- and twenty-first-century novels of formation, self-formation continues to be represented in gendered terms—in relation to some norm of gender expression—even if other aspects of identity may also be important. In focusing my analysis within those terms, my aim is not to delineate a separate female tradition but rather to trace within the genre of the novel of formation *one* of the trajectories of identification that subtends it—a relay of reading and recasting that travels partly along a network of shared, deeply felt, but not exclusively defining gender identities. The novels I discuss themselves exhibit doubled or divided ends: the representation of shared features of women's formation as subjects, on the one hand, and a conception of subjectivity as fundamentally individual, on the other. While they represent the individual's formation, and obstacles to it, as specifically gendered, they also implicitly and explicitly insist that their female protagonists' experience and emotions have a claim on the human universal. Gender identity is often, but not always, the most prominent aspect of self-construction and trajectory of identification represented in these narratives; other group-level aspects of identity, such as sexuality, race, class, or national belonging may be equally or more important; the narratives may not address an exclusively or predominantly female readership; and they may draw to varying degrees on conventions of realism. Nevertheless, in their representations of the formation of female characters through relations of identification, in their invitations to readers to identify with those narratives through shared experiences and psychic structures of gender, and in the readerly and authorial identifications with other women's narratives embedded within them, these novels reproduce, across almost two centuries, certain rhetorical strategies and challenges. Without denying difference and distinction, I hope to demonstrate the continued importance of the novel of formation to writing by women, and of identification to the novel of formation.

In unfolding these claims, I draw on more than thirty years of study of English narratives of female formation from the points of view first of feminist, lesbian, and ethnic studies and latterly of queer and postcolonial studies, beginning with such foundational works as *The Voyage In: Fictions of Female Formation,* edited by Elizabeth Abel, Marianne Hirsch, and Elizabeth Langland. Studies of such fictions from the 1970s and 1980s often emphasize the deviation of narratives of female formation from a human norm and fictional tradition identified as masculine, white, European—the norm still called to mind by the term "Bildungsroman." For more recent critics, the contributions of several decades of feminist analysis, as well as the continued production of fictional narratives of female formation, have dislodged the authority of masculine narratives of formation sufficiently that they no longer provide a central reference point for the discussion of female development. Despite these differences, the work done by several generations of feminist critics has enabled me to take for granted in my own study that representations of female formation, ranging across literary-historical and national boundaries (e.g., among Victorian, Modern, and contemporary literatures, and among English, European, and postcolonial texts) and among works by canonical, emerging, and popular authors, present a broad and varied scope of inquiry in themselves, without needing to be set in relation to a presumptive masculine norm. My study is thus organized not by questions of gender difference but by a focus on the paths of transmission, through the identification of readers in a variety of circumstances with characters and authors. I highlight relations of identification in, and around, novels of formation by women, beginning with the nineteenth-century English novel and extending across its continental and colonial spheres of influence in the twentieth and twenty-first centuries, uncovering the shared narrative features of a multivalent and multidirectional tradition through what I call "literary identification."

By the term "literary identification" I mean to indicate an occurrence emerging from the encounter of the psyche of a reader and the rhetorical construction of a narrative by its author. "Identification" and its cousin "sympathy" have been used casually, often interchangeably or in tandem (as in common references to "sympathetic identification"), in twentieth-century literary criticism and theory to describe a reader's involvement with the represented emotions of a fictional character, her willingness to animate a fictional character's actions and relationships with her own affects.[6] I intend my use of the term to be more focused, drawing (as detailed in the following chapter) on the model of subject formation proposed by Freud and later developed in different directions by twentieth-century schools of psychoanalytic thought and by many feminist and queer literary theorists. I use "literary identification" to indicate three ontologically distinct kinds of relations depending on the interaction of real and fictional female subjects: relationships between characters within novels; responses of readers to characters rhetorically invited by the text or actually recorded elsewhere (in other texts); relations between readers and authors sponsored or mediated by textual representations. My terminological expansiveness is intended to capture the intricate relations among readers, characters, and authors of the novel of formation, and the way in which these roles can be transferred through identification. None of these forms of literary identification fits the model of a Freudian "primary" identification, that is, an early, unconscious, and preverbal relation. These literary identifications are, in Freudian terms, "secondary" or "partial," rhetorically constructed and accessible to consciousness, but, I contend, they can powerfully mimic, supplement, and shape the reader's relations with real (non-textual) as well as fictive others.

The text is the arena in which these relations occur; the reader is the subject who identifies, whether with a textually represented character or with the figure of the author. In some cases, the reading subject may also be the object of representation, as in autodiegetic memoirs, such as Lynne Sharon Schwartz's *Ruined by Reading* (discussed in the next chapter) or Beauvoir's *Memoirs of a Dutiful Daughter*, or at moments within novels, as in the case of Maggie Tulliver's reading in *The Mill on the Floss* (discussed in Chapter Two). In these cases, the force of the term "reader" is more or less unproblematically deictic: the reader is Schwartz or Beauvoir or Maggie. But difficulties arise in speaking more generally of, say, "the reader" of *The Mill on the Floss,* where the definite pronoun implies a normative or paradigmatic figure. Where does the norm come from; who establishes the paradigm? If it is the critic, might she not be mistaking her own (particular) reading habits and responses to a text for those of the (abstract) figure of "the reader" of that text? She might turn to testimonials or studies of actual readers, as Janice Radway does with great subtlety in *Reading the Romance,* a pioneering ethnographic study of reading and identification in the particular genre of the romance. As Radway suggests, however, her study is ultimately an investigation of "the way romance reading as a form of behavior operated as a complex intervention in the ongoing social life of actual social subjects" (7)—that is, empirical readers and the way they interpret their activity of reading a particularly homogeneous genre. She observes of her interviewees, "Because the women always responded to my query about their reasons for reading with comments about the pleasures of the act itself rather than about their liking for the particulars of the romantic plot, I soon realized I would have to give up my obsession with textual features and narrative details if I wanted to understand their view of romance reading" (86). Is it possible to posit an abstract figure of "the reader" in the context of a more heterogeneous set of texts, distributed more broadly in space and time, while maintaining a critical orientation toward the rhetorical features of text itself?

Reader-response theory and some strains of narratology have attempted to hypothesize such abstractable readers who can be posited as the subjects of an act of reading not only in default of but even in distinction from embodied, socially located readers. The most relevant set of such terms for my purposes are those that posit readers in the first instance as rhetorical effects of the text; examples include the "implied reader" the "mock reader," and the "narratee."[7] Like the "reasonable person" of legal discourse, these fictional subjects attain their analytic purity at the expense of social, physical, or psychological specificity. They pose difficulties for analyses interested in situated or transactional accounts of reading—ones in which readers are particular subjects located within particular cultural, political, or affective situations.[8] On the one hand, there is no *necessary* correspondence between even the most painstaking critical construction or textual projection of a reader and the situation or experience of any actual reader. As James Phelan points out, "As anyone who has followed the reader-response movement even in passing must already recognize . . . different readers bring different subjectivities to texts and therefore sometimes have different experiences of the same textual phenomena" (231). On the other hand, there must always be at least *one* actual reader present to recognize the textual address to or construction of the reader—that is, the critic. Forming a data set of one, the critic will always run the risk of oversampling his or her own competencies and responses in hypothesizing those of a model reader. This limitation may have political and ethical consequences, since particularly situated critics might read into, or out of, the text the impact of subjective differences, such as those of gender. Patrocinio Schweickart, for example, observes, "It is but a small step from the thesis that the reader is an active producer of meaning to the recognition that there are many different kinds of readers, and that women—because of their numbers if nothing else—constitute an essential class. Reader-response critics cannot take refuge in the objectivity of the text, or even in the idea that a gender-neutral criticism is possible" (38). Even the "essential class" of women readers is itself not indivisible, and the figure of "the woman reader" runs the same risks of totalization as the figure of "the reader" itself.

To conceptualize "the reader" abstractly, in other words, can often be tendentious rather than illuminating. And yet, as Phelan goes on to point out, "to celebrate difference and argue for the incommensurability of different accounts of the reading experience . . . though it has the advantage of validating different responses, has the significant disadvantage of endorsing a prison-house of subjectivity" (231), making it difficult to generate any hypotheses or speculations about reader response. If concepts such as "the implied reader" risk reducing the reader to an epiphenomenon of the text, affective, identity-based, or political approaches risk subordinating the text to the experiences of individual readers or classes of readers.[9] To navigate between the rock of overgeneralization and the hard place of overspecification, Phelan proposes an account of the reader as a unique subject but one addressed and positioned in particular ways by generalizable rhetorical performances of a given text. To describe this reader, he turns to the concept of the "authorial audience" posited by Peter Rabinowitz, on which I shall also draw.

Rabinowitz's tripartite construction of the reader begins with the "actual audience"—the "flesh-and-blood people who read the book." As Rabinowitz points out, this is the audience over whom the author has the least "control," since "each member of the actual audience . . . reads in his or her own way, with a distance from other readers depending upon such variables as class, gender, race, personality, training, culture and historical situation" (20–21).[10] This fluctuating, asymptotic "actual audience" is functionally replaced, in Rabinowitz's paradigm, by the "authorial audience." The authorial audience is "some more or less specific *hypothetical* audience" (21; emphasis in original) constituted by its recognition and "acceptance of the author's invitation to read in a particular socially constituted way that is shared by the author and his or her expected readers" (22). This "invitation" can be facilitated by the presence *within* the narrative by a third, separate but overlapping, set of readers that Rabinowitz calls "the narrative audience" (95)—another hypothetical audience, for whom a novel's data are not fictional but "real." In *The Mill on the Floss,* for example, the "authorial audience" shares Eliot's familiarity with the plots and cultural status of Madame de Staël's novel *Corinne* and Sir Walter Scott's novel *Ivanhoe,* as well as Maggie Tulliver's familiarity with the conventional fates of literary heroines (and probably corresponds quite well with a sizable contemporary "actual audience"). The "narrative audience" knows these things and additionally "knows," along with Maggie Tulliver, that her ontological status (as a "real" person) differs from that of Corinne or *Ivanhoe*'s Rebecca (as fictional characters). (I discuss this example further in Chapter Two.) The acceptance of this distinction by the narrative audience encourages the authorial audience to accept it as well.

Rabinowitz's model enables him to navigate between overspecification of the reader (Phelan's "prison-house of subjectivity") and underspecification (for example, what Schweickart identifies as the "pretense of gender-neutral criticism"). Relatedly, the model's transactional nature—according to which relations between readerly interpretations and authorial intentions, as embodied in texts, are mediated by a shared context of literary conventions—keeps simultaneously in view the text, the reader, and the social situation of both. Rabinowitz's actual/authorial/narrative distinction locates the reading transaction across the three levels that are key to my own analysis: *within the text,* where the narrative audience, as I will argue, often models the kinds of reading the reader should do (or avoid); *within the reader,* who is the object of the text's invitation to read in a particular way, and who has the power to accept or reject that invitation (and sometimes to testify, in her own acts of authorship, about her acceptance or rejection); and *within the author,* conceived of less as a biographical subject than as an ethical or aesthetic intention behind the arrangement of the text—the sender of its invitation, the other party to the transaction. In what follows, when I speak of "the reader," I will most frequently have in view a version of Rabinowitz's "authorial audience." I have also taken the liberty of adapting Rabinowitz's "narrative audience" to my purposes. Like Rabinowitz's, my narrative reader is located within the text and instantiates its epistemological assumptions, but she does so literally by being *a reader.* That is, the "narrative reader" in my analysis will refer to those characters in the text who *model* the act of reading for the authorial reader. I also choose to speak of the "reader" rather than the audience, since part of the invitation of a novel of formation is to make the authorial reader feel addressed more individually and intimately than the word "audience," with its collective and theatrical implications, suggests.

In fact, the term "identification" calls to mind a particular unit of intimacy—the pair. As their titles—"Coming Together," "Coming Apart," and "Coming Out"—suggest, each of the three main sections of this book is partly structured by intimate intersubjective encounters among pairs. The first, introductory, chapter outlines the way in which these intimate encounters are constructed and analyzed within some strands of psychoanalytic theory. In settings ranging from provincial Victorian England to pre–World War II Paris to late-colonial Rhodesia, the three narratives of the second chapter, "Coming Together," dramatize questions about the ethical relations between self and other through the psychological oscillations of identification and disavowal between women with close ties and shared ambitions. In the third chapter, "Coming Apart," the protagonists share, also across different temporal, geographical, and political circumstances (nineteenth-century Europe, the twentieth-century United States, and post-independence Zimbabwe), the trauma of *not* being recognized as subjects, but rather mobilized as representations of abject otherness, a distorted mirror image, by more fortunately situated other women. And the fourth chapter, "Coming Out," considers three twentieth-century novels of formation that both invite and deflect relationships of queer identification among characters and between readers and authors.

The pair in a different sense—the textual pair—has become a prominent feature of literature syllabi and scholarly analysis over the last several decades, encouraged by critical and literary developments. Postmodern writers and critics have found in the revision of canonical works of literature a method of revelation and critique, often giving voice to previously obscured subjects—for example, Jean Rhys's *Wide Sargasso Sea* (1966), whose revision of *Jane Eyre* quickly became part of the feminist pedagogical canon; J. M. Coetzee's *Foe* (1986), which revisits *Robinson Crusoe;* Peter Carey's *Jack Maggs* (1997), which recasts *Great Expectations;* Michael Cunningham's homage to Virginia Woolf and *Mrs. Dalloway* in *The Hours* (1998). Julie Sanders suggests that "in the late twentieth century, as the postmodernist movement developed its own interest in metafiction and writing which acknowledged its sources in a more explicit and deconstructive mode than previously, the Victorian era offered a diverse range of genres and methodologies to examine and appropriate" (122). Such revisions, as theorists of adaptation suggest, offer intrinsic textual pleasures—"the tension between the familiar and the new, and the recognition both of similarity and difference, between ourselves and between texts" (J. Sanders 14)—that, because they provide their own context, may be more easily conveyed in the classroom than certain kinds of literary history or critical methodology. Further, students often want to read contemporary literature, even as English departments continue to value knowledge of canonical texts. Pairing classic texts and contemporary adaptations answers the wishes of both groups.

From a critical perspective, however, the very familiarity of the pair, its aptness for relations of comparison and contrast, can limit its interpretive effects. The high-relief of comparison and contrast can, certainly, be revelatory. The juxtaposition of *Jane Eyre* and *Wide Sargasso Sea* in Gayatri Spivak's seminal essay "Three Women's Texts and a Critique of Imperialism," for example, makes vivid the dependence of Jane's subjectivity, as a British proto-feminist proto-citizen, on Bertha Mason's complementary disintegration, as the "native" female unworthy of human inclusion. As Julie Sanders observes, "The study of appropriations in an academic context has in part been spurred on by the recognized ability of adaptation to respond or write back to an informing original from a new or revised political and cultural position. . . . Many appropriations have a joint political and literary investment in giving voice to those characters or subject-positions they perceive to have been oppressed or repressed in the original" (98). But such comparisons can also enshrine hierarchical relations between texts. Juxtapositions of earlier exclusions and later voicings of textual "others" (Brontë's Bertha Mason, Defoe's Friday, Dickens's Magwich) can easily shift from analysis of prior textual and ideological assumptions to disdain for their apparent inability to see what is clear to present-day readers. It is perhaps to work against such a smug teleology that Spivak, having drawn a sharp contrast between Brontë's and Rhys's representations of Bertha Mason/Antoinette Cosway, triangulates her reading, closing with a third novel, Mary Shelley's *Frankenstein* (1818). *Frankenstein* has a less directly intertextual relation to either of the other novels than they do to each other, but in Spivak's analysis it is the antecedent author, Shelley, who provides the most suggestive critique of the liberal-imperial project of "soul-making."[11]

Against the potential Manichaeism of the pair then, my study is also structured by the figure of the trio. Dyadic interactions between characters are counterposed with triangulated relationships among authors, characters, and readers; likewise each chapter analyzes intertextual relationships among not a pair but a triad of texts. These triadic groupings, I hope, will disrupt hierarchies that might array texts according to relationships of priority and belatedness, origin and imitation, error and correction. The relationships among texts, as I will emphasize, are not unidirectional or even reversible (as a paired model cannot help suggesting) but rather multidirectional and sometimes indirect. Though the overall arc of the study moves from the nineteenth century to the twenty-first, the texts are grouped together on the basis of their intertextual relations rather than by literary historical periods (which also are three: Victorian, Modern, postmodern). I hope this syncopated chronology makes visible the novel of formation's own struggle with a logic of chronological unfolding: the projection of a version of a future self enabled or impeded by identification with a version of a past self. I also wish to emphasize the extent to which struggles over the role, effect, and limits of identification—among characters, between reader and character, between reader and author—are not new developments (i.e., of Modernist reflexivity or postmodern metafictional practice) but have marked the novel of formation from early in its career. Relationships of identification in the novel of formation, both of characters within novels and of readers with their characters and authors, have always been vexed. Protagonists who struggle with their existential debts to characters who embody developmental alternatives; narratives that indict the social inequities shaping psychological opportunities; authors ambivalent about the readerly identification they encourage—these effects of the novel of formation recur across centuries and in new contexts.

In the sense that literary identification has something to do with the way that the novel of formation as a genre reproduces itself, the final triangulation of this study might be that of my phrase, "literary identification," with two more familiar terms: "influence" and "intertextuality." What analytic or categorical shifts does my new term enable? In essence, I have attempted to steer a middle course between strongly author-centered, psychoanalytic accounts of authorial influence (such as those of Harold Bloom in *The Anxiety of Influence* and Sandra Gilbert and Susan Gubar's feminist revisions of Bloom's model in *The Madwoman in the Attic* and *No Man's Land*) and author-decentering, postructuralist accounts focused on intertextual relations, such as those of Roland Barthes ("The Death of the Author"), Julia Kristeva (*Desire in Language*), and Gérard Genette (*Palimpsests*). The concept of the author—and not just of the author, but of *selves* in general, including characters within the work—seems inevitably central to the novel of formation. Regardless of the actual or apparent degree of overlap between events in the author's life and those in the protagonist's, the biographical structure of a novel of formation emphasizes the significance of singular authorship to the life story. Readers of novels of formation may project beyond the text an author who becomes an object of identification; and authors may return the projection. Yet these relations between biographical authors and "actual" readers, whether instantiated (e.g. in letters or meetings) or not, do not supersede relations of readers to characters, or of texts to their precursors. Rather, all these vectors of intimacy, on different ontological planes, compose the web of readerly and intertextual relays whose effects I hope to capture under the heading of "literary identification."

ONE

The Novel of Formation and Literary Identification

EXPERIENCING LITERARY IDENTIFICATION

> There were some books I wanted to possess even more intimately than by reading. I would clutch them to my heart and long to break through the chest wall, making them part of me, or else press my body into them, to burrow between the pages. When I was eight I felt this passion—androgynous, seeking both to penetrate and encompass—for *Little Women*, which I had read several times. Frustrated, I began copying it into a notebook. With the first few pages I felt delirious, but the project quickly palled. It was just words, the same words I had read over and over; writing them down did not bring me into closer possession. Only later did I understand that I wanted to have written *Little Women*, conceived and gestated it and felt its words delivered from my own pen. . . . I did not want to feel and think like Louisa May Alcott, however, or even to know more about her. I wanted to write my version of *Little Women*, what Louisa May Alcott would write were she in my place, or if I were she, yet living my life. (Schwartz, *Ruined by Reading* 67)

This passage from Lynne Sharon Schwartz's memoir, *Ruined by Reading: A Life in Books* (1996), demonstrates concisely many aspects of literary identification. The first aspect is the centrality of representations of literary identification to the diegesis of narratives of formation, both fictional and autobiographical: here, Schwartz's youthful possession by a novel of formation, Alcott's *Little Women* (1868–69), introduces her narrative of her own formation as a reader. The second is its aspirational trajectory: although Schwartz may, like many young readers of the novel, have identified with Jo March, she represents herself here as identifying not with any of the novel's characters or immediately with the author, but rather with what she understands (without having any particular biographical information) the author to represent: a proleptic authorial self, a future Lynne Schwartz who inhabits the possibilities adumbrated by Alcott.[1]

At the same time, the passage exhibits as its third characteristic a quality of recursiveness in tension with that project of self-formation, drawing the reader into a narrative *mise-en-abîme*. Schwartz identifies with the authorial presence of Alcott; at the beginning of *Little Women,* Alcott herself advertises her own prior identifications, in a "Preface" that consists of twelve lines of verse adapted from the second part of John Bunyan's *Pilgrim's Progress:* "Go then, my little book, and show to all / That entertain and bid thee welcome shall, / What thou dost keep close shut up in thy breast; / And wish what thou does show them may be blest / To them for good" (preface). This part of *Pilgrim's Progress* narrates the pilgrimage of Christian's wife, Christiana, and their children, suggesting that in producing her own didactic novel of female coming of age, Alcott imagines herself as writing what Bunyan might have written, were he Alcott, and living her life. Beneath the attempts of the subject to project herself in the future as an agent of narrative runs a current that threatens to pull her back into subjection to textual representation.

Finally, Schwartz and Alcott together illustrate the association, not definitive but definite, of literary identification with an aesthetic identified with middlebrow or popular culture and with female and young readers. Many novels of formation belong simultaneously to, or migrate among, high-culture canons, pedagogical canons, and what Catharine Stimpson calls "paracanons." The paracanon, Stimpson suggests, "embraces both canonical and non-canonical works. In this respect, it is like a 'women's tradition,' which, in English, includes both a George Eliot and the silly female novelists she despised" (965). Taking *Little Women* as her exemplary paracanonical text, Stimpson observes that such a text "may or may not have 'literary value,' however critics define that term. Its worth exists in its capacity to inspire love. . . . We are grateful to the beloved text for being there. If it were not, how might we connect with it? Even cathect to it?" (958). The "cathexis" to which Stimpson here refers is one aspect of what I am calling "literary identification"—the passionate sense of connection to the text that "seek[s] both to penetrate and to encompass," to inhabit the text and to create it.[2] This association of literary identification with readers and reading practices conceived of as "passionate" rather than reflective has obscured the complexity of literary identification as both a response and a textual property.

Schwartz's title teasingly and ironically invokes eighteenth- and nineteenth-century anxieties (discussed further below) about the reading of fiction as a practice that, inflaming the imagination, can "ruin" the reader—especially the female reader—in the same way that women can be "ruined" by erotic knowledge or experience. In *Ruined by Reading,* on the contrary, Schwartz both downplays the power that such analyses impute to affective reading and credits it with being not the ruin, but the making, of her. "If no girl was ever ruined by a book," she asserts, "none was ever saved by one either" (114). This sounds dismissive, but only a few pages later, Schwartz affirms: "All the reading I did as a child, behind closed doors, sitting on the bed while the darkness fell around me, was an act of reclamation. This and only this I did for myself. This was the way to make my life my own" (119). Here, it is the act of reading itself as much as the content of what is read—the independent choice to direct her attention toward, and invest her emotions in, *these* objects and not others—that transforms Schwartz into a "self."

The fictional selves that Schwartz grows up to "make" as a writer testify to the productive rather than the ruinous impact of literary identification. Readers of *Ruined by Reading* likely know that the child passionately transcribing *Little Women* will become a novelist, one whose work includes novels of formation and domestic fictions that might well be described as "what Louisa May Alcott would write were she in my place, or if I were she, yet living my life." But Schwartz's twentieth-century novels redirect the conventional nineteenth-century associations among intellectual curiosity, erotic experience, and female "ruin." Schwartz's early novel *Leaving Brooklyn* (1989), for example, is a retrospective narrative of the first-person protagonist's ambivalently experienced seduction, in her fifteenth year, by a Manhattan ophthalmologist. The undisguised erotic curiosity of the protagonist, Audrey, is linked to her intellectual exploration as an avid reader: "What I was doing now," she reflects about their sexual encounters, "what was being done to me, was as vivid and insistent as any book and gave the same relief of arrival at a resting place, a bedrock reality. It was even like a book, with new passages rolling through me rhythmically, each bearing its multitude of sensations" (74). This sexual transgression wounds and alters her but also releases her into adult life as a writer: "I left Brooklyn. . . . I didn't become an actress in the end, but instead this I who makes up stories" (145). It does not bring about the "ruin" associated with illicit sexuality in nineteenth-century novels such as *Anna Karenina,* which Audrey reads on the subway ride home from her last visit to the doctor, and adumbrated even in juvenile literature such as *Little Women,* in which Jo March's pseudonymous career as a writer of sensational short fiction causes her to "delve[] in the dust of ancient times for facts or fictions so old that they were as good as new, and introduce[] herself to folly, sin, and misery, as well as her limited opportunities allowed" and thus "begin[s] to desecrate some of the womanliest attributes of a woman's character" (396). This decline is halted by the disapproving intervention of Professor Bhaer, at whose behest she burns her manuscripts and whom she ultimately marries. (The burning or other destruction of the protagonist's books, by or at the behest of an authority figure, recurs as a topos: we will encounter it in Brontë's work, in Kincaid's, and in Winterson's.) Jo's sister Amy, similarly, gives up her ambition of becoming an artist, and Laurie Lawrence, the girls' suitor (and ultimately Amy's husband) gives up his of becoming a composer. Alcott solicits her authorial readers' identification with artistic ambition, but she ultimately redirects that identification toward the inhibition of artistic in favor of social (familial) reproduction.[3]

Jo's attempt to write herself into an identity that is not hers (literally, since unknown to Jo, the newspaper editor is willing to publish her work because "one of his hacks, on being offered higher wages, had basely left him in the lurch" [348]) anticipates Schwartz's attempt to occupy the position of authorial privilege represented by *Little Women* itself. But the difference between their responses to the shadow of sexual "ruin" demonstrates that authorial interdictions can come to function, perversely, as incitements. As Schwartz represents it, the shape of her identification with Alcott's words—"clutch[ing] them to my heart and long[ing] to break through the chest wall, making them part of me, or else press[ing] my body into them, to burrow between the pages"—almost parodically exemplifies the kind of assimilative identification that Freud variously identified as primary, narcissistic, or melancholic, in which the ego wishes "to incorporate this [lost] object into itself, and, in accordance with the oral or cannibalistic phase of libidinal development in which it is, it wants to do so by devouring it" (qtd. in Barzilai 118). But its ultimate impact is more conscious and more productive than this representation suggests. In *Leaving Brooklyn*, Schwartz teases the reader with the possibility that the narrative of "libidinal development" is itself a convention as much as a revelation. If Audrey's early seduction transformed her into "this I who makes up stories," then perhaps the story of the seduction is itself made up. As Stimpson suggests, "Generations of female readers, lucky enough to have books, have maneuvered themselves around Alcott's most obviously constrictive maneuvers. They have continued to tutor themselves in unfeminine will through choosing which parts of *Little Women* and which Jo they will imitate, or, at the very least, find enchanting. Recidivists of reading, they return again and again to the far naughtier beginning and middle of the narrative" (969). Beyond the disappointment of *Little Women*'s characters (who give up their art) and its author (whose own less conventional life disappears into her moralized representation), a reader like Schwartz identifies with, and refuses to lose or let go, the image of authorial power that Alcott cannot quite disguise: the power to *produce the moral*—which is also the power to revise, reject, or replace it.

The relationship to Alcott that Schwartz recalls thus illustrates the ambivalent nature of literary identification. My study contends that, while novels of formation may not ruin or save their readers, they do attempt, through relations of identification, to counsel them; that their counsel points to the limits, as often as it exploits the pleasures, of identification; and that the chain of narrative identifications into which they introduce their readers—in which authors become characters, characters become readers, and readers in their turn become authors—may be productive as well as recursive and may serve to inaugurate new narrative directions as well as to reproduce old narrative patterns.

UNDERSTANDING LITERARY IDENTIFICATION

Connections between novel-reading and affective response, in particular identification with literary characters, accompany the emergence of the English novel out of the various literary fields of the eighteenth century. That identification with others is a central feature of the self and of social relations and that it is in the first instance a *narrative* function of imagination—a story we tell ourselves—were propositions central to the theories of eighteenth-century philosophers of mind such as David Hume in the *Enquiry Concerning Human Understanding* (1748) and Adam Smith in *The Theory of Moral Sentiments* (1759). Taking Hume's discussion of the limitations of sympathy as a lens through which to "reveal[] why fictional characters were uniquely suitable objects of compassion" (168), Catherine Gallagher argues that the novel as a genre coalesces around the philosophical question of how far and how deeply identification and sympathy can extend in our relation to fictional others. According to Gallagher, fictional characters elicit identification precisely because a fictional character is "nobody"—no real person—and therefore makes no demands on the reader's sympathy that might run counter to any material interest: "Fiction, then, stimulates sympathy because, with very few exceptions, *it is easier to identify with nobody's story and share nobody's sentiments than to identify with anybody else's story and share anybody else's sentiments.* . . . Nobody [i.e. a fictional character] was eligible to be the universally preferred anybody because nobody, unlike somebody, was never anybody *else*" (*Nobody's Story* 172; my emphasis). Gallagher concludes that "A similarly strong sense both of the impediments to sympathizing with other actual people and of the attenuation of otherness as a result of sympathy lies at the heart of the novel's most important formal trait: its overt fictionality" (173). Both identification with imaginary others, then, and a fictional character's ("nobody's") life story as a locus for that identification, are central to the novel.

The rise of the novel and its encouragement of emotional involvement with overtly fictional others aroused cultural anxieties as well as enthusiasm. The same feature that could make fiction didactically useful—its emotional appeal—could also make it dangerous, especially when addressed to those readers whose emotional lability was understood to be greater than their powers of reasoning—women, children, and later working-class readers. Kate Flint has traced the nineteenth-century history of the association among women, the novel, and identification in English culture, noting that "the woman reader was expected [by nineteenth-century critics and educators], according to the terms of the contemporary psychological and physiological tenets which stressed her innate capacity for sympathy, to find it far easier than a man would do to identify with characters and incidents from her reading material" (38). This impressionability made novel-reading alluring and also dangerous for women readers. Flint quotes the Victorian conduct writer Sarah Stickney Ellis in *The Mothers of England:* "A novel read in secret is a dangerous thing; but there are many works of taste and fancy, which, when accompanied by the remarks of a feeling and judicious mother, may be rendered improving to the mind, and beneficial to the character altogether" (qtd. in Flint 83).[4] In this conjunction of secrecy, danger, and female readers, we see the apprehension of moral "ruin" by reading to which Schwartz alludes.

Through the nineteenth century, then, the experience of identification was increasingly associated with the novel and its particular power, whether for good or ill. William Hazlitt was more positive about affective responses, including identification. He criticizes French tragic drama (which he approaches largely as a form of narrative rather than performance) by asserting that "The true [dramatic] poet identifies the reader with the characters he represents; the French poet only identifies him with himself. . . . We never get at that something more, which is what we are in search of, namely, *what we ourselves should feel in the same situation*" (qtd. in Heller 98; my emphasis). At the beginning of the nineteenth century, Hazlitt had already begun to construct a European canon of fiction, or "good novels and romances" (in which category he included Cervantes's *Don Quixote,* Lesage's *Gil Blas,* and works by Fielding, Richardson, and Scott), asserting that "there are few works to which we oftener turn for profit or delight" (Hazlitt 6: 106), and he had already begun to locate readers' affective response to fictional characters at the heart of that canon.[5]

With such encouragement, by the beginning of the Victorian period the general stigma attached to novels and the overtly affective reading styles they fostered had been redirected toward specifically disfavored genres, defined sometimes by subject and style (Gothic novels and their descendants, "sensation" and "New Woman" novels; French novels; "shilling shockers"; newspaper serials and "railway novels"); by the readership associated with them (e.g., working-class, "mass," and female readers); and by the methods and motivations of their consumption (such as Ellis's novels read "in secret"). Elevated above these genres, readers, and motivations to a mode of social critique as they were by Charles Dickens or of ethical instruction as they were by George Eliot, novels could be viewed as appropriate reading for cultivated readers of both sexes and could be harnessed to the more general project, perceived as increasingly urgent, of enlightenment through the spread of a demotic literary culture. Readers' identifications with fictional others in this context could represent not a residue of disfavored sentimental affect but rather a positive resource for the cultivation of morality.

This possibility is both suggested and delimited in Eliot's well-known manifesto for realist fiction in "The Natural History of German Life" (1856):

> The greatest benefit we owe to the artist, whether painter, poet, or novelist, is the extension of our sympathies. . . . A picture of human life such as a great artist can give, surprises even the trivial and the selfish into that attention to what is apart from themselves, which may be called the raw material of moral sentiment. . . . Art is the nearest thing

> to life; it is a mode of amplifying experience and extending our contact with our fellow-men beyond the bounds of our personal lot. (*Selected Essays* 110)

In Eliot's essay, the individuated emotional responsiveness to literature that Hazlitt describes as "something more . . . what we ourselves should feel in the same situation," is brought out of the realm of aesthetics and into that of ethics, "amplif[ied]" beyond its immediate source in the literary experience to become "the raw material of moral sentiment," that is, the foundation of a moralized fictional realism.

To this moral sentiment Eliot famously attaches the word "sympathy," which develops in her conception from a largely innate faculty to a strenuously cultivable moral achievement. The paradoxical result of Eliot's elevation of sympathy in fiction, however, is that in her novels, the recognition of similitude (identification), which had previously been important not in itself but as the *a priori* basis of sympathy, takes over as a primary effect of the reading experience. The route to this transformation is complex. In embracing sympathy as the basis for the development of a morally directed fictional realism, Eliot needs to dissociate it from the other more overtly didactic sentimental forms of fictional representation in which it flourished. In "The Natural History of German Life," she does this by attacking as sentimental and melodramatic Dickens's sympathetic representation of working-class altruism:

> But for the precious salt of his humor . . . [Dickens's] preternaturally virtuous poor children and artisans, his melodramatic boatmen and courtesans, would be as noxious as Eugène Sue's idealized proletaires in encouraging the miserable fallacy that high morality and refined sentiment can grow out of harsh social relations, ignorance, and want; or that the working classes are in a condition to enter at once into a millennial state of *altruism,* wherein everyone is caring for everyone else, and no one for himself. (*Selected Essays* 111)

Eliot suggests that Dickens falsifies these characters, and therefore the reader's emotional response to them, in two ways. On the one hand, when it is possible simply to assimilate characters (such as "poor children and artisans") to middle-class conceptions of virtue and the displays of "high morality and refined sentiment" on which authorial readers might pique themselves, Dickens does so, an elimination of difference that eases identification and thus the extension of sympathy. On the other hand, characters for whom assertions of similarity might be rejected—"courtesans and boatmen"—become melodramatic spectacles of difference.[6] Judging themselves, and judged by others, according to standards they do not meet, they would *like* to be like us but are not; they appeal to our sympathies through their self-abjection at the spectacle of their own difference. Thus Little Em'ly in *David Copperfield,* seduced by Steerforth, first hopes that he will "[bring] me back a lady" (419)—that she will become like the reader in (imputed) social class and virtue. When, instead, her sexual fall conventionally destroys the possibility of likeness between herself and the virtuous reader, Em'ly can reassert her claim to sympathy only by making herself the author of her own chastisement: "Oh dear, dear uncle, if you ever could have known the agony your love would cause me when I fell away from good, you never would have shown it to me so constant . . . but would have been angry to me, at least once in my life, that I might have had some comfort!" (661). In her disavowal of her former self, Em'ly becomes realigned with the moral values that her readers are supposed to hold, while maintaining the reassuring social and ethical distance indexed by her narrative banishment to Australia.

The problem with such methods for establishing sympathy, from Eliot's point of view, is that with either the elimination or the exaggeration of differences between readers and characters, readers' existing habits of feeling and response are not challenged, and the representations don't have the effect of "amplifying our experience and extending our contact with our fellow-men beyond the bounds of our personal lot." As Rachel Ablow suggests (in a discussion of Eliot's propensity to create pain for her characters), "Insofar as sympathy threatens to make the other into merely an extension of the self—or the self into an extension of the other—it is inimical to" the creation of ethical relationships (71). For Eliot, "amplif[ication]" and "exten[sion]" mean not the emotional amplification of the sentimental tradition or the depiction of out-of-bounds experiences such as those of melodrama but rather a greater immersion in and openness to ordinary feelings and events—in short, in what we have come to know as fictional realism. This program leads to the creation of characters such as the Rev. Amos Barton, who embodies "the eighty out of a hundred of your adult male fellow-Britons returned in the last census, [who] are neither extraordinarily silly, nor extraordinarily wicked, nor extraordinarily wise," who yet "bear a conscience, and have felt the sublime prompting to do the painful right; . . . have their unspoken sorrows, and their sacred joys" (36, 37). Eliot remains aware, however, that readers are likely to require direct authorial intervention to sympathize with characters such as Amos Barton (as with, later, Edward Casaubon); and her convictions never fully exempt her from some "idealized" portrayals of "artisans" (think of Adam Bede or Felix Holt) and flashes of the "melodrama" associated with "boatmen and courtesans" (Caterina Sarti and her dagger in "Mr. Gilfil's Love Story," the actress Laure stabbing her husband onstage in *Middlemarch*), that sometimes illuminate them.

Particularly in her major female protagonists, Eliot develops an alternative model of readerly involvement that elicits readerly identification *as against* sympathy. Eliot devotes her most detailed character portrayal and analysis to characters such as Maggie Tulliver and Dorothea Brooke, whose primary concerns are with their relations with others and who demonstrate considerable complexity—including error, confusion, hesitation, and doubt—in the development of those relations. These protagonists are represented, *inter alia,* as readers of texts, but as important, they are represented as "readers"—interpreters, analysts—directly of persons and relationships. These characteristics align them with the reader herself and magnify the moral importance of "reading" in both senses. Further, climactic moments of these characters' development always include powerful demonstrations of sympathy with others—such as Dinah Morris's solicitation of Hetty Sorrel's confession and Dorothea Brooke's visit of marital counsel to Rosamond Vincy—that suggest the attitude toward others that will ideally emerge from such reading.

At the same time, Eliot overwhelmingly emphasizes the difficulty, even the anguish, for her protagonists of achieving such sympathy.[7] When Maggie Tulliver, having resigned her claim on Stephen Guest, assures the abandoned Lucy Deane that Stephen "will come back to you," Eliot describes these words as "wrung forth from Maggie's deepest soul, with an effort like the convulsed clutch of a drowning man" (Eliot, *The Mill on the Floss* [hereafter *MoF*] 510). Because Maggie, the protagonist, with whose moral and emotional development the reader has detailed familiarity, is depicted as experiencing even *greater* emotional pain than the ostensible object of sympathy, the less fully drawn Lucy, the function of sympathy here is to reinforce, rather than transform, the authorial reader's experience of identification: It is Maggie, not Lucy, we mourn for; it is her agony in inflicting pain, not Lucy's in feeling it, that we experience. Despite Eliot's insistence on sympathy as the basis of moral art, to the very degree that she succeeds in drawing a reader into the intellectual and emotional processes by which her protagonists develop their sympathies with others, identification tends to remain in tension with, rather than ground, the sympathetic response.[8]

Nevertheless, if Eliot ends up separating a nascent conception of identification (not named as such) from sympathy and emphasizing a tension between them, both responses still function for her—as they did for Dickens—in the service of a primarily ethical conception of the self. An important ethical and structural shift in conceptions of sympathy and identification occurs at the end of the nineteenth century, via Freud's psychoanalytic theory. Freud begins to systematize a theory of identification—naming it, attempting to disentangle it from sympathy, and further moving the narrative of subject-formation out of the prescriptive, deontological realm of the "ought" and into the descriptive, aspirationally scientific realm of the "is."[9] As Diana Fuss writes, "[For Freud] identification replaces 'sympathy,' 'imagination,' and 'suggestion' to describe, in more 'scientific' fashion, the phenomenon of how subjects act upon one another" (4). Subjects can "act upon one another," of course, in a variety of ways, but the "act[ions]" encompassed by the terms "sympathy" and "identification" are foundational and paradoxical relations that both define a self, or subject, as separate from the other and link the subject inescapably *to* the other. In Fuss's succinct formulation, Freudian identification is "the detour through the other that defines the self" (6). Freud's conception of identification revises the direction of self-other relations posited in eighteenth- and nineteenth-century theories of sympathy. According to these theories, identification, underlying sympathy, allows us to reach out to selves outside our own, and thus at least implicitly maintains the value of the other. According to Freud's theory, identification allows us to bring others inside us—to assimilate or introject them, a direction that does not require a particular ethical stance toward, or attachment of value to, the other.[10]

Freud's ideas about identification are formulated and revisited in a number of essays over many years, including *The Interpretation of Dreams* (1900), *Mourning and Melancholia* (1917), *Group Psychology and the Analysis of the Ego* (1921), and *The Ego and the Id* (1923); as his many interpreters and critics have noted, there is no single, systematic theory of identification. Shuli Barzilai, for example, observes that

> Freud . . . did not provide a definitive and systematic description of this mental operation in his writings. Quite the contrary, his usage over the years is richly nuanced and also abounds in inconsistencies. . . . As variously described by Freud, identification could be any of the following: primary (the earliest form of emotional tie), regressive (the object-choice is introjected back into the ego), narcissistic (the self is taken as

> a model), and hysterical (the patient's symptom expresses an unconscious assimilation of the experiences, usually sexual, of other people). (113)

Most generally, Freud is inconsistent about whether and when identification is fundamental to all subjects or characteristic of pathological ones, and whether its origin is drive-related (internal to the subject) or relational (founded on the social orientation of the subject).[11] What is important for my purposes is not the specific content of Freud's conflicting formulations but rather a particular tension in the conception of the subject that they instantiate, which, I will argue, also structures the narrative of the self in novels of formation. That tension is between a concept of subject as fundamentally autonomous, developing in the context of social relations but established previous to or apart from them, and a subject as fundamentally social, relationally shaped from its earliest moments and in its deepest recesses.

Stephen Mitchell, in an important synthesis of later twentieth-century "relational-model theories" (such as British object-relations and various American interpersonal schools), describes how they shift Freud's emphasis: "Freud views mind as fundamentally monadic; something inherent, wired in, prestructured, is pushing from within. Mind for Freud emerges in the form of endogenous pressures. Relational-model theories view mind as fundamentally dyadic and *interactive;* above all else, mind seeks contact, engagement with other minds" (3). Against this monadism, however, many theorists, including Freud himself, have noted the foundational populousness of the Freudian psyche. "In the individual's mental life," Freud writes, describing identification at the beginning of *Group Psychology and the Analysis of the Ego,* "someone else is invariably involved, as a model, as an object, as a helper, as an opponent; *and so from the very first individual psychology . . . is at the same time social psychology as well*" (1; my emphasis). Tim Dean asserts, more dramatically, "As his theory of identification became progressively complex . . . Freud saw more than four people in even the most conventional coupling. No longer a question of constitutional bisexuality but of an individual's identifications with and ambivalence toward his or her parents of both sexes, every sexual encounter involves multiple generations, as well as multiple ghosts. The Freudian bedroom is a densely populated space. We might say that when classical psychoanalysis pictures people having sex, it can't resist conjuring a gang bang" (141). The shaping presence of others in the individual psyche does not quite make Freud's conception of the self fundamentally relational in Mitchell's sense, in which "embededness is endemic to the human experience—I become the person I am in interaction with specific others. The way I feel it necessary to be with them is the person I take myself to be" (276). While populous, the Freudian psyche is not necessarily sociable. Rather, it is precisely because they maintain, in their very inconsistencies and conflicts, an emphasis on the tense but utterly central relationship between "the person I am" and "interaction with specific others" that Freudian as well as more consistently relational psychoanalytic models of subject-formation can be employed to capture the tense dynamics of identification in narratives of formation.

If psychoanalytic subjects, viewed through a relational lens, share with fictional protagonists a narrative construction that emphasizes interactions of the self with others, they also share the feature of being embedded in retrospective narratives that retrace those interactions in order to understand the subject's formation. Peter Brooks, for example, suggests that "the kind of explanation in which psychoanalysis deals is inherently narrative, claiming an enhanced understanding of the present—and even a change in it—through histories of the past" (47–48). Freud himself is notoriously ambivalent about this unscientific resemblance between case history and novel. "There are many physicians," he concedes, "who (revolting though it may seem) choose to read a case history of this kind [i.e., *Dora*] not as a contribution to the psychopathology of neuroses, but as a *roman à clef* designed for their private delectation" (Freud, *Dora* 23). "Revolting" though such a reading may be, in Freud's narrative interpretations of memories, dreams, fantasies, and case studies, the patient's "symbolic positionalities" and obscure desires acquire imaginative *mises-en-scène;* Brooks suggests that Dora "reads as a kind of failed Edwardian novel, one that can never reach a satisfactory dénouement" (50).[12] As Mikkel Borch-Jacobsen observes, "Even in its crudest, most stereotyped forms (as in his 'Child is Being Beaten,' for example), a [Freudian] fantasy unfailingly calls up an entire scene complete with protagonists—dramatic personae—and plot. This minimal dramatization is simply amplified in dreams that rework the material of unconscious fantasy, in the fantastic genealogies of 'family romance,' in the stories of daydreams, and also in literary fiction, which originates, according to Freud, in fantasy" (17).[13] Perhaps reflecting his uneasiness about the relation of psychoanalytic to literary, rather than scientific, narrative, Freud's own theoretical accounts of the generative relationship between fiction and fantasy are notoriously simplistic. In "Creative Writers and Daydreaming," for example, he chooses to focus on what Stimpson might call "paracanonical" literature:

> Not the writers most highly esteemed by the critics, but the less pretentious authors of novels, romances and short stories, who nevertheless have the widest and most eager circle of readers of both sexes. One feature above all cannot fail to strike us about the creations of these story-writers: each of them has a hero who is the center of interest, for whom the writer tries to win our sympathy by every possible means and whom he seems to place under the protection of a special providence. . . . It is the true heroic feeling, which one of our best writers has expressed in an inimitable phrase: "Nothing can happen to me!" It seems to me, however, that through this revealing characteristic of invulnerability we can immediately recognize His Majesty the Ego, the hero alike of every daydream and of every story. (9–10)

Freud here represents literary identification as the occasion for crude wish-fulfillment. But as his own interpretations of his patients' "daydream[s] and stor[ies]" suggest, it is not always "immediately" easy to reveal their traces of "His Majesty the Ego"; and the expectation of fantasy that "Nothing can happen to me!" is disappointed, in the case histories as well as in novels, more frequently than it is fulfilled.

Important reconceptualizations of Freudian identification have emerged from feminist and queer psychoanalytic, literary, and cultural studies. Beginning in the 1970s, English, French, and American feminist psychoanalytic theorists, such as Juliet Mitchell, Hélène Cixous, and Nancy Chodorow, placed pressure on the gendering of identification and desire within the Freudian Oedipal narrative, the place at which, for Freud, both emerge. As Freud represents it, identification at the Oedipal stage is above all a recognition of *gendered* sameness and difference. Ideally, for Freud, identification operates symmetrically with object-choice, or desire, within the scenario of the Oedipal complex, to produce a heterosexual orientation: the subject identifies with (wishes to be) the parent of the same sex and orients his or her desire toward (wishes to have) the parent of the opposite sex. For the male child, this process requires sublimating an initial rivalry with the father for the mother's love into an identification with the father and a desire oriented toward women who will replace the mother. For the little girl, on Freud's account, the process is more complex and indirect, requiring her to accept an identification with the inferior ("castrated") position of the mother and orient herself toward the male who can supply her with a replacement for the penis in the form of a baby. Feminist psychoanalytic writers such as object-relations theorist Nancy Chodorow and the Lacanian Jane Gallop developed paradigms that made the female subject central and transvalued her complex relations of identification to the mother (Chodorow) and the father (Gallop). Feminist literary theorists such as Sandra Gilbert and Susan Gubar and Margaret Homans drew on psychoanalytic models to consider the complexities of literary identification and influence for female readers and writers in a male-defined literary canon.

Beginning in the 1980s, a further challenge to the Oedipal model of the opposition of identification and desire emerged from psychoanalytically inflected queer theory. Freud concedes that the "normal positive Oedipus complex" (*The Ego and the Id* [*hereafter EI*] 29), with its binary gendered and heterosexual outcome, is by no means the most likely resolution of the "Oedipus situation," which is complicated by its "triangular character . . . and the constitutional bisexuality of each individual" (26). Whether male or female, the child has available alternative objects (male and female) of identification and desire, and there is no *prima facie* reason to suppose that he or she will assort them in the ways that produce a "normal positive" outcome or that identification and desire are mutually exclusive responses to the other (*EI* 29, 26). Freud temporizes about how the Oedipus complex and its identifications do produce a gendered outcome: "In both sexes the relative strength of the masculine and feminine sexual dispositions is what determines whether the outcome of the Oedipus situation shall be an identification with the father or the mother" (*EI* 28). Freud tends to present such observations as minor qualifications that do not significantly alter the logic of his argument; but in this case, since "masculine and feminine sexual dispositions" are what Freud presents the Oedipus complex as *producing*, it is unclear what can ground the *prior* existence of those "dispositions."[14] Judith Butler, Diana Fuss, Eve Kosofsky Sedgwick, Kaja Silverman, and Michael Warner, among others, have taken up the tautologies, contradictions, and gaps in Freud's account of identification, using them to produce alternative versions that erode the boundaries between masculine and feminine and between homo- and heterosexual identities and that thus call into question the naturalization the heterosexual subject and the "heterosexual matrix" anchored by that subject. This aspect of queer theory has not abandoned the Freudian account of the subject as produced by identification and desire, or of those affects as grounded in kinship, but it has dislodged the heterosexual subject, female or male, from its position as embodying *the* identity formation in relation to which other identities are imitations or aberrations.[15] This conceptual shift brings into view not only the expressly queer subjects of some of the twentieth-century and contemporary narratives of formation in this study, including Radcylffe Hall's *Well of Loneliness* and Jeanette Winterson's *Oranges Are Not the Only Fruit,* but also the ambiguity and inconclusiveness of gendered and sexual subjectivity in narratives not ostensibly or primarily queer, such as *The Mill on the Floss,* Virginia Woolf's *Voyage Out,* and Simone de Beauvoir's *Memoirs of a Dutiful Daughter.*

As productive as dislodging identification and desire as the grounding of a "heterosexual matrix" has been questioning the very distinction between the two forms of the subject's relation to an other. In a discussion of Freud's characterization of identification in *Group Psychology and the Analysis of the Ego,* for example, Eva Badowska suggests that

> The introduction [by Freud] of the distinction between "having" and "being" has a twofold effect. Its positive effect is to draw attention to identification as a form of being; as the very ground of subjectivity. But its negative effect . . . is to insist that identification must—had better—be different from object-cathexis, even as identification is construed [by Freud] as an "emotional tie." . . . Notwithstanding Freud's nice formula for distinguishing between object-love ("having") and identification ("being"), the notion of identification as "emotional tie" undercuts the possibility of such distinctions by revealing that identification too is a way of "having"—relating to, or loving and hating—an object. Despite Freud's protestations, identification and desire, like two ghosts, occupy one place and keep fluidly morphing into one another. (966, 967)

In Badowska's account, identification and desire "fluidly [morph]" into one another at such a rate that the distinction threatens to vanish altogether. Badowska cites Borch-Jacobsen's post-structuralist rereading of Freudian identification: "Following René Girard (1965), [Borch-Jacobsen] believes that desire has no essential connection to an object and is essentially mimetic." In Badowska's words, the aim of the wish expressed by desire is no different from that expressed by identification—to occupy the place of another as a way of fulfilling "a wish to be a subject, to position [oneself] and [one's] desire" (960). This metapsychological point does not, presumably, deny a felt distinction for the subject between alignments of self and other that are experienced as primarily erotic (desire) and those that are experienced as primarily emulative (identification). It does suggest that these experiences are not mutually exclusive—or even easily separated. It also suggests, like the analysis from the point of view of queer theory cited above, that the predominance of identification or desire in any relationship, or phase of a relationship, cannot be predicted by the gender, or even the sexuality, of subject or object. As Fuss asks, since "psychoanalysis's basic distinction between wanting to be the other and wanting to have the other is a precarious one at best, its epistemological validity seriously open to question. . . . Why assume . . . that any subject's sexuality is structured in terms of pairs?" (11). My own emphasis in this study reverses these terms: Why assume that any pair is structured in terms of its subjects' sexuality? That is, in the readings of self/other relationships that follow, I do not take the "wish to be a subject" that binds these pairs as primarily a wish about object choice. I read desire largely in terms of identification: as desire to be, rather than to have, a particular kind of subject—sometimes, but not always, including a particular kind of sexual subject.

Further challenges to conventional psychoanalytic accounts of the vectors and consequences of identification for sexuality and gender identity have come from theorists, such as José Muñoz, in *Disidentifications,* Heather Love, in *Feeling Backward,* and Kathryn Bond Stockton, in *Beautiful Bottom, Beautiful Shame,* who draw on recent interest in negative affects such as shame, loss, and disidentification to challenge not the classic division between identification and desire but another slippery Freudian division, between progressive or formative instances of identification and those (often associated with narcissism or melancholia) that are apparently regressive or disintegrative. Love, for example, suggests that queer theory's "relation to the queer past is suffused not only by feelings of regret, despair, and loss but also by the shame of identification" with those negative feelings; in response "queer critics and historians have . . . disavowed the difficulties of the queer past, arguing that our true history has not been written" (32). By contrast, she suggests the necessity of allowing scope to "negative or ambivalent identifications with the [queer] past [that] can serve to disrupt the present" (45). Muñoz addresses the question of how subjects with racially as well as sexually minoritized identities—queers of color—experience "disidentification" as a response that does not simply disavow "ruined or spoiled" identities or desires but rather that "negotiates strategies of resistance within the flux of discourse and power" (19), particularly through performance art that reworks the representation of both ideal and stigmatized objects of identification.

Important redirections and rethinkings of Freudian schemata in the context of race studies and postcolonial studies have also come from outside queer theory, from seminal works such as Frantz Fanon's *Black*

Skin, White Masks to more recent analyses such as Paul Gilroy's *Postcolonial Melancholia* and Anne Anlin Cheng's *The Melancholy of Race.* Like Fanon, Cheng insists on the inseparability of a psychic mechanism of identification from the social context that makes possible or forecloses identifications, asking "What are the ontological conditions under which 'identify' can take place?. . . . How do we separate ontic and familial 'selves' (an assumption and a preoccupation inherited from psychoanalysis) from the subject positions invented by society, culture, and politics? . . . Social forms of compulsion and oppression may have their hold precisely because they mime or invoke ontic modes of identification" (27). Such challenges to the distinctions between the psychic and the social are visible in the representations in novels of formation of protagonists in situations of racial or national oppression and conflict, as in Jamaica Kincaid's *Lucy* and Tsitsi Dangarembga's *Nervous Conditions* and *The Book of Not.*

DEFENDING LITERARY IDENTIFICATION

Suspicion of reading and readers associated with identification did not disappear in the twentieth century, or with the rise of psychoanalytic models. With the emergence of Modernism and an avant-garde aesthetic in the first decades of the twentieth century, the narrative and reading practices associated with Victorian and Edwardian realist fiction, including their encouragement of readerly identification, began to be viewed as old-fashioned and were associated with a numerically impressive but culturally less prestigious readership that came to be defined, derogatorily, as "middlebrow."[16] As Kate Flint points out, the view of women readers as psychosocially inclined toward identificatory reading continues to influence twentieth- and twenty-first-century readers and critics (31–37); women readers and women's fiction are middlebrow unless proven otherwise. The susceptibility of a text to literary identification often functions as a mark of middlebrow or feminized status. As Suzanne Keen writes in a discussion of Oprah Winfrey's Book Club, which propels book sales by "grant[ing] middlebrow status to works that would otherwise seem either too difficult or beneath notice," writers, particularly male writers, who aspire to definitively literary stature may have mixed feelings about such aid: "For a [Don] DeLillo *manqué,* increased readership does not necessarily compensate for the association with the topicality and emotional invitation that Oprah books promise their empathetic readership" (104).

At the same time, as the reading public appears to decline, cultural anxieties about the consumption of text now most frequently attach to the growth of digital and visual media and the loss of traditional reading practices.[17] As Keen points out, "bold claims have been made for the positive consequences of novel reading, and these contentions grow more urgent as the practice of literary reading in Anglo-American culture undergoes startling declines" (xv). Some scholars and critics in a variety of fields—Keen instances the philosopher Martha Nussbaum, the historian Lynn Hunt, and the evolutionary psychologist Steven Pinker—have revived assertions that, through readers' sympathetic identification with characters, "novel reading cultivates empathy that produces good citizens for the world" (xv) and thus achieves desirable social ends. This humanist defense of literature as culturally valuable implicitly equates fiction with *realist* fictions, which classically invites responses of identification and sympathy. It also explicitly equates reading with moral pedagogy.

The implicit or explicit celebration of literary identification is open to empirical, aesthetic, and political objections. From an empirical point of view, as Keen points out, "Whether novels on their own can actually extend readers' empathetic imagination and make prosocial action more likely remains uncertain" (116).[18] From an aesthetic point of view, an advocacy of literature based primarily on assumptions about its moral function and effect can seem to devalue or at least misrecognize the creative enterprise. Such advocacy makes no claims for, and indeed may be incompatible with, rhetorical and narrative modes that do not invite identification. It may be hostile to any textual practices whose aims are not primarily realist, ethical, or socially oriented, and to postmodernist fictions that break with both nineteenth-century realism and Modernist experimentalism—metafictive or metaphysical modes (such as can be found in the work of Paul Auster); parodic or ironic modes (such as can be found the work of Kathy Acker or Jasper Fforde); magical realist modes (as in, for example, novels by Angela Carter or Salman Rushdie); and the anomic or confrontational vision of authors such as Denis Cooper or Rebecca Brown.

From the point of view of political critique, the strong pedagogical and ethical claims made on behalf of fictional realism—based partly on its imputed ability to create sympathy for real others on the model of the identifications it encourages with fictional ones—are equally open to question. If identification takes a "detour through the other," as Fuss says, its final destination is always the self. This autocentrism is all the more pronounced in identification with literary characters (rather than real persons), since in some sense their attributes, to which the reader responds, can only be those that the reader has already lent, and since (as Catherine Gallagher points out) literary characters cannot, unlike actual other persons, evade, resist, or pose counter-claims to our assimilations of them. Many political objections can be raised against the supposed ethical value of literary identification: it may be seen to encourage subjective, emotional responses to situations that would be better served by activism; to serve as a medium for the reproduction of bourgeois subjectivity; and to indulge readers in solipsistic fantasies of sympathy and solidarity that do nothing to improve their responsiveness to real others, and in particular do nothing to engender social or political change.[19] Such reservations echo the concerns of eighteenth- and nineteenth-century thinkers about the possibly self-indulgent and fantastical nature of emotional response to fictional others. But where those concerns were broadly ethical in nature and often allied to conservative social views (for example about the intellectual capacities of women or working-class subjects), these contemporary critiques are generally politically progressive, shaped by almost a century of Marxist and post-Marxist aesthetics that is generally wary of the immersive effects of aesthetic representation. Bertolt Brecht, for example, found both nineteenth-century fictional realism and traditional naturalistic drama equally illusionistic and reactionary in their aesthetics of character identification. According to Etienne Balibar and Pierre Macherey, Brecht's theory of identification demonstrates how "the ideological effects of literature . . . materialise via an identification process between the reader or the audience and the hero or anti-hero, the simultaneous constitution of the fictive 'consciousness' of the character with the ideological 'consciousness' of the reader" (90).[20]

In this ideological functioning, literary identification becomes an instance, in the aesthetic field, of what Louis Althusser defines as "interpellation": a "hailing" of the subject by ideology, which "has the function (which defines it) of 'constituting' concrete individuals as subjects" (171). Althusser does not address literature in this essay; it is not a "state apparatus" at the level of his other examples, which include the state educational system and the Church. Balibar and Macherey's "On Literature as an Ideological Form," however, explicitly attempts to extend his conception of ideology as a system of social practices to the function of literature in interpellating subjects:

> There is [in literary texts] only ever identification of one subject with another (potentially with "oneself": "Madame Bovary, c'est moi,"

> familiar example, signed Gustave Flaubert). . . . Through the endless functioning of its texts, literature unceasingly "produces" subjects, on display for everyone. . . . Literature endlessly transforms (concrete) individuals into subjects and endows them with a quasi-real hallucinatory individuality. (93)

Balibar and Macherey conclude that "class struggle is not abolished in the literary text and the literary effects which it produces. They bring about the reproduction, as dominant, of the ideology of the dominant class" (93), through the identification-effect among other effects.

For Marxist and post-Marxist critics, nineteenth-century realist fiction is a *locus classicus* for the at best ambiguous, and at worst reactionary, tendencies of literary identification in relation to social change. Raymond Williams finds, in Victorian authors attempting to depict working-class experience, such as Elizabeth Gaskell, George Eliot, and George Gissing, that a "negative identification"—an "imaginative recoil" (90) from the potential disaffection, violence, and cultural difference of working-class protagonist with whom, up to a point, these authors also experience "imaginative identification" (88)—ultimately vitiates the representation and resolution of class struggle. "When she touches . . . the lives and the problems of working people," Williams observes of Eliot, "her personal observation and conclusion surrender, virtually without a fight, to the general structure of feeling which was the common property of her generation" (109): Eliot's authorial identification with a protagonist cannot overcome her class identification with her own class interests and "structure of feeling."[21] In *Scenes of Sympathy: Identity and Representation in Victorian Fiction,* Audrey Jaffe returns to a similar contretemps. She argues that because sympathy and identification in many Victorian novels depend on a previous recognition of similarity, the novels function ideologically not to bridge but to exclude and minimize experiences of difference. In a discussion of *Daniel Deronda,* Jaffe argues that because Daniel first sympathizes with Jews and subsequently discovers that he *is* a Jew, "what is represented [by Eliot] as sympathy with the other turns out to be sympathy with the self" (133); thus "rather than promoting sympathy as a means toward understanding difference, then—indeed, strikingly rejecting that principle in Deronda's rejection of Gwendolen—the novel valorizes sympathy as an identification with and affirmation of similarity" (141). These repeated discoveries of the self-same in an apparent other, Jaffe argues, sharply undercut the proffer of disinterested tolerance, if not sympathy, that the novels, in a liberal humanist mode, understand themselves to be making. Regenia Gagnier suggests that such obliterating responses similarly characterize the present-day readers of Victorian novels of proletarian experience such as those by Hardy and Gissing: "Middle-class students today . . . want to 'identify' with characters, and the only characters they can identify with are those with subjectivities (introspective, self-conscious, self-interested subjectivities) like their own. . . . If literature does not give 'us'—the status quo—ourselves, we do not identify with it and it is not canonical" (136). In other words, according to Gagnier, literary identification leads not to Eliot's hoped-for "extension" of sympathies but rather to their sclerosis and to a reproduction, through canon-formation, of dominant ideologies.

Yet if literary identification can function to interpellate bourgeois subjects, reproduce the status quo, and negate rather than address social difference, those effects do not foreclose more radical or liberatory possibilities. The response of a reader to the text's invitation to identification is not predictable or predetermined, even in these cases. Jaffe persuasively demonstrates that the moral argument of *Daniel Deronda* about Judaism depends on a construction of similitude that eliminates rather than tolerates the possibility of ethnic difference within national borders. But one might respond that the novel and its title character have hardly commanded much enthusiasm, let alone identification, from readers then or now—"Daniel Deronda, *c'est moi*" is not a common response. F. R. Leavis captures a widespread impatience when he famously advocates eliminating Deronda altogether. Indeed, the novel's division of attention among Daniel, Gwendolyn, and even Mira Lapidoth, along with its other rhetorical features (such as its swatches of historical and ethnographic exposition), militate against readerly identification with a single character.[22] As for the canonicity of Hardy and Gissing: although Hardy may have ended his life as a literary lion, the Victorian response to his political provocations was not uniformly welcoming; and Gissing has fared better in contemporary editions and on syllabi, than, say, George Meredith, a less politically provocative writer. What I mean to emphasize here is that readers are not so reliably swept away by the rhetoric or affect of identification as to render them incapable of discrimination both in individual reading practices and over the history of reception. The pleasure in literary identification is not necessarily opposed to a capacity for analysis; it is not a swoon of the intellect but a changeable response, one that may be withheld, modified, reflected on; a detour, not a determination.

Further, readerly identification beyond the individual character—with authors and the act of authorship—may indicate prospects of thought and action not embodied within, and even counter to, a novel's diegesis. *Jane Eyre,* for example, is a novel whose trajectory of identification appears to be tightly controlled by the intensity of its first-person point of view, which makes it difficult, in Gayatri Spivak's resonant phrase, to "wrench oneself away from the mesmerizing focus of the 'subject-constitution' of the female individualist" (897). But even *Jane Eyre* offers more opportunities for distance and reflection than might first appear. For example, the eleventh chapter of Brontë's novel draws attention to the artifice of scene construction, as it metaleptically conflates the locations of author, reader, and character: "A new chapter in a novel is like a new scene in a play; and when I draw up the curtain this time, reader, you must fancy you see a room in the George Inn at Millcote. . . . All this is visible to you by the light of an oil-lamp hanging from the ceiling, and by that of an excellent fire, near which I sit in my cloak and bonnet; . . . I am warming away the numbness and chill contracted by sixteen hours' exposure to the rawness of an October day" (*Jane Eyre* 96). The ontological status of the pronoun "I," this novel's usual location of identification, shifts radically over these sentences. In the first sentence it must belong to someone we would call an author, Charlotte Brontë (or Currer Bell), who has written "a new chapter in a novel," and addresses an authorial reader. Subsequently, however, the "I" clearly belongs to the autodiegetic narrator, "Jane Eyre," who is, as that reader has just been reminded, a character *in* the novel. This "I" might be imagined as addressing a narrative reader, one for whom "the George Inn at Millcote" is a real location, and Jane a real speaker—but it would make no sense for such a Jane to locate herself or her address within "a new chapter in a novel." On the one hand, Brontë redoubles the imaginary nature of the scene through a simile that compares the novel to a theatrical performance. On the other, she asserts the equally material embodiment of all the parties to this readerly transaction—the author "draw[s] up the curtain," which requires a physical effort; the reader "views" the scene not metaphorically, in her mind's eye, but with the sense of sight, "by the light of an oil-lamp . . . and by that of an excellent fire"; and the character feels "warm[th]" succeeding "numbness and chill," through the sense of touch.

Such coexistence among author, reader, and character ought to register as paradoxical if not impossible, yet this moment is much less disruptive of realist illusion to read than it is to describe. Garrett Stewart describes this potentially paradoxical relationship of "the twin pulls on the subject reader of classic fiction. These are, on the one hand, the draw of a credible world and, on the other, the lure of assured readerly status with respect to that world. . . . Only the mutually compelling appeal . . . could keep in suspension their fields of force " (5). Brontë's scene illustrates the simultaneous appeal of, and appeal to, both these "fields of force"—Jane's "world" is credibly sensuous, but Brontë's direct invocation of a narrative reader reminds the authorial reader of her status *as* reader. Brontë's and Jane's casual acknowledgment that she is a fictional construct seems to increase, rather than to interrupt, an authorial reader's intimacy with both figures. At the same time, it also reinforces that reader's autonomy in relation to Jane; our identification is partly chosen and willed, and thus remains under our control.

In all of these ways, literary identification not only offers readers the "mesmerizing" experience of "subject-constitution" but also draws attention to the limits and complexities of that autonomy. Which of these reading experiences predominates will be different for differently situated readers and even for individual readers at different times. In other words, to speak of a reader "identifying" with a character does not exhaust the possibility for different affects in and effects of this identification. As one of Eve Kosofsky Sedgwick's memorable "axioms" reminds us, "To identify *as* must always include multiple processes of identification *with*. It also involves identifying *as against;* but even did it not, the relations implicit in *identifying with* are, as psychoanalysis suggests, in themselves quite sufficiently fraught with intensities of incorporation, diminishment, inflation, threat, loss, reparation, and disavowal" (*Epistemology* 61). These "multiple processes" and "intensities" may offer different points of entry particularly to readers otherwise marginalized by a text or the cultural construction it represents. (Otherwise, there could have been no *Wide Sargasso Sea.*) In *Disidentifications,* Muñoz draws on Michel Pêcheux's elaboration of Althusser to theorize an aesthetics of "disidentification" within the aesthetic of performance by queers of color:

> [In Pêcheux's schema] the first mode is understood as "identification," where a "Good Subject" chooses the path of identification with discursive and ideological forms. "Bad Subjects" resist and attempt to reject the images and identificatory sites offered by dominant ideology and proceed to rebel, to "counteridentify" and turn against this symbolic system. . . . Disidentification is the third mode of dealing with dominant ideology, one that neither opts to assimilate within such a structure nor strictly opposes it; rather, disidentification is a strategy that works on and against dominant ideology. . . . [T]his 'working on and against' is a strategy that tries to transform a cultural logic from within, always laboring to enact permanent structural change while at

> the same time valuing the importance of local or everyday struggles of resistance. (12)

Muñoz's analysis focuses specifically on twentieth-century (post-Stonewall) visual and performance arts, often in a consciously political or activist context. Announced or explicit performances of such "disidentification" are less frequent in the novels of formation that I analyze, even those written by queer authors and authors of color, but the ways in which such writers use the inherited structure of the novel of formation to represent non-dominant forms of subjectivity can themselves be seen as "working on and against" writerly strategies. The range and variability of responses to, and within, identification suggested by Sedgwick, Pêcheux, and Muñoz will, I hope, be visible in the literary identifications I describe—a range and variability that allow such identifications to function in liberatory or life-enhancing ways as well as (I do not say "rather than") oppressive or conservative ones.

Finally, a representation of fictions of identification as appealing to readers only, or even primarily, on the basis of an *a priori* similarity seems to me incomplete. As described above, identification is not only assimilative but projective, involves not only recognition ("She's like me!") but also aspiration ("I could be like her!") and fear ("I could be like her!"); it requires not just familiarity but also a measure of otherness, a space of difference across which identification can take—or fail in—its synaptic leap. To varying degrees, and in different contexts, identification in all of the novels considered here involves these forms of negotiation and balance. Not only may the reader be invited to identify with characters whose spatial or historical location or subject positions she or he does not share, but also the narratives themselves often represent identification as difficult, partial, or occurring across difference.

Susan Bernstein distinguishes between "promiscuous identification" with a sympathetic protagonist (such as, in her example, Anne Frank), which involves an "unreflective assimilation of the read subject into an untroubled unitary reading self" (146) and "dissonant identification," which "captures the value of affective engagement as a strategy for approaching, for self-consciously apprehending, traumatic knowledge" (158–59). Certainly in the novels I discuss, literary identification is never simply mimetic and is often "dissonant"; it hinges on and points to what Sharon Marcus, also discussing Anne Frank, calls the "difference" that is "identification's ongoing condition" (105). And to the extent that these novels implicitly or explicitly represent their authors' own identifications with previous novels of formation and take those narratives in new directions, they exemplify the ways in which literary identification may produce innovation as often as recursion. Yet here I must register a final caveat. Bernstein's distinction revalues literary identification by disavowing its pleasurable or indulgent aspects, assigning them to the false consciousness of some *other, bad* identifying readers or reading practices and approving in their place a metacritical reading strategy ("self-consciously apprehending"). In other words, her defense of literary identification functions by reviving an attribution of moral efficacy to (particular kinds) of reading. (Even her use of the word "promiscuous" recalls the moralistic Victorian association between affective reading and sexual transgression.) In basing my own defense of literary identification in part on demonstrations of its complexity, productivity, and potential multiplicity, I also do not entirely escape the temptation to represent this practice as valuable by moral association (since our culture generally ascribes value, both aesthetic and ethical, to complexity), but in the chapters that follow, I have tried to avoid suggesting that literary identification necessarily makes readers morally better or politically freer, or that its pleasures and comforts can only be justified by such a claim. My goal is less to justify or to arraign than to account for the continued appeal of a genre and reading practice.

TWO

Coming Together

GEORGE ELIOT, SIMONE DE BEAUVOIR, AND TSITSI DANGAREMBGA

IN THE NARRATIVES discussed in this chapter—two partly autobiographical novels, George Eliot's *The Mill on the Floss* (1859–60) and Tstsi Dangarembga's *Nervous Conditions* (1988), and one volume of autobiography, Simone de Beauvoir's *Memoirs of a Dutiful Daughter* (1959)—relationships of identification within the narrative, among characters, raise ethical questions about the responsibility of the self toward an other that also echo in the relations between the authors and their readers. In the work of these authors, the *negative* eligibility of a fictional character for identification suggested in *Nobody's Story: The Vanishing Acts of Women Writers in the Marketplace,* Catherine Gallagher's analysis of the eighteenth-century novel—the fictional protagonist as a "nobody" with whom, therefore, *anybody* can (potentially) identify—is transformed into something more complex and conflicted. Each of these characters is emphatically a *somebody else,* located in a thickly described context, furnished with a plot that emphasizes causality, understanding, and the challenge of maintaining an ethical relation to another.

Not only does Eliot, for example, do everything she can to give Maggie Tulliver or a Dorothea Brooke the weight of a *somebody else,* but she also makes the difficulty—and the necessity—of identifying with "anybody else's story and shar[ing] anybody else's sentiments" (C. Gallagher, *Nobody's Story* 172) the central conflict of their narratives of formation. The realization, as Eliot famously puts it in *Middlemarch,* that the other has "an equivalent centre of self, whence the lights and shadows must always fall with a certain difference" (*Middlemarch* 173), both beckoning in its equivalence and unreachable in its difference, is central to the formation of the protagonists of each of these narratives. The protagonist of each begins as a dutiful daughter (a "jeune fille rangée," or well-behaved girl, in Beauvoir's French title), in a cultural context in which the daughter's duty is specifically that of the maintenance and continuation of the values of her family, clan, and class. These values must be upheld in the face of both competing internal desires (romantic, financial, or social) and external forces of historical change: the evolution, in early nineteenth-century England, from an agricultural and mercantile to an industrial and capitalist economy; the relative decline, in early twentieth-century France, in the power of the Catholic bourgeoisie; the increasingly cracking fault-lines of colonial rule in 1960s Rhodesia in *Nervous Conditions.* In each case, the protagonist's conflict is routed through an intimate relationship with a counterpart—Maggie's cousin Lucy Deane in *The Mill on the Floss;* Simone's best friend Zaza Mabille in *Memoirs of a Dutiful Daughter,* and Tambudzai's cousin Nyasha Sigauke in *Nervous Conditions*—who represents an alternative trajectory of female formation. This counterpart not only serves as an object of identification in the service of the protagonist's self-construction but also, as their trajectories proceed in parallel and at cross-purposes, comes to embody the challenge of ethical responsibility toward the other. The conflict represented in the relationship between them—between identification as primarily self-affirmation and identification as the anchor of an ethical orientation toward the other—is echoed in the relationship between readers and authors, that is, in the reception of these texts.

As an element of narrative structure, the relationship between the protagonist and her counterpart in these texts signifies in multiple registers. Most simply the pairings represent allegorically divisions that exist within the psyche or situation of the protagonist: in *The Mill on the Floss* and *Memoirs of a Dutiful Daughter,* Lucy and Zaza embody an untroubled relation to femininity that Maggie and Simone can neither fully dismiss nor fully attain; in *Nervous Conditions,* contrarily, Nyasha manifests overtly the rebellion that Tambudzai strives to repress. Maggie, Simone, and Tambudzai are all in more straitened material circumstances than Lucy, Zaza, and Nyasha. In each narrative the relationships between the two women encompass the blend of emulation, rivalry, and desire that constitutes identification in its fullest sense. These relations of identification are always represented from the point of view of the protagonist (which is part of how we recognize her as the protagonist). But the relationship between the two women is not simply that of protagonist and foil, with the counterpart highlighting aspects of the protagonist's formation. Rather, the self-other relationship between the two women bears the ethical weight of the narrative; morally and psychologically, it *is* the story of the protagonist's formation.

Each narrative concludes with the protagonist's acknowledgment of responsibility toward her counterpart based on her identification with the counterpart's struggles: Maggie sacrifices her own love—and ultimately her life—rather than enjoy it at Lucy's expense; Simone dedicates herself to a struggle against the family structure that she holds responsible for her friend's death; Tambudzai asserts herself against Nyasha's father, the family patriarch, to get her troubled cousin the psychiatric help that she requires. The inherent self-referentiality of relations of identification in each case—"the detour through the other that defines the self" (Fuss 6)—is brought into confrontation with the countervailing ethic of altruism, of orientation toward the other. However, the gestures toward the other are not easily undertaken or necessarily successful: Maggie all but destroys Lucy's life before giving Stephen up; Simone cannot save Zaza's; Tambudzai supplants Nyasha in Nyasha's family and cannot arrest her mental disintegration. To the extent that the counterpart's tragic narrative is incorporated into that of the protagonist as a sign or cause of her own development, this incorporation demonstrates the appropriative violence of identification and of a subjectivity built on lost objects.

I have adopted the term "counterpart" (*semblable*), which Jacques Lacan uses to describe the role of the other in a child's identification with his or her siblings, to describe these texts' other women, who as cousins or peers bear a similarly lateral relationship to the protagonists. As Dylan Evans explains,

> The term "counterpart" . . . designates other people in whom the subject perceives a likeness to himself (principally a visual likeness). . . . The emphasis here is on likeness; the child identifies with his siblings on the basis of the recognition of bodily similarity. . . . It is this identification that gives rise to the "imago of the counterpart" (Evans 28)

In the essay by Lacan to which Evans refers, "Les complexes familiaux dans la formation de l'individu," the counterpart is represented particularly as belonging to what Lacan calls the "intrusion complex [*complexe de l'intrusion*]," which "represents the experience that brings into being the primitive subject, most often when he sees one or another of his counterparts participate with him in domestic life, in other words, when he recognizes his siblings. . . . The critical point revealed by these investigations [into sibling rivalry] is that jealousy, at its roots, represents not an active rivalry [*rivalité vitale*] but a mental identification" (Lacan, "Complexes" 35–36; my translation).[1] In "The Mirror Stage," Lacan equates the counterpart with the aspirational vision of his or her own body that the infant beholds in the mirror: "The imago of the counterpart is interchangeable with the image of the subject's own body, the specular image with which the subject identifies in the mirror stage, leading to the formation of the ego" (Lacan, "Mirror Stage," 28). In the narratives I discuss here, the "likeness" between protagonist and counterpart is based on their shared gender; the lateral structure of the sibling relationship is echoed in the relationship of cousin or best friend. But a cousin or a best friend is not quite a sibling, and the distinction both allows for and circumscribes the emergence of erotic attachment. The possibilities and frustrations of the not-quite—oscillations between sameness and difference, distance and desire—mark these relationships. The relationships between Maggie and Lucy, Simone and Zaza, and Tambudzai and Nyasha, all include physical and emotional intensifications that interrupt or pose alternatives to heterosexual pairings, but unlike the novels by Virginia Woolf, Radclyffe Hall, and Jeanette Winterson that I discuss in Chapter Three, none of these narratives consciously foregrounds such alternatives, and none of these protagonists defines herself as lesbian or queer. Further, the plot structure of heterosexual female rivalry remains to some degree in place for all of them, however strongly they resist it.

It is on account, rather than in spite, of this irresolution that these narratives can productively be viewed through the lenses of contemporary queer theory, particularly in its psychoanalytic inflection, which has done so much to make such oscillations visible even—and perhaps especially—when they cannot be stabilized in one libidinal posture (homo- or heterosexual) or one form of cathexis (identification or desire). Judith Butler, for example, asks, "What is to restrict any given individual to a single identification? Identifications are multiple and contestatory, and it may be that we desire most strongly those individuals who reflect in a dense or saturated way the possibilities of multiple and simultaneous substitutions. . . . Insofar as a number of such fantasies can come to constitute and saturate a site of desire, it follows that we are not in the position of *either* identifying with a given sex *or* desiring someone else of that sex; indeed, we are not, more generally, in a position of finding identification and desire to be mutually exclusive phenomena" (*Bodies that Matter* 99). The possibilities of fluctuation that Butler identifies here—of "multiple and contestatory" identifications; of "multiple and simultaneous substitutions" subtending our responses to others; and of the mutual implication of the "phenomena" of identification and desire—are central to the relationships of protagonist and counterpart in the narratives I discuss in this chapter.

In thus bringing to bear a psychoanalytic schema, I do not mean to suggest that any or all of these authors construct their characters primarily as psychoanalytic case studies. But they do, within the norms of their particular historical moments and cultural contexts, emphasize the intricate relationships for their protagonists between demands perceived as internal (emotional, affective) and those perceived as external (familial, religious, institutional). Maggie Tulliver—driving nails into the "Fetish which she punished for all her misfortunes . . . the trunk of a large wooden doll" (Eliot, *MoF* 28); pushing her cousin Lucy into the mud; forming an attachment to Philip Wakem, the son of her father's enemy; gliding down the river with Stephen Guest, "hardly conscious of having said or done anything decisive" (467)—is certainly readable as a pre-eminently Freudian subject *avant la lettre*. Her ego, her rational and socially-directed mind, seems under siege by the barely containable countermovement of unsocial hostilities and desires signified for Freud by the id, and constantly chastened by the socially sanctioned ethical norms that he identifies with the superego. In *The Mill on the Floss,* the intensity of Maggie's psychological conflict comes close to overwhelming its repeatedly asserted ethical signification (e.g., that "faithfulness and constancy mean something else besides doing what is easiest and pleasantest to ourselves" [475]) and her ability to function as a moral sign in a providential plot. In other words, *The Mill on the Floss* takes a long step toward the Freudian shift of emphasis from the *ought* of the deontological individual to the *is* of the psychological subject, and (as a result) from the strains of allegorical and providential character construction that linger within Victorian fictional realism to the Modernist emphasis on affective and subjective elements of character interaction.[2]

GEORGE ELIOT

DARK WOMAN, DUTIFUL DAUGHTER

The beginning of such a shift is evident, for example, in the use Eliot makes of Thomas à Kempis's account of the progress of the Christian soul, *De Imitatione Christi,* for humanist rather than doctrinal moral ends. In her representation the text is not homiletic but a relatively unmediated form of life-writing, "written down by a hand that waited for the heart's prompting . . . the chronicle of a solitary, hidden anguish, struggle, trust and triumph . . . a lasting record of human needs and human consolations" (Eliot, *MoF* 291). As Eliot displaces moral conflict from an arena of doctrinal or theological to one of psychological struggle, Freud will relocate it still more deeply within human consciousness. In Freud's schema of consciousness, it is the superego—an authority that "retains the character of the father" and is later reinforced by "the influence of authority, religious teaching, school, and reading" (*Ego and the Id* 30)—that takes on the function attributed by Eliot to Thomas à Kempis's Christian humanism (which itself is in contradiction with Maggie's parental authorities—her father's desire for vengeance, her mother's reverence for social convention). Each re-interpretation significantly lessens the deontological impact of such authority. It is precisely the resistance to "[patriarchal] authority, religious teaching, school, and reading" that becomes a source of struggle in the two twentieth-century texts, *Memoirs of a Dutiful Daughter* and *Nervous Conditions,* that, as I argue, share a narrative pattern and set of ethical concerns with Eliot's. In *Memoirs of a Dutiful Daughter,* Simone, enjoying the privileges of her family's bourgeois status, both identifies with her book-loving father and then, as she sees the stultification and breakdown of Zaza, comes to resist the family system of which he remains the head. In *Nervous Conditions,* a number of characters, including Tambudzai, her mother, Mai, and Nyasha, at different times experience psychological breakdowns. It is Nyasha who most clearly evinces colonial subjectivity as a "nervous condition," but Tambudzai's narrative also emphasizes the social and material oppression underlying the novel's psychological disorders. Beauvoir cites Eliot and *The Mill on the Floss,* along with other French, English, and American works, as formative; while Dangarembga does not allude to Beauvoir or Eliot specifically, her protagonist is represented as reading classic English literature, and the novel's title and epigraph, adapted from Jean-Paul Sartre's introduction to Franz Fanon's polemic *The Wretched of the Earth* (1961), link her to the intellectual heritage of Sartre and Beauvoir. With all their differences, then, these three narratives of female formation share an organizing structure that magnifies both oscillations of identification and desire within each character, and the binarization of the female role (dutiful/rebellious daughter) within each social context, by recasting and repeating them between protagonist and counterpart.

In *The Mill on the Floss,* Maggie, as a narrative reader, models for the authorial reader the pitfalls of literary identification and the difficulty of moving through identification to sympathy and change, whether in fictional, personal, or social narratives. In a scene of reading at the center of the novel, Maggie refuses to finish another novel, Madame de Staël's novel *Corinne* (1807), loaned to her by her would-be suitor, Philip Wakem:

> As soon as I came to the blond-haired young lady reading in the park, I shut it up and determined to read no further. I foresaw that that light complexioned girl would win away all the love from Corinne and make her miserable. I'm determined to read no more books where the blond haired women carry away all the happiness. . . . If you could give me some story, now, where the dark woman triumphs, it would restore the balance. I want to avenge Rebecca and Flora MacIvor, and Minna and all the rest of the dark unhappy ones. (Eliot, *MoF* 332)

In the passage in *Corinne* to which Maggie refers, we learn that the narrative reader within Staël's text—Corinne's half sister Lucile—is "very engrossed in her reading" (*Corinne* 317) but not what the book is, and Lucile lays it aside when she meets Oswald, whom she will marry. The figure of the narrative reader here does not oppose but opens into the trajectory of the heterosexual romance plot.[3] Within this fictional plot, to which Maggie objects but which she also, as she puts the book down, repeats, the reward for female conformity is the attainment not only of the subjective state of "love" but also, more important, its public coordinate in marriage; the punishment for female eccentricity or rebellion, on the other hand, is a loss of love and social death (exile, ostracism) or actual death.

Maggie recognizes in *Corinne* a fictional counterpart; her anxious disavowal of Staël's plot reminds us that these outcomes were already axiomatic to nineteenth-century novel readers, even those whose circumstances, like Maggie's, limited their access to books. Indeed, Maggie correctly imagines *Corinne*'s outcome: The eponymous dark-haired protagonist, who has achieved fame as a poet and orator, loses her lover, Oswald Nelvil, to her more domesticated, conventional half-sister Lucile and dies of grief. Despite warning echoes, however—of her cousin Lucy's name in that of Staël's character Lucile; of the relation of half-sister in that of cousin; of the book eternally unfinished in Staël's novel and in Maggie's hands—Maggie is less astute about her own implication in social and fictional norms. When Philip imputes to her a desire to "avenge the dark women in [her] own person" she backs away from her original identification with Corinne—"'Philip, that is not pretty of you, to apply my nonsense to anything real'" (Eliot, *MoF* 333)—and shifts questions of identification from sororal likeness *to* other "dark women" to more general sympathy *for* them: "I thought you wanted to remind me that I am vain, and wish every one to admire me most. But it isn't for that, that I'm jealous for the dark women—not because I'm dark myself. It's because I always care the most about the unhappy people; if the blond girl was forsaken, I should like *her* best" (333). Maggie acknowledges her desire for attention (which she shares with Corinne, the poet and performer) only to disown it; she disclaims a primary, narcissistic identification (caring about Corinne because she is "dark [her]self") in favor of what sounds like an other-directed sympathy ("car[ing] most about the unhappy people"). Although this shift aligns Maggie with Eliot's explicitly favored ethical modes, of renunciation and sympathy, it proves difficult for her to sustain, partly because Maggie herself is one of the "unhappy people." The remainder of the novel's plot is driven by Maggie's increasingly frantic oscillation between other- and self-directed impulses, between renunciation of pleasure and a desire to be happily beloved. This ambivalence ends only as the two impulses are united in death; sacrificing herself to rescue her brother Tom, Maggie earns again the long-withheld regard of her earliest beloved object.[4]

As Staël's Lucile is Corinne's counterpart, so Lucy, in *The Mill on the Floss,* is Maggie's. Although Lucy is a secondary character, from the beginning of the novel, the reader is invited to view the two girls as a study in contrast. The narrative contrast is often overtly presented, through other characters' points of view, in terms of their appearance or behavior. The narrator, however, also alerts the reader (though not the other characters) to the emotional and psychological implications of Maggie's relation to Lucy. Eliot's "authorial reader," in Rabinowitz's terms—one who accepts "the author's invitation to read in a particular socially constituted way that is shared by the author and his or her expected readers" (Rabinowitz 22)—must share with Maggie what the elders of the Dodson clan largely do not: a sense of the self as structured by conflicting and ambivalent motivations. (Eliot takes pains to establish the literal-mindedness and obtuseness of the Dodsons. For example, she observes, of Mrs. Tulliver's failed attempt to dissuade lawyer Wakem from purchasing Dorlcote Mill, that "fly-fishers fail in preparing their bait so as to make it alluring in the right quarter, for want of a due acquaintance with the subjectivity of fishes" [Eliot, *MoF* 254]). For the authorial reader that Eliot could hypothesize based on her contemporaries, the vocabulary for representing that conflicted interiority would have been essentially ethical or theological; for the reader of our own day, it may additionally or instead be, as mine is here, psychoanalytic. Whatever the vocabulary, however, the authorial reader then or now responds to a call to distinguish between surface and depth and to understand that the "subjectivity" of the other will always be both difficult and necessary to imagine.

Contemporary readers may, for example, see in the oscillations of Maggie's relation to Lucy ambivalent shifts between identification and desire and between sympathy and rivalry.[5] These oscillations appear within a single paragraph in the narrative introduction of Lucy:

> Certainly the contrast between the cousins was conspicuous and to superficial eyes was very much to the disadvantage of Maggie, though a connoisseur might have seen "points" in her which had a higher promise for maturity than Lucy's natty completeness: it was like the contrast between a rough, dark, overgrown puppy and a white kitten. . . . [Lucy] looked up with shy pleasure at Maggie, taller by the head, though scarcely a year older. Maggie always looked at Lucy with delight. She was fond of fancying a world where the people never got any larger than children of their own age, and she made a queen of it just like Lucy. . . . only the queen was Maggie herself in Lucy's form. (Eliot, *MoF* 61)

The emphasis on vision here recalls the spectatorial emphasis of Lacan's description of the counterpart (which itself recalls the visual emphasis of Freud's formulation of the discovery of sexual difference). But the look here, and its conclusion in favor of Lucy's femininity, are located within "*superficial* eyes" (my emphasis). The clear caddishness of the position of a "connoisseur" evaluating the girls' "points" as if they were horseflesh simultaneously raises the possibility of and warns the reader away from such a schematic and superficial reading. As Tess Cosslett points out, Mrs. Tulliver is also prone to this way of contrasting the two girls—"Our first introduction to Lucy is through Mrs. Tulliver's perception of her as the ideal daughter, the image against which Maggie is measured and found wanting" (24). The fact that a comically imperceptive character such as Mrs. Tulliver continually recurs to this external contrast ("I'm sure [Lucy's] more like *my* child than sister Deane's, for she'd allays a very poor colour for one of our family, sister Deane had" [Eliot, *MoF* 43]) should alert us to its inapplicability. As the passage's free indirect discourse moves from both of these dismissed spectatorial points of view into Lucy's ("shy pleasure") and then Maggie's ("delight"), the emphasis turns from contrast to mutual admiration, and finally, finishing in Maggie's consciousness, to a possessive identification ("the queen was Maggie herself in Lucy's form") that is, however, also a form of rivalry: There can, after all, be only one monarch. Subsequently, a competition for Tom's attention (anticipating later competition for Stephen Guest's attention) tips the balance back toward heterosexual rivalry. "I wish Lucy was *my* sister," Tom tells Maggie (86), who avenges the insult by pushing "poor little pink-and-white Lucy" into the mud with a "fierce thrust of her small brown arm" (101). "Anger and jealousy can no more bear to lose sight of their objects than love," Eliot observes (sounding rather Freudian), "and that Tom and Lucy should do or see anything of which she was ignorant would have been an intolerable idea to Maggie" (100).[6] Turning the initially "pink-and-white" Lucy even darker than Maggie's own frequently remarked-on "brown" self, Maggie moves from projecting herself into Lucy's exalted position to debasing Lucy to her own degraded one. Tom punishes her with "two smart slaps" on the offending arm. Maggie's aggression toward Lucy here and Tom's response to it prefigure her later treatment of Lucy (in running away with Stephen) and the dragging of her own reputation through the mud. The apparently passing references to Maggie's arm—aggressive, "brown," subject to Tom's punitive attention—recur more forcefully later in the figuration of the erotic attraction of Maggie and Stephen largely through a focus on their arms.[7]

From its beginning, then, the relationship between Maggie and Lucy is one in which imitation and attraction, mirroring and opposition, are thoroughly entwined. When the two are brought together again as young women, after Maggie has been earning her living teaching and Lucy occupying herself as a dutiful and cherished daughter at home (with Maggie's now-widowed mother as her housekeeper), all but engaged to Stephen Guest, the same oscillations reappear. Maggie and Lucy admire each other's contrasting qualities: Maggie finds Lucy a "dear tiny thing" and appreciates her enjoyment of "other people's happiness" (Eliot, *MoF* 373), while Lucy reciprocally is drawn to Maggie's passionate enjoyment of music, so that on one listening occasion she "could not resist the impulse to steal up to her and kiss her" (417). Lucy is described by the narrator as "loving and thoughtful for other women, not giving them Judas-kisses with eyes askance on their welcome defects, but with real care and vision for their half-hidden pains and mortifications, with long ruminating enjoyment of little pleasures prepared for them" (370); while Maggie muses, "I don't enjoy [other people's] happiness as much as you do—else I should be more contented. I do feel for them when they are in trouble; I don't think I could ever bear to make any one *un*happy; and yet I often hate myself, because I get angry sometimes at the sight of happy people" (373). While Maggie's self-assessment is accurate—she does indeed both resent Lucy's happiness and suffer in causing her sorrow—the narrative attribution to Lucy of "care and vision" seems ironic, since the pleasure that she supplies for Maggie, in the person of Stephen, is one that Lucy never anticipated and cannot enjoy. (Lucy's obliviousness to the state of feeling between Maggie and Stephen, though apparently testifying to her naïve goodwill, might less generously be viewed as manifesting the privileged ignorance of the powerful; much as Lucy admires her cousin, it never occurs to her that Maggie could be a rival.) Maggie's abortive, semi-voluntary flight with Stephen down the river Floss repeats more dramatically her childhood attack on Lucy, though it reverses, and transforms into metaphor, the sullying effects of that scene. The attraction between Maggie and Stephen and her subsequent renunciation of him in favor of Lucy's claims provide her with the opportunity first to "avenge the dark women" by knocking Lucy from the ranks of "happy people" and then, once Lucy has been "forsaken," to demonstrate her sympathy with the unhappy ones. After Lucy recovers from the illness caused by this betrayal, she visits Maggie secretly; the two women cry in each other's arms and part with "a last embrace" (511)—Maggie's last embrace with anyone before her death in Tom's arms. As in the childhood scene, Maggie reduces the distance and difference between herself and Lucy, first by usurping her position as Stephen's queen, and then by sharing in Lucy's misery in his loss.

These oscillations complicate the completion of the heterosexual romance plot. Consummation of most of the romantic couplings that have surfaced throughout the narrative (between Maggie and Stephen, Maggie and Philip, and implicitly Lucy and Tom, who has loved her silently) is made impossible by the deaths of Maggie and Tom. True, the novel does conclude with a vision of a heterosexual couple, presumably a reunited Stephen and Lucy: "One [man] visited the tomb [of Maggie and Tom] again with a sweet face beside him—but that was years after" (Eliot, *MoF* 522). But the periphrastic, and therefore vague, phrasing of this vision, along with the ineradicable taint of infidelity on Stephen's part, suggest a narratorial reluctance to cede the novel's conclusion to a conventional, exogamous heterosexuality; instead the novel's two concluding couples are implicitly incestuous (Tom and Maggie) and shopsoiled (Stephen and Lucy).[8]

Further, the scenes of mutual admiration and passionate reunion between Lucy and Maggie in Book Six adumbrate possibilities of a same-sex desire counter or alternative to the energies of the heterosexual couple. Such representations of emotional intimacy between women in Victorian novels, as Sharon Marcus has argued, are not *prima facie* evidence of the undermining of heterosexual convention, because female friendships in these novels are not only compatible with but also productive of marriage bonds: "In the plot of female amity, love between [female] friends develops the emotional disposition necessary for companionate marriage" (87). In suggesting that Maggie Tulliver is an exception that proves this rule, Marcus says that the novel emphasizes "contrasts and rivalry" between Maggie and Lucy and that Maggie in fact "lacks female allies" (80). But as my reading has suggested, the novel also emphasizes identification and desire between the two women, whose final meeting is one of mutual comfort and forgiveness. "When I come back, and am strong, they will let me do as I like. I shall come to you when I please then," Lucy tells Maggie (Eliot, *MoF* 510). Cosslett, in a discussion of female friendship that anticipates aspects of Marcus's argument, considers *The Mill on the Floss* an example of, rather than an exception to, the centrality of women's relationships to heterosexual closing unions. As she points out, Lucy's visit of reconciliation to Maggie "sets a seal of approval on Maggie's action in leaving Stephen—it *does* restore Lucy to her, and win Lucy's admiration. . . . As in *Middlemarch* and *Aurora Leigh,* a scene in which two women affirm their friendship, and one gives up a man to the other, is necessary before the final male-female coming together. Instead of the man choosing between the two female 'rivals,' it is the women who arrange between themselves who is to have him" (Cosslett 36–37). In the absence of Stephen himself, this act of "arrang[ing]" also seems to cement the bond between the two women. Since Eve Kosofsky Sedgwick's identification of the "between men" narrative triangle, in which women function as often expendable conduits for an array of male homosocial relations, critics (beginning with Sedgwick herself) have agreed that no simple gender reversal for this structure is possible, because "in any male-dominated society, there is a special relationship between male homosocial (*including* homosexual) desire and the structures for maintaining and transmitting patriarchal power: a relationship founded on an inherent and potentially active structural congruence" (Sedgwick, *Between Men* 25). Nevertheless, over the outcome of the Maggie/ Stephen/Lucy triangle hovers the faintest ghost of a different conclusion, in which the disappearance of the unworthy male suitor (Stephen departs for Holland in the aftermath of the boat-trip) enables a newly strengthened ethical and emotional bond between two women. (This ghost also hovers over the rapprochement between Esther and Mrs. Transome in *Felix Holt,* and takes on substance in Romola's rescue of Tessa in *Romola.*)[9]

But the novel's resistance to the triumph of the heterosexual couple and of female rivalry is truncated. If Maggie escapes the conventional outcome of heterosexual coupling, she does so by fatally recommitting herself to her family of origin, both immediate (Tom) and extended (Lucy). Maggie's flight with Stephen Guest, who can offer her "love, wealth, ease, refinement, all that her nature craved" (Eliot, *MoF* 458), expresses her desire not only for attention and admiration but also for the escape from a closed society offered by exogamous marriage. In the end, however, she turns away from the deracination expressed not only by Stephen's last name but also by his association with cosmopolitan mercantilism (when we first meet him, he is wearing "attar of roses," an imported product) and back toward the autochthonous, literally stifling embrace of her family, as represented by the passionate "clasp" in which she and Tom drown. At the same time, because one woman's death secures the other's marriage, the structure of a plot of female formation based on division rather than identification remains in place. (Later in Eliot's career, the conclusion of *Romola* dispatches not one but two male objects of desire [Tito Melema and Savanarola] to death, and brings Tessa, Romola, and Tessa's children together as a kind of counter-family. But Tessa's helplessness and dependence on Romola, exacerbating the class difference between them, positions her more as a third child herself than as a possible object of desire or romantic attachment for Romola.)

Maggie's end suggests a cautionary conclusion about reading and identification. The reader of Maggie's narrative, Eliot suggests, should think twice if she is tempted to feel that she may do better than Maggie in altering the conventional outcome of gendered social narratives. After all, to disavow a similarity to Maggie is, paradoxically, to identify with her by repeating the error that Maggie makes about *Corinne.* The moral of this *mise-en-abîme* seems to be that authorial readers equate reality with narrative freedom at our peril. We are not entitled to assume, because the realist novel gives fictitious form to social conventions, that social conventions are therefore fictitious, in the sense that we may alter their plotting at will. Indeed, as I have just suggested, Eliot herself, like Maggie, remains unable entirely to escape the overwhelming binary logic of a construction of femininity in which the attainment of conventional womanhood—here, as in *Corinne,* the achievement of heterosexual love and marriage—

demands the sacrifice of alternative modes of desire and achievement. She consistently returns to the female protagonist/counterpart structure in her novels, varying outcomes but always conforming to an either/or logic that pivots around one character's renunciation. The protagonist is ultimately identified with the roles of *both* the dutiful daughter (the one who devotes herself to familial and endogamous claims) *and* the passionate nonconformist. Her capacity for passion is transformed over the course of the narrative into a passion for duty; and by the novel's end, the counterpart becomes narratively marginalized as a repository for disavowed desires less easily assimilated to the ethical scheme (e.g. for social advancement or sexual conquest). As the conclusion of *The Mill on the Floss* demonstrates, for a fictional character, diegetic survival isn't everything: Lucy lives within the novel, but Maggie lives beyond it, an object of identification for future readers who also serves as a warning of the dangers of identifying with fictional lives.

This ending has, however, been notoriously unsatisfying to readers and critics from Eliot's time to our own. Eliot's contemporaries—particularly male reviewers—were troubled by Maggie's attraction to Stephen Guest. "The hideous transformation," fulminates Algernon Charles Swinburne, "by which Maggie is debased—were it but for an hour—into the willing or yielding companion of Swinburne's flight would probably and deservedly have been resented as a brutal and vulgar outrage on the part of a male novelist. . . . But the man never lived, I do believe, who could have done such a thing as this" (Carroll 165). Leslie Stephen, in his volume on Eliot for the "English Men of Letters" series, suggests the potential intimacy of the reader's bond with both Eliot and her protagonist: "The novelist speaks for us because he speaks for himself" (88); and "if the test of a heroine's merits be the reader's disposition to fall in love with her (and that, I confess, is my own), I hold that Maggie is worth a wilderness of Dinah [Morrises]" (89). But this very bond gives Maggie's subsequent behavior the flavor of a personal betrayal: "We might even have forgiven [Maggie] if, after being a little overpowered by the dandified Stephen, she had shown some power of perceiving what a very poor animal he was. The affair jars upon us, because it is not a development of her previous aspirations, but suddenly throws a fresh and unpleasant light on her character" (103). Swinburne's and Stephen's reactions evidence the intermingling of impulses to "be" and to "have," the possibilities of ownership and loss, that mark identification.

For many twentieth-century readers, the problem with the end of *The Mill on the Floss,* and with the outcomes for many of Eliot's female protagonists, is different one. Eliot's repeated representation of specifically female experience and betrayal made her an important writer for second-wave feminist criticism beginning in the 1970s. But the distance between the success that Eliot found in unconventional paths of love and work, and the sufferings she visited on protagonists such as Maggie who sought the same, seem to obstruct routes to identification with author or protagonist and undermine the social critique that a feminist reader might hope to find in the protagonist's life story. In Kate Millett's resonant phrase, "'Living in sin,' George Eliot lived the revolution as well, perhaps, but she did not write of it" (192). The ambivalence of Eliot's relationship with Victorian feminism has been well canvassed, but what interests me more here is her concomitant ambivalence about her own position as a public object of emulation.[10] Her reticence suggests that part of what she fears about political pronouncements is the way they might fix her as a member of a class rather than an exceptional individual. "The peculiarities of my own lot have caused me to have idiosyncrasies rather than an average judgment" (Eliot, *Letters* 4: 364) she insists in a letter on the topic of female suffrage, and it is a claim that she makes, in different words, many times in the letters.

She finds more inviting direct correspondence with many of her most admiring readers, female and male, such as the young Scotsman Alexander Main. In Rosemarie Bodenheimer's account: "After Alexander Main entered into correspondence with her, Marian wrote to him that he was 'a friend of the only sort I now desire much to acquire: one who takes into his own life the spiritual outcome of mine' (5:229). Such a definition of friendship—as a kind of extraphysical fertilization of the younger by the elder—makes it clear that what she valued most was the private absorption of her narrative voice" (241). In Main, Eliot could see her "spiritual" legacy reproduced, in all its individual "idionsycracies," by a kind of introjection. At the same time, Eliot gave her blessing to Main's plan to produce of a compilation of quotations from her work, *The Wise, Witty, and Tender Sayings of George Eliot* (1872)—a much more public projection of that legacy, circulating precisely the voice of "pronouncement" that Eliot elsewhere eschews. Contemplating the dubious literary merits of this project, Bodenheimer concludes, "The key to the episode remains ambiguous: Marian's desire to cultivate reverence in the 'affectionate labours' of the young is supported by her unacknowledged yearning to be heard as the preacher lurking within the artist" (247). Bodenheimer's terms, "The artist" and "the preacher," both, of course, refer to public identities, but "the artist" in this sense names the author in her apparently more intimate, reciprocal relationship with a reader, while "the preacher" invokes a more impressively large but less directly reachable audience. For Eliot, as for many of the writers in this study, a balance between reciprocity and control, between inviting readers' intimacy and becoming subject to readers' projections and expectations, remains an elusive goal.

SIMONE DE BEAUVOIR

MY FREEDOM, HER DEATH

The Mill on the Floss is often called Eliot's most autobiographical novel; some of her own childhood circumstances and early intellectual development are clearly visible within the narrative of Maggie's formation.[11] Eliot was dubious about nonfiction life narrative—biography and autobiography—and even in her fiction eschewed the autodiegetic voice developed so powerfully by Brontë and Dickens. To say, as Eliot does in "The Natural History of German Life," that "art" is "nearest" to life is also to acknowledge that the two are not identical. As Janice Carlisle points out, in this definition Eliot "avoids the more radical claims that her fiction would like to suggest: that art is experience, that aesthetic apprehension is coterminous with life" (*Audience* 23). It is, Carlisle argues, the gap between the ideal and the actual relation between life and art that generates, for mid-Victorian novelists including Eliot, what she calls the "analogical" bonds among readers, authors, and characters to create a "linked chain of morally forceful relations" (25), and bring about the moral transformations that justify the practice of realist fiction. Eliot's purpose as an author is not to solicit a reader's direct identification with her own experience, which in any case she understood as exceptional, but to create narratives that enable the reader to move through identification into a relation to an other recognized *as* an other.

As Eliot was an iconic English Victorian female intellectual, also read and admired on the Continent and in the United States, so Simone de Beauvoir was, in Toril Moi's words, "the emblematic [European] intellectual woman of the twentieth century" (1). Like Eliot, Beauvoir was a successful novelist—her second novel, *The Mandarins* (1954), won the Prix Goncourt. Unlike Eliot, however, she regarded fiction as but one mode of representing experience and "life," and it was her memoirs, as well as her persona as a public intellectual, that captured the imagination of several generations of English, American, and European readers in the mid-twentieth century. Describing the gestation of *The Mandarins,* itself a highly autobiographical novel, Beauvoir suggests that "one of the essential purposes of literature" is to capture the multifariousness of lived experience:

> to make manifest the equivocal, separate, contradictory truths that no one moment represents in their totality, either inside or outside myself; in certain cases one can only succeed in grouping them all together by inscribing them within the unity of an imaginary object. Only a novel, it seemed to me, could reveal the multiple and intricately spun meanings of that changed world to which I awoke in August 1944. . . . We were intellectuals, a race apart with whom novelists are advised to have nothing to do. . . . [But] after all, we were human beings, just a little more concerned than most people with giving our lives an integument of words. . . . I felt situated at a point in space and time at which each of the sounds that I could draw from myself had a chance to awaken echoes in a great many other hearts. (*Force of Circumstance* [hereafter *FC*] 263)

The goals of Eliot's and Beauvoir's fictional realism clearly belong to the same tradition; Beauvoir, like Eliot, aims for a form of "amplifying experience . . . and extending our contact with our fellow-men," an ethical act aimed at inspiring ethical action in others. But their moral orientations—Eliot's deontological humanism, which stresses the suppression of the self in relation to the claims of the other, and Beauvoir's Existentialism, which emphasizes the autonomy of the self as the basis for the relation to the other—differ in their evaluations of the self–other relationship and, as a result, in how they represent this relationship through textual relations of identification.

As Ursula Tidd writes, "The ethical parameters of the Self–Other relation were a source of philosophical concern to Simone de Beauvoir from the beginning of her career. All of her literary and philosophical writing can be described as marked by a concern to map an ethical relation with the Other" (163). For Beauvoir, however, the existence of the self is always the starting point for the relation to the other, and as a result, in her writing, she is always the fundamental subject of representation: "Whether it is a question of a novel, an autobiography, an essay, an historical work or no matter what, the writer attempts to set up communication with others by the uniqueness of his personal experience" (*All Said and Done* [hereafter *ASD*] 115). Autobiography, a more unmediated form of representation because it need not provide the "unity of the imaginary object" of fiction, becomes her preferred mode of communication.[12] "[My autobiography]," she asserts in a typical pronouncement, "is not a work of art, but my life with its enthusiasms and disappointments, its convulsions, my life attempting to express itself and not to serve as a pretext for elegance" (*FC* 1: vi–vii). At the same time, however, she acknowledges the structural fictiveness of all self-representation that many theorists of life-writing have noted. Indeed, her readers' failure to recognize the gap between life and life-writing often irritates her—an irritation that, characteristically, she records, noting for example that readers of *Force of Circumstance* "did not fully realize the distance that lies between the flesh-and-blood writer and the character he brings into existence by the act of writing—a character endowed with a fictitious constitution" (*ASD* 115). In Beauvoir's writings, events seem less to occur then to *re*cur: represented and rerepresented in fiction and in memoir, their initial representation and their reception becoming the retrospective subjects of further representation—a *mise-en-abîme* more dizzying than Maggie's. But Beauvoir and Eliot both assume that the ideal approached, however unevenly, by different forms of representation is the author's communication of lived experience that both possesses "uniqueness" and may "awaken echoes3 in . . . other hearts"; that both resists mere imitation and offers opportunities for the potentially transformative experience of identification.

That tension between the unique and the common is, as Catherine Gallagher points out, "coiled at the heart of the novel genre," since "the founding claim of the form . . . was the insistence that the referent of the text was a generalization about, and not an extra-textual, embodied instance of, a 'species'" ("George Eliot" 61). Certainly *Memoirs of a Dutiful Daughter,* unlike *The Mill on the Floss,* seems to offer precisely an "extra-textual, embodied instance," as suggested in the name shared by author, narrator, and protagonist: Beauvoir's memoir undertakes to narrate not the plots of fictional characters but the lives of real persons. But if autobiography may resemble fiction in creating characters "endowed with a fictitious constitution," this resemblance is particularly pronounced, according to Beauvoir, in *Memoirs of a Dutiful Daughter:*

> All through my childhood and my young days, my life had a distinct meaning: its goal and its motive was to reach the adult age. . . . For my people and for me, my duty as a child and an adolescent consisted of forming the woman I was to be tomorrow. (That is why *Memoirs of a Dutiful Daughter* has a fiction-like unity lacking in the later volumes. As it does in novels dealing with apprenticeship to life [*les romans d'apprentissage*], in that book time runs straight on from beginning to end.) (*ASD* 14)

In this account, her life story has the "fiction-like unity" of a novel of formation not because Beauvoir has retrospectively "endowed" it with that unity but because autobiographical fidelity demands that the memoir be novelistic, since the young Simone conceives of her life in novelistic terms. The fictional conception, in other words, precedes the non-fiction representation of the memoir. This intermingling is emphasized by those parts of *Memoirs of a Dutiful Daughter* that take the form of a reader's memoir.

Thus, one model of "fiction-like unity" for Beauvoir is *The Mill on the Floss,* the reading of which is represented as a central moment in Simone's youthful intellectual formation.[13] Maggie Tulliver as an adolescent identifies with the protagonist of *Corinne;* so Simone, though with greater confidence in herself, identifies with Maggie Tulliver:

> George Eliot's *The Mill on the Floss* made an even deeper impression upon me than *Little Women.* I read it in English, at Meyrignac, lying on the mossy floor of a chestnut plantation. Maggie Tulliver, like myself, was torn between others and herself: I recognized myself in her. She too was dark, loved nature, and books and life, was too headstrong to be able to observe the conventions of her respectable surroundings. . . . The others condemned her because she was superior to them; I resembled her. . . . [But] I couldn't see myself dying of solitude. Through [Maggie], I identified myself with the author: one day other adolescents would bathe with their tears a novel in which I would tell my own sad story. (*Memoirs of a Dutiful Daughter* [hereafter *MDD*] 140)

As Christina Angelfors observes, "Il semblerait donc que la fiction offre à la jeune Simone de Beauvoir de meilleurs modèles d'identification que la réalité. De là à transformer la réalité en fiction et elle-même en un personnage de cette fiction, il n'y a qu'un pas" ("It would thus seem that fiction offers the young Simone de Beauvoir better models of identification than reality. From there to transforming reality into fiction and herself into a character in this fiction is but a step"; 68). In *Memoirs of a Dutiful Daughter,* Beauvoir aims to reformulate, not reject, the conventions and the outcome of the novel of female formation with which Maggie identifies in *Mill on the Floss.* To a point, she is successful. Rebellious Simone, unlike Maggie, avenges the "dark women": she reads what she wants to read, negotiates the plot of heterosexual romance without losing her intellectual or sexual freedom, and survives to write her own story. In this sense a generic distinction between novel and memoir re-emerges as important: The detailed account that Beauvoir provides in *Memoirs of a Dutiful Daughter* of her youthful intellectual development casts that development, retrospectively, as the root of her historical status as a celebrated intellectual woman; her attainment of that status is simultaneously the narrative's *raison d'être* and the story it tells. The memoir asserts, by its existence as well as in the events it narrates, a potentially redemptive distinction between literature and life, or convention and action. By producing hundreds of pages on the subject of her own intellectual development and transgressive life choices, Beauvoir makes her autobiographical rejection and revision of feminine plots explicitly available to a variety of readers in a way that Eliot does not. By making her own experience simultaneously the subject and object of representation, Beauvoir aims in the act of producing autobiographical writing to correct and transcend not only Maggie's plot but also Eliot's pessimism about altering it.[14]

If the turn from fiction to autobiography cannot guarantee a move from representation to truth, however, so too—as Eliot warns at the end of *The Mill on the Floss*—it cannot guarantee a transformation from oppression to liberty. Cultures like genres have discourses, including discourses of gender, that constrain individual will and action. Like *The Mill on the Floss, Memoirs of a Dutiful Daughter* intertwines the narrative of the survival of one woman with that of the death of another—in this case, Simone's best friend, Zaza Mabille.[15] To the extent that Simone's relationship to Zaza is in part a rewriting of the Maggie/Lucy plot in *The Mill on the Floss,* Beauvoir's narrative does not escape the gender conventions of that plot. Beauvoir's relationship with Sartre will, as she insistently represents it, attempt to recast the conventional heterosexual plot, but this volume ends with their relationship barely begun. The conclusion of *Memoirs of a Dutiful Daughter* instead highlights Zaza's death and Simone's guilt over it. Simone as protagonist evades the murderous intention of revenge that haunts Maggie, but her narrative does not evade its outcome, expressive at once of a homicidal rage (inasmuch as the "other" woman is destroyed) and a suicidal desperation (inasmuch as Beauvoir represents this "other" woman as an avatar of the self). *Memoirs of a Dutiful Daughter* certainly pushes much further than *The Mill on the Floss* in its representation of female homosocial and homoerotic relationships, and thus in its challenge to the heterosexual plot; but that challenge comes at a cost that haunts both the protagonist of *Memoirs of a Dutiful Daughter* and Beauvoir as a writer.[16]

Simone's childhood reading of *The Mill on the Floss* escapes an otherwise stringent parental supervision: "Sometimes, before giving me a book to read, my mother would pin a few pages together; in [H. G.] Wells's *The War of the* Worlds I found a whole chapter placed under the ban" (*MDD* 83). After Simone reads *Silas Marner* at school, however, her mother buys her a copy of *Adam Bede,* unaware of its plot of unwed motherhood and infanticide. Simone conceals Eliot's unsuitability, reading *The Mill on the Floss* in English, in the summer, alone in the woods, when she has begun to lose her religious faith. What Simone reads is a description of a social order different from hers, belonging to another country, century, and class of people, yet recognizable enough to allow her identification with Maggie's own struggles as a dutiful daughter. Etienne Balibar and Pierre Macherey, applying Althusser's theory of the social reproduction of ideology specifically to literary production, emphasize that it is the location of literature within national linguistic and educational practices that enables it to reproduce the dominant bourgeois ideology (96–97). Simone's mother's attempted censorship extends such practices into the home, but Simone's reading of *The Mill on the Floss,* taking place outside of the schoolroom, the family home, and the national tongue, places her identification with Maggie in a context of transgression—just as Maggie's reading of the borrowed *Corinne* (also, for Maggie, a foreign text, though a translated one) represents a transgression against the familial strictures embodied in her brother, who has forbidden her to meet Philip Wakem. As Beauvoir observes, such transgressions are limited: "As for the rest, my freedom consisted of accepting the lot laid down for me, and of accepting it cheerfully, even zealously. My piety had ardour in it; and straight away I became the best pupil at the Cours Désir. . . . I was passionately devoted to books. I loved my father and my father loved books: he had filled my mother with a religious respect for them. They satisfied my curiosity—a curiosity that was active in me as far back as I can remember and that has never faded" (*MDD* 7). Beauvoir writes elsewhere of her adolescent reading that it was "the key that opened the world to me. It foretold my future: I identified myself with the heroines of novels, and through them I caught glimpses of what my life would be" (*ASD* 138). In identifying with Maggie she is interpellated as a particular kind of female subject—the "dark" or rebellious woman. The literary characteristics of that figure, though certainly not transcultural or transhistorical, are constant enough from Victorian, Protestant, petty bourgeois, provincial England to 1920s Catholic, bourgeois, provincial France to make Maggie recognizable to Simone—just as Corinne, incarnating the values of yet another culture, time, and place, is recognizable to Maggie.[17]

As is the case for Maggie, Simone's parents' reduced circumstances, and the attendant loss of a promising dowry, necessitate her planning for work rather than marriage (see *ASD* 12). The young Simone, however, has more opportunities than Maggie (including the opportunity of a university education) and is both a more naïve and a more aggressive reader than Maggie. If she disavows her likeness to Maggie less sharply than Maggie does hers to Corinne, that is partly because she does not hesitate to engage in some enthusiastic misreading. First, Simone, already losing her religious faith, ignores the growing Evangelical fervor that causes Maggie (as it had caused Eliot in her own youth) to reject novels entirely because they might "make [her] long to see and know many things" (Eliot, *MoF* 402). Simone consistently understands Maggie as less ambivalent in her resistance than Maggie conceives herself to be. This (mis)interpretation allows Simone to continue to identify with Maggie even when their values are not shared. It also means that that identification is already being routed, covertly, through author rather than protagonist, since Eliot, in writing a novel, seems to have transcended Maggie's ambivalence about reading one. Second, Simone's interpretation of Maggie's death is strained: Maggie dies not of or in solitude, but as a result of her decision to attempt to rescue her mother and brother. She dies in the latter's arms, and the novel memorializes sister and brother with the biblical David's epigraph for the warring Saul and Jonathan: "In their death they were not divided" (657).[18] Maggie's death thus turns her away from the artistic isolation that Simone envisions and back toward not only the Bible but also the embrace of her family of origin, the Dodsons. Eliot represents this return as a tragic but transcendent reconciliation; by contrast, *Memoirs of a Dutiful Daughter* ends with Simone not only about to leave her own family but also repudiating the family of her best friend, Zaza, who has succumbed, like Maggie, to the family's fatal clasp.

Simone's final misrecognition lies in extending to her identification a transitive power: "Through [Maggie]," she writes, "I identified myself with the author" (*MDD* 140). She assumes that, just as Maggie's fictionality makes her available to Simone's appropriation, the author's biographical existence makes her a representative of relatively unconstrained historical agency. In the second volume of her memoirs, *The Prime of Life* (*La force de l'âge,* 1960; trans. 1962), Beauvoir acknowledges this conversion in discussing her difficulties in writing her first novel: "I passionately wanted the public to like my work; therefore like George Eliot, *who had become identified in my mind with Maggie Tulliver,* I would myself become an imaginary character, armed with beauty, desirability, and a sort of shimmering transparent loveliness" (441; my emphasis; hereafter *PL*). In *Memoirs,* then, for the first but not the last time, Beauvoir imagines herself transcending the distinction between representation and action: "My life," she declares, "would be a beautiful story come true, a story I would make up as I went along" (169). Such an assumption is consistent with Beauvoir's later commitment to Existentialism, with its emphasis on individual agency; in the identification with Eliot, however, it is ironic as well as astute. It is astute because in leaving behind her birth identity as provincial, pious, petit-bourgeois Mary Anne Evans to construct a series of new identities—first as the free-thinking Anonymous, translator of Strauss and Feuerbach and editor of the *Westminster* review; scandalously as Marian Evans Lewes, companion of a married man; famously as George Eliot, novelist and moralist; and most conventionally as Mary Ann Cross (the name sharing space with "George Eliot" on her tombstone), wife of John—Eliot certainly also "made her life up as she went along." It is ironic because the ontological status of Simone's object of identification, "George Eliot," is more necessarily a *construction* even than is usual for that elusive persona, the implied author. The name is a public fiction whose announced gender is at odds with the gender of the biographical person to whom it is attached; and the "real" name used, for example in signing her letters, by the person behind the pseudonym—Marian Evans Lewes—is equally fictitious, with no legal, and only a precarious social, existence.[19]

Just as Maggie Tulliver's moment of identification with the fictional Corinne is elaborated in her relationship with Lucy Deane, so too Simone's recognition of herself in the fictional Maggie and the autobiographical George Eliot is both subordinated to, and elaborated in, her relationship with Zaza. Zaza, the daughter of a large Catholic family wealthier and more socially prominent than Simone's, joins her class at school when Simone is ten. Immediately, she becomes an object of identification for Simone: "In Zaza," Beauvoir writes: "I could glimpse a presence, flashing as a spring of water, solid as a block of marble, and as firmly drawn as a portrait by Dürer. I compared this with my own inner void, and despised myself" *MDD* 112); "I loved Zaza so much that she seemed to be more real than myself: I was her negative; instead of laying claim on my own characteristics, I had to have them thrust upon me which I supported with ill grace" (113).

This relationship between a "negative" or inchoate self and a "solid" counterpart might be read psychoanalytically to suggest that Simone's relationship with Zaza represents an iteration of her connection to her mother. Catherine Portuges, for example, analyzes "the formative influence of Simone de Beauvoir's relationship with her mother—and the mothering elements of other, subsequent attachments—on her own psyche and view of women" (110); and Alex Hughes reads Zaza as an image of "the phallic mother . . . the one means by which Simone hopes (erroneously) to elude the mother-related anguish evoked in Part I whilst avoiding the 'exile' to which she knows definitive mother/daughter separation condemns her" (126–27). But reading Zaza as an avatar of the mother can have the effect of displacing the libidinal energy of the Simone–Zaza coupling chronologically and developmentally backwards; emphasizing the maternal relation has the effect of disavowing Beauvoir's childhood and adolescent representation of desire for Zaza herself. As Beauvoir remarks defensively in another context, "In the eyes of (psychoanalytic) doctrinaires, adult relationships are nonexistent: they take no note of that dialectic process which from childhood to maturity—starting with roots the deep importance of which I am very far from misconceiving—works a slow transformation upon one's emotional ties with other people" (*PL* 443). Although psychoanalytic readings capture the aspects of the relationship between Simone and Zaza that mark it as a rehearsal of a foundational scene of identification, in other words, they obscure those aspects that make it available to interpretation as itself a foundational scene of homoerotic desire—in this text, a potential and, as we will see, ultimately foreclosed, path out of the *mise-en-abîme* created by literary identification. Indeed, Simone's early identification with Zaza is inseparable from both desire for her and aggression toward her; their relationship exemplifies the mutually constitutive, rather than oppositional, relationship of identification and desire emphasized by current queer theory. As Judith Butler argues, for example, "To identify is not to oppose desire. Identification is a phantasmatic trajectory and resolution of desire; an assumption of place; a territorializing of an object which enables identity through the temporary resolution of desire, but which remains desire, if only in its repudiated form" (*Bodies* 99). This combination of identification, desire, and aggression will lead Simone, at the end of the narrative, to take on a guilt caused by her assumption of Zaza's "place" as the surviving and flourishing female subject.

Beauvoir's revised plot thus more thoroughly than *The Mill on the Floss* blurs the boundaries between identification and desire, challenging, though not abandoning, the requirements of the heterosexual romance plot. Although Beauvoir did have sexual as well as emotional attachments to some women, a lesbian or even bisexual sexual identity was never part of her public presentation, and on occasion she categorically denied it. Nevertheless, *Memoirs of a Dutiful Daughter,* particularly by contrast with *The Mill on the Floss,* certainly undermines the opposition between identification and desire that structures a more general narrative of heterosexual identity.[20]

Initially, Simone's attraction to Zaza, like her identification with Maggie, seems to have its basis in the kind of "jubilant" identification with an aspirational version of the self that Jacques Lacan discusses in "The Mirror Stage." Zaza is Simone writ large. "Zaza, like myself, liked books and studying," Beauvoir writes:

> In addition, she was endowed with a host of talents to which I could lay no claim. Sometimes when I called [at] the rue de Varennes I would find her busy making shortbread or caramels. . . . She used to hectograph a dozen or so copies of a *Family Chronicle* which she edited and produced herself each week. . . . She took a few piano lessons with me, but very soon became more proficient and moved up into a higher grade. . . . [W]hen the first fine days of spring came along . . . Zaza would run into a field and do the cartwheel, the splits, the crab, and all kinds of other tricks. . . . In everything she did, she displayed an easy mastery which always amazed me. (*MDD* 93)

If Zaza displays tomboyish "mastery" of gymnastics, she also incorporates intellectual achievements (the production of the *Family Chronicle*) and more conventionally domestic accomplishments (cooking, playing the piano). She both more clearly repudiates conventional femininity than Simone, and more closely attains it. With her established familial and personal position, she represents the subject who can afford deviations from the norm precisely because she is confident in being its incarnation.

In the remainder of the narrative, however, the *mores* of Zaza and Simone's social world, Simone's own attitude toward Zaza, and Beauvoir's retrospective narrative will all conspire to deprive Zaza of her display of "easy mastery." Zaza's apparently effortless incarnation of both feminine and tomboyish attributes exceeds the boundaries of the mastering identification that Simone can feel with literary others such as Maggie. Her relationship with Zaza threatens from the start to tip from the mode of pleasurable recognition into more disruptive modes of disavowal, aggression, and desire. She repeatedly asserts her independence from and impregnability to Zaza: "Love is not envy. I could think of nothing better in the world than being myself, and loving Zaza" (*MDD* 96); "If it had been suggested that I should be Zaza, I should have refused; I preferred owning the universe to having a single face" (114). As Alex Hughes points out, Simone imagines Zaza's death twice before it actually arrives, suggesting a wish-fulfillment fantasy: "For all her idealization of Zaza, Beauvoir's narrator/heroine is manifesting . . . an implicit but powerful need to remove a resented obstacle to her own autonomy" (128). If Simone's submerged hostility toward Zaza has psychoanalytic antecedents in familial structures of identification, it also has literary precedents in Maggie's disavowed aggression toward Lucy—pushing her into the mud as a child and eloping with Stephen as a young woman.

If Simone's hostility toward Zaza is not quite acknowledged as such, the intensity of her desire for her friend is at first also unintelligible to her: "Zaza was my best friend: and that was all. In a well-regulated human heart friendship occupies an honourable position, but it has neither the mysterious splendour of love, nor the sacred dignity of filial devotion. And I never called this hierarchy of the emotions into question" (*MDD* 94). Nevertheless, Simone soon realizes that "I loved Zaza with an intensity which could not be accounted for by any established set of rules and conventions" (118). She fetishizes objects associated with Zaza: "I could touch all the objects that were expressions of her presence; but they did not give her up to me." Since "we both kept well within the bounds of modesty, for we were both of the opinion that our innermost feelings should not be exposed" (118), Simone cannot know whether Zaza shares her feelings, and she suffers because Zaza remains unreachable: "I would not even admit to myself with what fevered torment I paid for the happiness she gave me" (120). What Simone "will not admit to herself," the "intensity which could not be accounted for by any established set of rules and conventions," may be read both as homoerotic desire and as a strong identification that embodies her passion for her *own* existence and autonomy. Her portrayal of her willful ignorance of her own feelings and of Zaza's echoes a claim Freud makes in "The Psychogenesis of a Case of Homosexuality in a Woman." He expresses his

> astonishment that human beings can go through such great and momentous phases of their love-life without heeding them much, sometimes even, indeed, without having the faintest suspicion of them: or else that, when they do become aware of these phases, they deceive themselves so thoroughly in their judgment of them. . . . One must agree that the poets are right who are so fond of portraying people in love without knowing it, or uncertain whether they do love, or who think that they hate when in reality they love. It would seem that the knowledge received by our consciousness of what is happening to our love-instincts is especially liable to be incomplete, full of gaps, and falsified. (153–54)

Fondling objects associated with Zaza, using the florid language of love poetry—"mysterious splendor," "fevered torment"—and stressing her own conscious ignorance of her feelings, Simone does, indeed, appear to be "in love without knowing it."

As the memoir draws toward its conclusion, however, difference is reinforced against both identification and desire. Simone is headed to university; Zaza, whose mother has forbidden her further study, struggles with the expectation that she make an arranged marriage within the Catholic bourgeoisie. It is at this moment of divergence that Simone's passion for Zaza receives its only physical recognition. One evening Simone watches her play a Chopin piece, "this passionate music which really expressed [Zaza's] true self," and reflects:

> There was that mother and all that family between us, and perhaps one day she would disown her real self, and I would lose her. I felt such piercing sadness that I got up, left the room and went to bed in tears. The door opened; Zaza entered and came over to my bed, leaned over me and kissed me. Our friendship had always been such an undemonstrative one that her action filled me with joy. (*MDD* 281)

The scene recalls a similar association in *The Mill on the Floss* between music and erotic longing, when Philip Wakem plays the piano for Maggie, Lucy, and Stephen:

> The thought that Stephen knew how much she cared for his singing, was one that no longer roused a merely playful resistance. . . . But it was of no use: she soon threw her work down, and all her intentions were lost in the vague state of emotion produced by the inspiring duet—emotion that seemed to make her at once strong and weak, strong for all enjoyment, weak for all resistance. . . . Poor Maggie! She looked very beautiful when her soul was being played on in this way by the inexorable power of sound. You might have seen the slightest perceptible quivering through her whole frame as she leaned a little forward, clasping her hands as if to steady herself. . . . Lucy . . . could not resist the impulse to steal up to her and kiss her. (416)

In both cases, desire—Simone's for Zaza, Maggie's and Stephen's for each other, potentially Lucy's for Maggie—comes up against specifically familial obstacles to its realization. In *Memoirs of a Dutiful Daughter,* the silent kiss has no sequel, but when Simone leaves Zaza, she has "decided to fight with all my strength to prevent her life becoming a living death" (282)—from the stifling Catholic-bourgeois conventions of the world of the Mabille family, with its arranged marriages and distrust of the intellect, particularly in women, which is also near, but not quite identical, to the strictures of Simone's own family.

Simone's rage at the Mabilles, contrasted with her growing attachment to Jean-Paul Sartre, reproduces a conventional strategy of the heterosexual romance plot: A potential critique of the compulsory quality of heterosexuality *in general* becomes a critique of particular enforcements (by family or church) of *specific* heterosexual arrangements—here, the arranged marriage. (Eliot's representation of Dorothea's misguided motives in marrying Casaubon in *Middlemarch,* contrasted with the apparently redemptive marriage to Ladislaw, follows this pattern.) Simone's attitude somewhat resembles Philip Wakem's toward Maggie, when he brings her books and upbraids her for "narrow self-delusive fanaticism" (Eliot, *MoF* 427). As a woman Simone cannot fully or finally, in Beauvoir's conception, take on the role of rescuer with success (a disability that she shares with the feminized Philip Wakem), and the relationship between Simone and Zaza, despite its intensity, never seriously challenges the narrative power of the heterosexual plot.

Instead, as the memoir draws to a close, the two women begin to occupy roles both parallel (progressing toward heterosexual partnerships) and divergent (Zaza overcome by the demands of conventional femininity, Simone successfully fighting them). Once out of her charmed adolescence, Zaza becomes both the representative and the victim of conventional femininity, torn between her sense of duty and her potential for self-expression:

> Doubtless it was her Christian duty to obey her mother in everything; but . . . by allowing herself to be diminished and her intelligence to be misused, was she not acting contrary to God's will? . . . She was afraid of the sin of pride if she surrendered to her own judgment, and of being cowardly if she gave in to pressure from outside. (*MDD* 276–77)

Zaza's struggle recapitulates Maggie's arguments with Philip Wakem and Stephen Guest about what Eliot calls "the great problem of the shifting relation between passion and duty" (*MoF* 497). Beauvoir maintains that "Zaza and I agreed on almost everything" (*MDD* 281), but Simone consciously resents Zaza's continuing familial attachment and religious devotion: "I could no longer accept such a division of personality. By not coming over to my side, Zaza was throwing in her lot with enemies who were set on destroying me, and that made me feel resentful towards her" (287). Yet Beauvoir recognizes her younger self's own continuing attachment to one central value—female chastity—of her clan: "Sexual taboos still haunted me to such an extent that I longed to become a drug-addict or an alcoholic, but never for a moment did I contemplate sexual indulgence" (308). If she does not experience herself as subject to "division" in the way that Zaza is, the reason is partly that Zaza enacts that conflict for both of them. In doing so, however, she begins to embody precisely that aspect of bourgeois female subjectivity—the equation of moral action with social convention—that Simone has become determined to disavow.

In their last summer together, the two women both find male suitors—for Beauvoir, Sartre, and for Zaza, "Jean Pradelle" (the name Beauvoir gives to Maurice Merleau-Ponty). In one scene, the two women and Pradelle go boating together, recapitulating the setting of the abortive elopement of Stephen and Maggie. As the relationship between Zaza and Pradelle proceeds toward the conventional conclusion of romance, Simone, despite her interest in Sartre, is represented, though briefly and benignly, as a rival who must be overcome. An occasion arrives on which Zaza confesses her happiness that "for the first time . . . she had not felt like an intruder with Pradelle and me. . . . The same day, Pradelle told me how highly he thought of my friend. . . . One of my dearest dreams was about to be realized: Zaza's life would be a happy one!" (*MDD* 330). After this climax, Beauvoir writes, "I still went out frequently with Pradelle and Zaza, and now it was I who began to feel I was an intruder" (332). Pradelle has assumed the role of Stephen Guest—a catalyst for exogamous heterosexual desire—and Simone and Zaza contract into the roles of Maggie and Lucy.

To a greater degree than Eliot, Beauvoir complicates the representation of female rivalry: Simone's description simultaneously opposes the two women, makes them parallel, and finally collapses them into one. Each at some point feels herself to be an "intruder" in the other's relationship with Pradelle, so that even their opposition stresses their likeness; then, in a remarkable elision, *Zaza's* happiness becomes *Simone's* dearest dream. This substitution begs the question of whether Zaza's happiness will in fact interfere with Simone's dreams, either by removing Zaza as her companion or by arrogating to Zaza the narrative outcome of a successful heterosexual union. Simone, meanwhile, begins to find her own happiness with Sartre, who "corresponded exactly to the dream-companion I had longed for since I was fifteen: he was the double in whom I found all my burning aspiration raised to the pitch of incandescence" (*MDD* 345). This description makes clear the extent to which this heterosexual doubling both inherits and replaces the earlier, now disappointing, bond with Zaza.[21] At the same time, however, it demonstrates Beauvoir's refusal to observe conventional oppositions between, and gender assignments of, identification and desire. Within both relationships, identification and desire seem virtually inseparable, and Zaza's ultimate unsuitability as a reflection of "burning aspiration" emerges from the socially determined stunting of her own ambitions rather than from an essential (feminine) deficit.

Simone's dream of Zaza's happiness does not come true: Pradelle's passivity and parental opposition undermine the relationship between Pradelle and Zaza. Zaza succumbs to a mysterious illness that Beauvoir represents as the somatic manifestation of thwarted desire:

> The doctors called it meningitis, encephalitis; no one was quite sure. Had it been a contagious disease, or an accident? Or had Zaza succumbed to exhaustion and anxiety? She has often appeared to me at night, her face all yellow under a pink sun-bonnet, and seeming to gaze reproachfully at me. We had fought together against the revolting fate [*le destin fangeux*] that had lain ahead of us, and for a long time I believed that I had paid for my own freedom with her death. (*MDD* 360)[22]

In these, the last words of the memoir, the jaundiced Zaza grotesquely recalls the "light-complexioned" heroine on whom Maggie Tulliver could not quite imagine exacting revenge. Simone does not cause Zaza's death, but she is unable to save her. In that death, the two women *are* divided. The dutiful daughter's memoirs can be written only when the dutiful daughter—the role that Zaza has taken over—has been expelled from the text. In *All Said and Done,* Beauvoir reflects, "From the time I was sixteen my own family filled me with a longing for escape, with anger and resentment; but it was through Zaza that I discovered how odious the bourgeoisie really was. . . . For me Zaza's murder by her environment, her milieu, was an overwhelming, unforgettable experience" (9–10), and one that echoes through her life and work.

Since *Memoirs of a Dutiful Daughter* is the first of four volumes of autobiography, however, Beauvoir's narrative only pauses, rather than ends, with Zaza's death. In her preface to *The Prime of Life,* Beauvoir explains why she decided to continue the project:

> When I had completed my *Memoirs of a Dutiful Daughter* no voice spoke to me out of my past, urging me to continue the story. . . . [But] little by little I became convinced that, from my own point of view, the

> first volume of my *Memoirs* required a sequel. There was no point in having described how my vocation as a writer was acquired unless I then went on to show its realization. (5–6)

This description casts Beauvoir's "vocation as a writer" not in Eliot's hieratic vocabulary but rather with an emphasis on self-determination and worldly activity. The "sequel[s]" that Beauvoir produces—four further volumes of memoir as well as autobiographical narratives such as *America Day by Day* (1948; trans. 1952), *A Very Easy Death* (1964; trans. 1983), and *Farewell to Sartre* (1981; trans. 1986); the collections of letters to Sartre (1990; trans. 1991) and to Nelson Algren (1997); and interviews, including those with Alice Schwarzer collected in *After the Second Sex: Conversations with Simone de Beauvoir* (1983; trans. 1984)—seem to embody Beauvoir's triumph over Maggie Tulliver's unfulfilled trajectory, through demonstration of her "vocation as a writer" and as exhaustive records of material activities of writing, travel, political resistance and erotic intimacy.

One result of this textual productivity is that, as Toril Moi observes, "Simone de Beauvoir" becomes for her readers more than usually a textual figure: "The intertextual network of fictional, philosophical, autobiographical and epistolary texts that she left us *is* our Simone de Beauvoir" (4). This textual "Simone de Beauvoir" becomes a complicated object of readerly identification. "Many readers," Beauvoir observes in *All Said and Done,* "turn me into an image and at the same time identify themselves with me" (116). But Beauvoir strains against her readers' expectations that her female protagonists—whether the autobiographical "I" or fictional creations—will embody the most vigorous, successful, emancipated aspects of their creator and will thus offer positive objects of identification. Instead, Beauvoir's fictional female characters, like George Eliot's, are often limited by their gender roles and participate in their own confinement or destruction. Thus with the publication of *Les Belles Images* (1966; trans. 1985), an attack on "this technocratic society" in which "no character could speak in my name [because] in order to display [this world] I had to stand back and view it from a certain distance" (*ASD* 122), readers were "disappointed . . . that they could not identify themselves with any of the characters" (123). Beauvoir's next novella, "The Woman Destroyed," a grim study of a an "emotionally intrusive" (124) housewife who falls apart when her husband leaves her, indicts its title character as much as the straying husband for her habits of dependency and helplessness. On its publication, Beauvoir writes, "Immediately I was overwhelmed with letters from women. They identified themselves with the heroine. . . . Their partiality made it evident that as far as their husbands, their rivals and they themselves were concerned, they shared [the heroine's] blindness. Their reactions were based upon an immense incomprehension" (126).

In the exasperation that such readings provoke in Beauvoir, she may be forgetting her own enthusiastic identification with Maggie Tulliver. Yet the thrust of Beauvoir's complaint is that for such readers self-recognition becomes a reification ("they would like to think that I am immutably dedicated to serenity," she grumbles [*ASD* 116]) rather than a starting point for self-projection onto and intervention within a world historical stage. Some readers do respond in this way, however; as a result of the writing of *The Second Sex,* Beauvoir claims, she received "numberless testimonies" from women who "have found help in my work in their fight against images of themselves which revolted them, against myths by which they felt themselves crushed; they came to realize that their difficulties reflected not a disgrace peculiar to them, but a general condition. . . . If my book has helped women, it is because it expressed them, and they in turn gave it its truth" (*FC* 1: 192). Beauvoir's conflicting responses to her readers' identifications—finding them sometimes misguided and sometimes "expressive"—are echoed in readers' identifications themselves. In the film *Daughters of de Beauvoir,* which is made up of interviews with feminist scholars and authors influenced by Beauvoir, Ann Oakley expresses a nuanced view of such conflict: "A lot of her own autobiography is an attempt to present a rational view of her life, to make it into a project without contradictions, in which she does achieve this aim of being independent . . . [but] perhaps it is as much the contradictions that we identify with, because we feel them, and we live through them, and we can't find a solution either" (Sutton, n.p.). Beauvoir's memoirs, and Beauvoir as a female intellectual, no longer have the centrality they had just before and during the period of second-wave feminism, but the questions of identification they raise—in particular its trajectories and effects—remain salient.

In the political upheavals of the second half of the twentieth century, particularly the brutal French reaction to Algerian anti-imperialism, Beauvoir herself finds that national identifications, as well as gender identifications, have conventions that are not easily rewritten or disavowed: "Whether I wanted to be or not, I was an accomplice of these people I couldn't bear to be on the same street with. . . . I needed my self-esteem to go on living, and I was seeing myself through the eyes of women who had been raped twenty times, of men with broken bones, of crazed children: a Frenchwoman" (*FC* 2: 91). Beauvoir again draws on the power of authorship both to distance *herself* from, or reformulate, the identity of "a Frenchwoman" and to call attention to the experiences of the others through whose eyes she imagined herself being called to account. Most notably, in 1960, at the instigation of the French activist and lawyer Gisèle Halimi, she intervened in the case of Djamila Boupacha, a young Algerian woman imprisoned as a bombing suspect and tortured by French military forces. The case became a *cause célèbre,* and Beauvoir contributed an introduction to (and was the co-author of record of) Halimi's book about the case.[23] But in this case, as well, Beauvoir's relationship to the female subjectivity she hoped to "express" invited resistance as well as assent. Mary Caputi writes, for example, that "Ultimately, Halimi was unhappy about her collaboration with Beauvoir. . . . Halimi detected detachment on Beauvoir's part, and a tendency to treat the case in abstract terms . . . hers was not a hands-on approach that showed deep concern for another's concrete situation, but an abstract appraisal of the situation at large" (120). In Caputi's interpretation, Halimi is disappointed that Beauvoir chooses a philosophical distance—"abstract appraisal"—over a more direct identification with "another's concrete situation" (125). Caputi defends Beauvoir's involvement with the Boupacha case, arguing that her actions "remain true to her ethical mandate that, because each is bound to all, we must intervene in the fact of political struggle. We are responsible toward those who cannot enjoy the freedom, choice, and responsibility that are open to us, and we must extend the giving gesture toward the other" (125). But it seems difficult to deny that the object of that "gesture" may well register her construction as "the other" as something less than a gift—an identification imposed, and felt to be false.[24]

In *The Mill on the Floss,* Maggie Tulliver, the reading girl, becomes trapped in a circle of representation and identification, helpless to read differently or, therefore, to be differently read. Beauvoir writes to elude this trap, aiming beyond the narrative horizon altogether, toward the vanishing point at which experience and its representation become one. But her desire for unmediated communication leads inevitably and paradoxically to a dizzying proliferation of texts. She can never stop producing texts that comment on, repeat, and revise each other, since even texts that have the stylistic markers of direct address (memoirs, interviews) become, once published, representations in which "the I that speaks stands at a distance from the *I* that has been experienced" and thus open once again to the appropriations, enthusiastic or hostile, of readerly identification.

TSITSI DANGAREMBGA

SCHOOL STORIES

> I was not sorry when my brother died. Nor am I apologizing for my callousness, as you may define it, my lack of feeling. For it is not that at all. I feel many things these days. . . . Therefore I shall not apologise but begin by recalling the facts as I remember them that led up to my brother's death, the events that put me in a position to write this account. (Dangarembga, *Nervous Conditions* 1)

> Anybody may blame me who likes, when I add further, that, now and then, when I took a walk by myself in the grounds. . . . I longed for a power of vision which might overpass that limit. . . .
>
> Women are supposed to be very calm generally: but women feel just as men feel; . . . they suffer from too rigid a restraint, too absolute a stagnation precisely as men would suffer. (Brontë, *Jane Eyre* 114, 115)

"I was not sorry when my brother died"—the striking opening sentence of *Nervous Conditions* sets the novel's plot in motion. From this opening, the protagonist, Tambudzai (generally called Tambu) backs up to "[recall] the facts as I remember them that led up to my brother's death, the events that put me in a position to write this account" (Dangarembga, *Nervous Conditions* [hereafter *NC*] 1), and then moves past that death to its liberating effect on her. The novel recounts Tambu's early efforts to pursue her formal education, which founder on the inability of her parents, sunk in rural poverty, to cover her school fees and on their conviction that because Tambu is a girl, her "sharpness with books is no use because in the end it will benefit strangers" (56). (The position that Tambu's father takes here is similar to that of Maggie Tulliver's, who admires his daughter's cleverness but can only think it wasted: "It's a pity but what she'd been the lad—she'd ha' been a match for the lawyers, *she* would" [Eliot, *MoF* 19]. The two fathers also resemble each other in their fecklessness and inability to provide for their families.) Tambu's brother Nhamo is unsympathetic to her position—he steals the corn that she grows to raise money for school fees—and his own education alienates him from his family and makes him a "stranger to [her]" (55). Nhamo's death (of an unspecified illness contracted at the Mission school run by his uncle, Babamukuru) allows Tambu to succeed to his privilege of living with Babamukuru's family and attending his school. The novel recounts the effects of this social transformation and of Tambu's new intimacy with her rebellious and skeptical cousin Nyasha, who challenges Tambu's strong identification with the values embodied in the hard-pressed gentility of Babamukuru's family and the colonialist education of the Mission school. Because the novel (unlike *The Mill on the Floss* or *Memoirs of a Dutiful Daughter*) covers only two years of Tambu's life (beginning when she is thirteen) political conflict remains only incipient and largely invisible to Tambu herself, who is "young . . . and able to banish things" (203). Like Beauvoir, Dangarembga cannot contain the narrative of formation within a single iteration, because for both, formation is not a final occurrence but a series of *ref*ormations or *trans*formations. *Nervous Conditions* thus ends, like *Memoirs of a Dutiful Daughter,* with a gesture toward future action: "Quietly, unobtrusively and extremely fitfully, something in my mind began to assert itself, to question things and refuse to be brainwashed, bringing me to this time when I can set down this story. It was a long and painful process for me . . . whose events stretched over many years and would fill another volume" (204). That volume becomes the novel's sequel, *The Book of Not* (discussed in the next chapter).

From the opening sentence unfolds not only the novel's plot but also its complex, cross-cultural web of authorial echoes and identifications. One set of echoes and identifications points to psychoanalytic discourse and discourses of third-world solidarity. *Nervous Conditions,* the novel's title, is an adaptation of a phrase from Jean-Paul Sartre's preface to Frantz Fanon's study *The Wretched of the Earth* (1961). This epigraph connects Dangarembga to Sartre, Beauvoir, and their engagement with resistance to French colonialism, as well as to Fanon himself. At the same time, Dangarembga chose the title before she had actually read *The Wretched of the Earth* (Zwicker 10), and she redirects the male-oriented focus in Fanon's writing toward a female protagonist, and its Francophone context to the specificities of British imperialism in Rhodesia/Zimbabwe. Thus the title and epigraph are not straightforward references or homages but challenges, like the challenge that Caputi attributes to Gisèle Halimi in dialogue with Beauvoir, to colonialist intervention in anti-colonial struggle and to the role of gender in that struggle.

A second set of echoes and identifications thus points to the aspects and interpretations of novels of female formation that have challenged structures of male dominance. Like Simone's confident assertion that "I couldn't see myself dying of sorrow," Tambu's refusal to mourn her brother's death invokes through denegation the fictional and social conventions that represent women as subordinated by sibling or romantic relationships with men. For example, the strong causal relation suggested between the death of her brother Nhamo and Tambu's resulting access to an education that enables her to become a speaker or author might recall the fraternal determination of girl-children's fates happening just offstage in the lives of so many of Jane Austen's protagonists, who, because of patrilineal laws of primogeniture and entail, are equally disinherited by the presence or the absence of brothers. Tambu's defensiveness about her unfeminine "lack of feeling" also echoes and reverses Jane Eyre's dare to "anybody" to blame her for her unfeminine excess of passion, as her effort to continue her education echoes Jane's "long[ing]" for a greater "power of vision." Most directly, in the context of the argument of this chapter, Tambu's assertion may recall Maggie Tulliver's contrasting sorrow over her lost relationship with her brother and her eagerness not only to mourn for but even to die with him.

The novel's opening paradoxically functions, at least for English and American readers, to invoke familiar novelistic traditions amid unfamiliar cultural details. Some readings of the novel have emphasized its defamiliarizing functions. In an introduction to the American edition, Kwame Anthony Appiah posits that readers respond to the first sentence of the novel "in the light of the knowledge that the speaker, like the author, is a woman," and asks rhetorically, "Isn't there something especially shocking—something inhuman, unnatural—in a sister's coldness in the face of a brother's death?" (iii). But *Nervous Conditions* was first published by an independent feminist press, The Women's Press, in England (and by another feminist press, Seal, in the United States), and for many of its first readers in England and the United States, familiar in 1988 with several decades of feminist criticism and literature, any shock would as likely have registered as recognition and even (shockingly) pleasure. Both responses would arise from identification with the speaker's rejection of womanly tact and empathy, and from anticipation of the representation of a recognizable theme of twentieth-century women's writing—the covert or open expression of women's anger at or resistance to masculinist or patriarchal traditions—within a cultural context (that of Zimbabwe [then Rhodesia] in the late 1960s, just before the struggle for independence) probably new to most such readers. In "Cosmopolitan Reading," from which Appiah's introduction is drawn, he suggests the possibility of a more ethnocentric (Western) reading of Tambu's assertion: "You will probably find that your reading of the sentence is conditioned, too, by the thought that its author is an African woman, writing in the latter half of the twentieth century: for this will mean that you draw on a 'knowledge' that women are not well treated in Africa, so that a sister's hatred for her brother . . . is perhaps in these circumstances more natural than a brother's would be" (208). Appiah seems concerned that readers will judge Dangarembga as an angry writer—or, perhaps even worse, judge that her anger is "natural" to her national situation. I am suggesting that some feminist readers might experience the representation of a "sister's hatred for her brother" as an occasion for identification rather than for such distancing and condescending presuppositions.[25]

Within colleges and universities in the United States, the novel rapidly entered a pedagogical canon as an exemplar of African literature recognizable and teachable as the familiar, classroom-friendly genre of the coming-of-age story:

> *Nervous Conditions* has much to say to a first-year American college student in its story of a young person leaving home to obtain an education, a person who is eager to abandon her old life and develop a new self, a person who simultaneously finds herself homesick, nervous, awestruck, and skeptical upon entering a strange place. The transformation that Tambu envisions herself undergoing when she leaves home is not unlike the intellectual and physical liberation anticipated by many American college students. (S. Gallagher 63)

Critical attention to the novel, emphasizing feminist or postcolonial approaches singly or in combination, has also often started from a consideration of the novel's relation to the Bildungsroman tradition.[26] Many critics have read the novel's relationship to that tradition as most significantly one of contestation. Hershini Bhana Young, for example, argues that

> *Nervous Conditions* . . . shows the inadequacy of the bildungsroman form in a colonial context by pointing to the impossibility of the typical, eventual full integration into familial, religious, and educational systems. . . . Finally, the bildungsroman's linear structure in which the protagonist comes into consciousness is disrupted. *Nervous Conditions* does not tell a progressive story where Tambu grows to become more aware of her self and the institutions around her. Rather, the narrative is repeatedly interrupted by the voice of an older, more overtly politicized Tambu, who responds to and frames the responses of the less experienced Tambu. (136)

Joseph Slaughter, in a nuanced analysis of the relationship of *Nervous Conditions* to the Bildungsroman tradition, also suggests that the novel's "apparent generic conventionality" as a narrative devoted to "performing its traditional social work of demarginalizing the marginal subject—of enfranchising the individual as the normative, national citizen-subject" (229) is in fact a "literary feint, a preamble to a story of *Bildung* that remains unwritten—a process that is, the novel seems to suggest, systematically unwritable for a Shona girl in colonial Rhodesia and unassimilable to the conventions of the idealist *Bildungsroman,* whose democratic norms of citizenship do not match the forms of social and civil participation available either to the marginalized black majority generally or to native women specifically" (230). Certainly the narrative withholds, or at least defers, the representation of the historical events that have fostered the retrospectively narrating Tambu's more disenchanted and "overtly politicized" point of view. If this deferral, however, "makes readers responsible . . . for articulating the relations that an aphasic Tambu could not and for disabusing themselves of hyperbolic, ahistorical fantasies of unilateral self-determination" (245), it also has an arguably more "conventional" rhetorical effect: to allow the reader to inhabit, and perhaps even to identify with, the limited and partly uncomprehending point of view of Tambu *as she experiences* the events whose political and historical significance she cannot yet interpret.

In both Young's and Slaughter's readings, analyses of Dangarembga's complex address to the authorial reader risk overstating the univocality of earlier conventions of the Bildungsroman tradition and underestimating the extent to which Dangaremba adopts rather than diverges from those conventions. For example, the presence of an older, wiser narrative voice that "responds to and frames" the impressions of the "less experienced" self is a feature that *Nervous Conditions* shares with the first-person narratives of both *David Copperfield* and particularly *Great Expectations.* The older Pip frequently interposes observations on the moral error of his earlier self; close to the novel's end, for example, he reflects, "We owed so much to Herbert's ever cheerful industry and readiness, that I often wondered how I had conceived that old idea of his inaptitude, until I was one day enlightened by the reflection, that perhaps the inaptitude had never been in him at all, but had been in me" (480). For readers of both Dangarembga and Dickens, furthermore, such interruptions surely foster rather than disrupt the sense of a progressive story. Gesturing toward the future anterior, they remind the reader that the events being recounted *will have* transformed a callow subject protagonist into a more mature narrator—one who has undergone what Tambu calls a "process of expansion" (Dangarembga, *NC* 204). And events in *Nervous Conditions* in fact unfold with more linearity than do those in, say, *David Copperfield,* in which hidden plots distinct from David's development periodically burst into his own narrative, causing extended flashbacks and recalibrations of meaning and value (e.g., the Doctor/Annie Strong/Jack Maldon and Steerforth/Little Em'ly/Ham Peggoty triangles). If the time period covered by *Nervous Conditions* is more truncated and its ending less conclusive than those of many Victorian novels of formation, its concluding emphasis on the "process of expansion" that Tambu continues to undergo does suggest a trajectory of linear progress. It is also the case that in many of the apparently "linear" Victorian novels, such as *The Mill on the Floss, Villette,* and even *Great Expectations* as Dickens first conceived its ending, "full integration into familial, religious, and educational systems" turns out to be impossible for a protagonist even within the context of Victorian narrative and colonial power.

I would describe what Dangarembga does in *Nervous Conditions* less as critique or defamiliarization of the tradition of the narrative of female formation than as its use and extension in the only way a genre can ever remain alive—through continuing adaptation and redirection across time and place. Dangarembga frequently cites her readerly and authorial identification with this tradition and her commitment to producing new possibilities for the kinds of identification that it sponsors. When writing *Nervous Conditions,* for example, she "had been reading all the English classics, and you know how they give you a real sense of the time, of the passing of time and it just seemed to me that, well, there were people living in Zimbabwe or Rhodesia, and nobody knew about them, and if nobody set it down, then nobody would know about them" (George and Scott 311). This lack, Dangarembga suggests, has important implications because "with all the things you read, with everything that you're taught, you construct a kind of cognitive map for yourself that is comfortable. . . . I do think *Nervous Conditions* is serving this purpose for young girls in Zimbabwe. They call me on the telephone, you know, just to talk to me" (George and Scott 312). Like Beauvoir, who was "overwhelmed with letters from women" when she published *The Woman Destroyed,* Dangarembga registers the urgency of her readers' identification with both character and author; unlike Beauvoir, however, she does not regard them as having misread her text. To recall Diana Fuss's summary of identification as "the detour through the other that defines the self," in *Nervous Conditions,* the tradition of the English novel of formation, particularly female formation, provides one "detour through the other"—one point of literary identification—through which Dangarembga finds a narrative means to help her protagonist, and through the protagonist her readers, define a self.

The traces within *Nervous Conditions* of that tradition have the effect, I have suggested, of making the novel more welcoming to readers who may be less familiar with the social context of Rhodesia/Zimbabwe. That does not mean that the English novel of formation is the single or predominantly significant context for the novel or an analysis of it. The literary filiations that Dangarembga invokes, both within *Nervous Conditions* and in interviews discussing its composition, reflect a complex literary location and web of authorial identifications. Influences cited by Dangarembga run from schoolroom reading that included "the English classics: *Wuthering Heights* and *Romeo and Juliet*"; through African-American women writers, including Alice Walker, Toni Morrison, and Maya Angelou, who spoke to Dangarembga's later "quest as it were for the kinds of literature that I could really relate to, that could teach me something about myself and why I was and where I was and so forth" (Wilkinson 194); through black and white African authors, including Chinua Achebe, Ngugi wa Thiong'o, and Doris Lessing (195); to coming-of-age narratives such as *Catcher in the Rye, The Diary of a Young Girl,* and *To Kill a Mockingbird* (197).

The diversity and national range of these literary connections is not a utopian expression of multicultural reading practices but on the contrary the result of Dangarembga's location within and response to conditions of white Western domination of culture industries as well as other aspects of colonial society, including the imposition on African nations of a Eurocentric colonial education system; colonial and postcolonial oppression and resistance in Rhodesia/Zimbabwe; the resulting rise of postcolonial nationalism; and the domination of literary markets by Western metropolitan centers, which shapes the publishing opportunities of writers from formerly colonized countries.[27] The colonial education shared by Dangarembga and her characters Tambu and Nyasha, including their reading within and outside the classroom, intertwines inextricably conditions of oppression and those of expression. Dangarembga, for example, traces her generation's lack of a "cognitive map" to the operation of the Southern Rhodesia Literature Bureau, sponsored beginning in 1954 by both the colonial and the mission authorities, which "published all the African writing [i.e., in two native languages, Shona and Ndebele]. And they would only allow tales of traditional witchcraft, wives poisoning their husbands, you know, that kind of thing" (George and Scott 312).[28] In this context it is worth remembering that although Simone de Beauvoir read

The Mill on the Floss in English, it was available in French; in stepping across a national border into another national literature, she was nevertheless remaining within a shared European literary tradition already being constructed as such by the beginning of the nineteenth century; a tradition materially as well as thematically subtended by a shared history of colonial conquest. Dangarembga and Tambu, however, could not have read the "English classics" in Shona. Tambu's literary education, both formal and informal, likewise works to assimilate her, as her English-educated aunt and uncle have been assimilated, to colonialist ideologies of African inferiority, even as it speaks to her essential desires for knowledge and for an escape from her parents' grinding poverty.

Within the novel, as I have suggested above, Tambu does not fully develop a consciousness of this colonial context. At the outset she is thrilled to be at the mission school,

> meeting, outside myself, many things that I had thought about ambiguously; things that I had always known existed in other worlds although the knowledge was vague; things that had made my mother wonder whether I was quite myself, or whether I was carrying some other presence in me.
>
> It was good to be validated in this way. Most of it did not come from the lessons they taught at school but from Nyasha's various and extensive library. I read everything from Enid Blyton to the Brontë sisters, and responded to them all. Plunging into these books I knew I was being educated and I was filled with gratitude to the authors for introducing me to places where reason and inclination were not at odds. It was a centripetal time, with me as the centre, everything gravitating towards me. It was a time of sublimation with me as the sublimate. (Dangarembga, *NC* 93)

The ironies of the young Tambu's enjoyment will be apparent to some older readers—Enid Blyton's books are a byword for the overt racism and Anglocentric complacencies of some pre-1960s English children's literature, and Brontë's novels, in which the African continent appears only as a fever-dream, represent most women outside of white, Protestant England as metaphors for victimization.[29] To some degree the distinction that Tambu perceives between "lessons they taught at school" and "Nyasha's extensive and various library" is false, since in both cases the "lessons" are those of a colonialist curriculum. Even on their own terms, the traditions of representing girls and women that she is encountering have not always suggested, at least to feminist literary critics, that "reason and inclination" are easily reconciled. But as a young reader, Tambu—like Simone de Beauvoir reading *Little Women* or *The Mill on the Floss*—is not fully attuned to the national or literary histories, or even the nuances of the gender ideologies, in which these apparently questing and adventurous individual protagonists are embedded, and this lack of contextual knowledge perhaps produces some lasting as well as an illusory confirmation of self.

Only in the last sentence of this passage does a skeptical older voice seem to shadow the young Tambu's excitement, playing on the accrued meanings associated with the abstract noun "sublimation" and its adjective and verb forms. Tambu experiences a moment of "sublimation" presumably in the sense of "elevation to a higher state or plane of existence; transmutation into something higher, purer, or more sublime" (*OED*, "sublimation," def. 5a), with herself, as the "sublimate," a "refined and concentrated product" (*OED*, "sublimate," def. 1b). The concept of sublimation, however, includes more sinister implications—"converting a solid substance by means of heat into vapour" (def. 1a)—being, in other words, vaporized. The "sublimate" remains as a solid mass, but a virulent one: "mercury sublimate," the topic of *OED* definition 2, is a "violent poison." In *The Book of Not,* Tambu will discover some of the obliterating and poisonous aspects of her transformation; in *Nervous Conditions,* Nyasha warns her of them: "She could not hide, did not even try to hide, her disappointment when I told her how thrilled I was [about the opportunity to attend a convent school]. . . . It would be a marvellous opportunity, she said sarcastically, to forget. . . . The process, she said, was called assimilation, and that was what was intended for the precocious few who might prove a nuisance if left to themselves" (178–79). Perhaps the Freudian implications of "sublimation," which involves the redirection of self-gratifying instincts toward socially recognizable and acceptable behaviors, also hover, reinforcing the suggestion that Tambu's transformation involves forms of loss and redirection that are not entirely under her control and that may serve others' interests rather than her own. "Sublimation" in this sense is close to a synonym for Althusserian interpellation. Tambu's feeling that "everything is gravitating towards me" parallels Althusser's description of being "hailed" as a subject and, as with interpellation, what she experiences as individual recognition is in fact subjection to her role in a patriarchal, colonialist, and racist society.

Nyasha, by contrast, thoroughly understands this subjection and rejects the roles of the dutiful daughter and the reading girl. Nyasha, who has spent five years in England, where her parents have been studying for their MAs, has forgotten how to speak her native Shona, sneaks cigarettes, uses tampons, and dances with boys; she argues continuously with her parents, rejecting both the patriarchal rule of Babamukuru and the anxious subservience of her highly educated but deferential mother, Maiguru; and she questions the status quo both personal and public. She might initially seem to a Western reader a more familiar rebellious adolescent, preoccupied with personal autonomy and with a budding sexuality. But her rebellion is also against Western imperialism, whose systemic and hegemonic features are much more apparent to her than to Tambu. Although the Blytons and Brontës that Tambu reads are Nyasha's, she dismisses them: "When I tried to describe to Nyasha a little of what was happening in my world, she laughed and said I was reading too many fairy-tales. She preferred reality. She was going through a historical phase. . . . She read about Arabs on the east coast and the British on the west; about Nazis and Japanese and Hiroshima and Nagasaki" (Dangarembga, *NC* 93). Since Nyasha is clearly interested in the "reality" particularly of colonial or imperial aggression, her reading is also founded on a kind of identification, but with national rather than individual narratives. It might also be viewed it as an instance of "disidentification" in José Muñoz's sense, "a strategy that tries to transform a cultural logic from within, always laboring to enact permanent structural change while at the same time valuing the importance of local or everyday struggles of resistance" (11–12).

When Nyasha does read a novel, her shocking choice is *Lady Chatterley's Lover,* which her parents censure for its sexual impropriety. Nyasha, however, minimizes its significance: "I've read everything in the house that you say I can and there's not much of a library at school. What's all the fuss about anyway? It's only a *book* and I'm only *reading* it" (Dangarembga, *NC* 75). Nyasha's offhand dismissal of the impact of novel-reading recalls Lynne Sharon Schwartz's assertion that "If no girl was ever ruined by a book, none was ever saved by one either" (*Ruined by Reading* 114). But Nyasha, for all her precocious analysis of historical narrative, like Maggie Tulliver underestimates the power over her of existing, socially (and literarily) sanctioned plots, particularly those that divide the dutiful and "decent" from the rebellious daughter. For all her sophistication, she, like Tambu, has not yet lost the belief that there might be "places where reason and inclination were not at odds." In *The Second Sex,* Beauvoir argues that "it is regardless of sex that the existent seeks self-justification through transcendence—the very submission of women is proof of that statement. What they demand today is to be recognized as existents by the same right as men and not to subordinate existence to life" (73). Nyasha's understanding of herself, like that of Beauvoir's insurgent woman, is existentialist: Taking herself to be primarily a human and historical, rather than female and familial, individual, she sees her behavior as rational, not rebellious, and miscalculates (as Beauvoir does not) the opposition it will arouse. Whether opining airily that her mother "knew that tampons were offensive, that nice girls did not use them [but] would be pleased enough to know we were not pregnant to provide" (Dangarembga, *NC* 96) or disputing her father's censorship of her reading, she misreads gender codes as rationally disputable. That misunderstanding leads her to violent conflict with her father (she punches him in the eye when he accuses her of "behav[ing] like a whore" [114]), anorexia, and mental breakdown: by the end of the novel, while Tambu has triumphantly matriculated at the Sacred Heart convent, Nyasha has been institutionalized and drugged into lassitude.

Before her breakdown, however, it is she who most often causes Tambu to question her own dutiful role. When Tambu moves in to go to Babamukuru's school, the two girls become immediately intimate despite their differences:

> In fact it was more than friendship that developed between Nyasha and myself. The conversation that followed [on her first night with Nyasha] was a long, involved conversation, full of guileless openings up and intricate lettings out and lettings in. It was the sort of conversation that young girls have with their best friends, that lovers have under the influence of the novelty and uniqueness of their love, the kind of conversation that cousins have when they realise that they like each other in spite of not wanting to. You could say that my relationship with Nyasha was my first love-affair, the first time I grew to be fond of someone of whom I did not wholeheartedly approve. (Dangarembga, *NC* 78)

As this passage suggests, the relationship between Tambu and Nyasha, like those between Maggie and Lucy and Simone and Zaza, confounds distinctions among affective ties: friendship, family connection, and romantic or sexual attraction. Like those, too, it incorporates bonds of identification (the subjective interpenetration of "lettings out and lettings in"); desire; and repudiation ("lik[ing] each other in spite of not wanting to"; "not wholeheartedly approv[ing]"). Later, after Nyasha stays outside too long after a dance talking, alone, to a male friend, she has a vicious, bruising fistfight with her father. Tambu comforts Nyasha by "climb[ing] into her bed, where we cuddled up to each other and fell asleep." As with the kiss that Zaza bestows on Simone and the tearful embrace that Lucy and Maggie share, this moment of same-sex physical intimacy is associated with an outbreak of female desire that, despite its heterosexual object, is transgressive in its challenge to the dominance of the male-headed family of origin. The reaction of Nyasha's mother, who was "not very pleased the next morning when she found us in bed together, but . . . could not mind that Nyasha was beginning to feel better and so nothing was said" (119), offers the novel's only indication that physical intimacy between women might itself be perceived as transgressive.

Indeed, faced with the double bind of female sexuality in a partriarchal context—the demand for a total submission to heterosexual hierarchy coupled with the interdiction of any display of interest in sexuality—Tambu simply absents herself: "As far as boys were concerned, I was obviously uninterested," she asserts (Dangarembga, *NC* 94); marriage is something that she considers "in an abstract way . . . a very good idea" (180) while noting with distaste its invocation as a curb on her ambitions. She remains, we might say, focused on identification—who shall I be?—not as a form of, but to the exclusion of, desire (whom shall I have?). Although the more forward Nyasha also teaches Tambu to use tampons; comments on her appearance; and encourages her to attend a school dance, beckoning her toward greater (hetero)sexual sophistication, her greatest influence on Tambu remains intellectual: "I tried hard to understand, because Nyasha was very persuasive and also because I liked to think" (160). For her part, although she mocks Tambu's ambition to attend the Sacred Heart convent, Nyasha is equally driven by her own studies: "She worked late into the night to wake me up regularly and punctually at three o'clock with a problem—a chemical equation to balance, the number of amperes in a circuit to be calculated, or an irregular Latin verb to be conjugated. . . . 'I have to get it right' she would whisper with an apologetic smile" (200). Like that between Simone and Zaza, the relationship between Tambu and Nyasha is a complex blend of emulation and rivalry, desire and identification, attraction and recoil, all both intellectual and physical.

In the end, however, the relationship between Tambu and Nyasha, like the relationships between Zaza and Simone and (to a degree) Maggie and Lucy, cannot overcome a narrative structure of splitting and rivalry between protagonist and counterpart. As Tambu takes over the role of the dutiful daughter that Nyasha rejects, she visibly usurps her place in the family:

> I could see that my uncle was growing more and more disappointed with his daughter. . . . Beside Nyasha I was a paragon of feminine decorum, principally because I hardly ever talked unless spoken to. . . . Above all, I did not question things. . . . I was not concerned that freedom fighters were referred to as terrorists, did not demand proof of God's existence nor did I think that the missionaries, along with the other Whites in Rhodesia, ought to have stayed home. As a result of all these things that I did not think or do, Babamukuru thought I was the sort of young woman a daughter ought to be and lost no opportunity to impress this point of view upon Nyasha. (Dangarembga, *NC* 155)

We might recall that Maggie Tulliver's understanding of duty, too, involves a renunciation of over-ambitious "think[ing] and do[ing]." She has given up books, she explains to Philip, because reading "would make me in love with this world again, as I used to be; it would make me long to see and know many things—it would make me long for a full life" (Eliot, *MoF* 306); when Philip persuades her to borrow his books, she ends by wondering whether "what you call being benumbed was better" (335). For Tambu, unlike Maggie Tulliver, academic achievement is part of the dutiful daughter's role. But as suggested by her sardonic summary of Babamukuru's negative ideal of conduct—based on "all these things that I did not think or do"—that achievement functions not to encourage intellectual discovery or independent thought but to serve a kind of "benumbed" conformity.

Nyasha takes a mistakenly magnanimous view of this pernicious contrast and "would agree that, apart from being a little spineless (which she thought could be corrected), yes, I was an exemplary young lady" (Dangarembga, *NC* 155). While Tambu puts on weight in her uncle's well-stocked household and starts menstruating, Nyasha becomes bulimic and anorexic and increasingly at odds with her father's patriarchal regime. Brave as she is, Nyasha—like Zaza and Maggie—finally cannot sustain the conflict between her own desires and familial duties and values. She does not die, but she breaks down completely, raging in the girls' bedroom, "shredding her history book between her teeth . . . breaking mirrors, her clay pots, anything she could lay her hands on and jabbing the fragments viciously into her flesh, stripping the bedclothes, tearing her clothes from the wardrobe and trampling them underfoot" (201). Tambu also has a moment, earlier, of psychosomatic revolt, when her uncle insists on sponsoring a belated, and therefore humiliating, wedding for her parents: "The morning of the wedding, I found I could not get out of bed. I tried several times but my muscles simply refused to obey the half-hearted commands I was issuing to them" (166). But if this "half-hearted" rebellion mimics Nyasha's refusals of Babamukuru's authority and adumbrates her later breakdown, the severity of that breakdown enforces a cleavage rather than a parallel between protagonist and counterpart: Tambu's triumphant journey to the Sacred Heart convent is parallel to Nyasha's traumatic trip to a psychiatric clinic in Salisbury.

As in *Memoirs of a Dutiful Daughter* and *The Mill on the Floss,* the moment of separation is marked by a final, brief intensification of physical intimacy. "'Can I get into bed with you, Tambu?' [Nyasha] whispered, but when I rolled over to make room for her to climb in she shook her head and smiled. 'It's all right,' she said. 'I just wanted to see if you would let me.'" When Tambu nevertheless attempts a comforting touch, it backfires, providing the "trigger" for Nyasha's rage (Dangarembga, *NC* 200). The force of Nyasha's knowledge and anger, reflected in her repetition of the phrase "I'm not a good girl" (200, 201) cannot be corralled into a soothing homosociality or solidarity or made into an exhibit for the power of sympathy. Unlike either Eliot's heroines (Maggie, Dorothea, Dinah) or their anti-heroic counterparts (Lucy, Rosamond, Hetty), Nyasha is neither self-subduing nor repentant. Like the fever that consumes Zaza, Nyasha's internal struggle instead seems to become increasingly solitary and isolating, even as Tambu, like Simone, sees her own fate as linked with that of her counterpart: "If Nyasha who had everything could not make it, where could I expect to go? . . . Nyasha's progress was still in the balance, and so, as a result, was mine" (202). Though Nyasha does not die, she haunts Tambu as Zaza haunts Simone. By the end of the narrative "I was beginning to have a suspicion . . . that I had been too eager to leave the homestead and embrace the 'Englishness' of [the Mission and then of the Sacred Heart convent]. The suspicion remained for a few days, during which time it transformed itself into guilt, and then I had nightmares about Nhamo and Chido [Nyasha's brother] and Nyasha two nights in a row" (203).

Throughout most of the narrative, however, the stakes are too high for the young Tambu, just starting on a path that she believes will take her far from the poverty of her parents' home, for her to entertain any such "suspicion." She cannot identify with Nyasha's active disidentification with all of the available daughterly roles. In this sense, *Nervous Conditions* is as much about resisting knowledge and experience—of sexuality and of colonialist racism—as about acquiring it. Tambu clings, however precariously, to the conventional position of the reading heroine of the novel of formation, for whom books and education still promise liberation compatible with innocence. In her second year at the mission school, nuns from the Sacred Heart convent, "a prestigious private school that manufactured guaranteed young ladies" come to examine the girls for the "two places [available] for all the African Grade Seven girls in the country" (Dangarembga, *NC* 178). On this occasion

> Of course I was chosen first to recite a poem.
>
> "Hamelintown'sinBrunswickbyfamousHanoverCity," I began, raising a gasp of admiration from my class, who knew I was bright but not quite that bright, not bright enough to have learnt such a long poem, one they had never heard of before, and recite it so well. . . .
>
> Mr. Sanyati told us that the nuns had come all the way from their own mission to have us write this test and herded all the girls in Grade Seven A into the classroom to answer questions about Louisa M. Alcott and *Little Women,* to multiply seven acorns by twenty-three acorns by forty-eight acorns by no acorns and to pick the odd item out in a set of gumboots, galoshes, snow shoes and bedroom slippers. (177)

Such ironized exhibitions of Eurocentric pedagogy are frequent in postcolonial coming-of-age narratives that recall experiences of colonialist education. In a scene from Jamaica Kincaid's novel *Lucy* that I discuss below, ten-year-old Lucy recites Wordsworth's "Daffodils" for "an auditorium full of parents, teachers, and my fellow pupils," who "stood up and applauded with an enthusiasm that surprised me." If Lucy's audience is as impressed as Tambu's, however, her own attitude more closely resembles Nyasha's scorn for "fairytales": "I was then at the height of my two-facedness. . . . And so I made pleasant little noises that showed both modesty and appreciation, but inside I was making a vow to erase from my mind, line by line, every word of that poem" (Kincaid, *Lucy* 18). Tambu, by contrast, embraces the identity of the good student and is thrilled to find that she has "performed brilliantly in that entrance examination, thereby earning the privilege of associating with the elite of that time, the privilege of being admitted on an honorary basis into their culture" (Dangarembga, *NC* 178). Once again, Dangarembga does not overtly distance the older narrating voice from the younger Tambu's enthusiasm. The exploitation and injustice in this colonial educational structure must be inferred by the reader from the passage's unmarked dissonant information—the admission to Sacred Heart of only two "African" (that is, Black) students from among "all the African Grade Seven girls in the country"; the repetition of words—"privilege," "elite," "honorary"—that mark social hierarchies and inequities; and the ostentatious Eurocentrism and scorn for local geography displayed in the list of objects (acorns, gumboots, galoshes, snow shoes, and slippers) among which students are asked to make fine discriminations.

Tambu's choice of poem likewise might cause the authorial reader unease, even if it impresses her narrative audience. Dangarembga withholds the poem's title and author, perhaps separating the anglophile sheep from the merely anglophone goats among her Western readers: Robert Browning's "The Pied Piper of Hamelin" is a less widely known poem than Wordsworth's "Daffodils," and even readers who can call to mind all or part of "Daffodils" are unlikely to have the same familiarity with Browning's poem. Tambu does not explain how she chose the poem, but her high-speed gabble suggests that she may not fully have taken in its dark story: swindled out of payment for ridding the town of Hamelin of a plague of rats, the Piper uses his enchanting music to lure all the townsfolk's children away. Nevertheless, the Pied Piper's plot is a familiar nursery tale, and many authorial readers will perceive, at least, that Tambu is reciting a poem about promises broken and children lured away from their village homes. Such readers are invited to make a connection that Tambu does not, between the poem and the bitter response of Tambu's mother to Babamukuru's intervention: "What will I, your mother, say to you when you come home a stranger full of white ways and ideas? . . . I've had enough, I tell you, I've had enough of [Babamukuru] dividing me from my children" (Dangarembga, *NC* 184). Tambu is neither unobservant nor disloyal, but she refuses to allow herself to notice such dissonant resonances: "If you were clever, you slipped through any loophole you could find. I for one was going to take any opportunity that came my way" (179). Only at the end of the novel does she begin to doubt Babamukuru and the patriarchal regimes of power—both African and colonial—within which he attempts to maintain his standing. Even then, the white colonial power standing behind him remains less visible to her than her familial relationships.

Like Simone's narrative in *Memoirs of a Dutiful Daughter,* however, Tambu's story does not end with the end of this novel, but continues in its sequel, *The Book of Not* (discussed in the next chapter). Like Simone, Tambu will find that politics and national history do not keep their place on the far "horizon" of experience but explode into her most personal relationships and choices; the ethics of the self/other relation, adumbrated and begun by the relationship between protagonist and counterpart, cannot be confined to the private relations of family and to dilemmas of personal morality. Under the pressures of world war and of the violent collapse of European colonialism, the two twentieth-century narratives breach the boundary between personal and public narrative that *The Mill on the Floss* maintains largely by evacuating public or historical events. On the one hand, *The Mill on the Floss* is itself a national tale that consciously locates itself within not just passing but historical time, and not just English but European time. Beryl Gray asserts that "[Eliot's] presentation of St Ogg's and its inhabitants depends as much on the implications of her perspectives of the Rhône and the Rhine, on her allusions to Aristotle, Sophocles, and Homer, on her application of Greek and German mythology, and on her engagement with the German cultural historian, Wilhelm von Riehl, as it does on the sense of an intimately-recollected past that, in turn, recognizes the abiding spiritual, local presence of Roman, Saxon, and Dane" (138). On the other hand, the actual narrative of *The Mill on the Floss* is profoundly insular. (Tellingly, Gray's essay concerns Eliot's engagement not with history *per se* but with a pan-European discourse of *natural* history, a "culturally boundless" range of "animal analogy and animal metaphor" influenced by such figures as Riehl, Goldsmith, Buffon, and Pliny.) This is the novel in which the narrator asserts that "the happiest women, like the happiest nations, have no history" (Eliot, *MoF* 385); if the narrator can see Maggie's historical connection to the German peasant as well as to the spider and the toad, these wider views are not present to Maggie, trapped in the narrow ambit of the novel's *histoire*. As Neil McCaw observes, "Eliot narrates a landscape that is peculiarly English. Her liberal philosophy may seem to offer itself as inclusive to people of differing cultural backgrounds, and her scientism implies a universal historical process, yet it is notable how quintessentially English the novels are" (11). The modern world of intercontinental trade and empire, of desires gratified by the multiplication of consumer goods rather than intimate relations, all implied by the busy wharves of Stephen Guest's father and Stephen's exotic scent of attar of roses, is, from Maggie's perspective, a faint and ultimately injurious rumor.[30]

Memoirs of a Dutiful Daughter and *Nervous Conditions* also "narrate landscape[s] that are peculiarly" national, but the nation is not evident to their young protagonists as such. Practices, languages, ideologies that bespeak the nation are omnipresent, embodied within familial relations and naturalized as a transparent medium in which individual life takes place, more or less invisibly to their young protagonists, though not necessarily to the authorial reader (and certainly not to the critic or teacher). In identifying, and identifying with, narratives of national struggle rather than remaining within relations of personal identification, Nyasha is exceptional; she provides a narrative audience for Tambu's naiveté that also functions to clue the authorial reader in. But her illness lends credence to Eliot's connection between unhappiness and history: subdued at the end of the novel by doses of Largactil (Thorazine), she might well echo Stephen Dedalus's assertion that "History is a nightmare from which I am trying to escape," an early adumbration of colonial/postcolonial alienation.

Despite the generally tight focus on private, protagonist-counterpart relations that render national identity seamless because invisible, moments of sudden fissure appear in both twentieth-century narratives. For Simone, recognition of her parents' intellectual inconsistency or cowardice, and most strikingly the suffering of Zaza, makes the conventions of bourgeois, Catholic subjectivity visible and despicable; for Tambu, the education that begins to divide her from her family of origin, the occasional glimpses of white society as an occupying force, and Nyasha's dramatic enactment of self-division point toward the ultimately untenable status of Babamukuru's assimilationism. Most important, unlike *The Mill on the Floss, Memoirs of a Dutiful Daughter* and *Nervous Conditions* are not concluded stories, but first entries in multipart narratives, whose future volumes will project their protagonists into a world-historical stage, in which the ethics of self–other relations can no longer be contained within the context of individual, or even familial, morality, and in which the historical domination of African countries by European ones will have a decisive and, for Tambu, despoiling effect on those relations. In such contexts, as I will argue in the next chapter, identification may prove an inadequate or unattainable ground for such relations.

THREE

Coming Apart

CHARLOTTE BRONTË, JAMAICA KINCAID, AND TSITSI DANGAREMBGA

IN THE NARRATIVES discussed in the previous chapter, relations of identification between protagonist and counterpart serve as templates for thinking about the obligations of the self to others. The protagonist may not succeed, by the narrative's end, wholly in meeting those obligations, but the narrative trajectory suggests that she will continue to strive to do so, and that perhaps—as in the case of the sequels to *Memoirs of a Dutiful Daughter* and *Nervous Conditions*—she will grow to understand the relationship between self and other in broader, more public and political contexts. The plots of *Memoirs of a Dutiful Daughter* and *Nervous Conditions* do not come to closure; their young protagonists, though they have already begun to experience loss and moral conflict, continue to look forward. *The Mill on the Floss,* concluding with a more conventional Victorian accounting of deaths and marriages, brings Maggie's story to a bleaker end, and offers no sequel; but the narrative still (as Beauvoir's reading of it suggests) allows for a more hopeful readerly identification beyond its beleaguered protagonist, with the voice of the narrator, who appears to possess the backward-looking wisdom that Maggie would have gained had she lived.

Optimism about the self's capacity for autonomy and growth is a well-attested convention of novels of formation, and Brontë, Kincaid, and Dangarembga all wrote novels that display that optimism: Brontë's *Jane Eyre;* Kincaid's *Annie John;* Dangarembga's *Nervous Conditions.* Each of these novels was the author's first to be published and each has attracted wide readership, representation on syllabi, and significant critical attention, particularly from feminist scholars. In each case, however, a subsequent novel—Brontë's *Villette,* Kincaid's *Lucy,* and Dangarembga's *Book of Not*—retells or continues the narrative of formation in a way that, while it retains a connection to the structure of the novel of formation, clouds the optimism of the earlier effort and in particular expresses great skepticism about the productive possibilities of identification. *The Book of Not* is straightforwardly a sequel to *Nervous Conditions,* continuing Tambudzai's story from the point at which the earlier novel concluded and pursuing the development of the same characters as the earlier novel. Despite a difference in protagonist's name and destination between Kincaid's *Annie John* and her *Lucy* (at the conclusion of the first book, Annie is about depart for England; at the beginning of *Lucy,* the protagonist arrives in the United States), Lucy's past experiences and present trajectory seem continuous with Annie John's. *Villette* is not a sequel to *Jane Eyre,* but it reimagines the orphan's tale of the first novel through a different, and less enchanted, set of experiences. Inhabiting different temporal, geographical, and political circumstances, and facing different levels of immediate domination and danger, the protagonists of *Villette, Lucy,* and *The Book of Not* nevertheless share the traumatic situation of marginalized subjects whose claims to personhood are not recognized or are rejected by dominant subjects. Rather, their historical situations of social subordination, produced by varying combinations of gendered, socioeconomic, and racial domination, demand of them that they not only function as but fully identify with the role of the *other*—that which is disavowed and abjected by dominant subjects who occupy the position of "self."

The protagonists in this chapter, Brontë's Lucy Snowe, Kincaid's Lucy Potter, and Dangarembga's Tambu Sigauke, seem to stand alone amid hostile others—the school-world, in the case of Lucy Snowe and Tambu; a white, urban elite, in the case of Lucy Potter. At points, however, their narratives are shadowed by a kind of negative inversion of the protagonist/counterpart relation; rather than a singular counterpart, they face a series of female antagonists, other women who embody the social denial of recognition, and thus of selfhood. Recognition by the other as foundational to the self is central to many psychoanalytic paradigms. "The basic relational configurations [in pyschoanalytic theory]," Stephen Mitchell writes, "have, by definition, three dimensions—the self, the other, and the space between the two. There is no 'object' in a psychologically meaningful sense without some particular sense of oneself in relation to it" (33). For many psychoanalytic theorists, the earliest form of recognition is offered by a caregiver who reflects the subject back to him- or herself, thus consolidating a sense *of* self. Psychoanalytic theorists of childhood development who may otherwise differ in emphasis use similar vocabularies of reflection to capture this foundational moment. Melanie Klein, for example, suggests that "One element in [a successful] maternal attitude seems to be that the mother is capable of putting herself in the child's place and of looking at the situation from his point of view" (318). This ability is both the product of, and will in turn produce, a "capacity for identification with another person [that] is a most important element in human relationships in general, and is also a condition for real and strong feelings of love. . . . Ultimately, in making sacrifices for somebody we love and in identifying ourselves with the loved person, we play the part of a good parent, and behave towards this person as we felt at times the parents did to us—or as we wanted them to do" (311–12). Similarly, in his conception of the "good-enough mother," D. W. Winnicott (who trained with Klein) considers that "a key aspect of her role is reflecting back to the child his own appearance, his own being. The capacity to experience and to hold a sense of one's own being as real depends on the mother's doing so first, mirroring back to the child who he is and what he is like" (Mitchell 32). Often, of course, this ideal mirroring situation fails (perhaps to be recreated and recuperated later through psychoanalytic intervention), but in these constructions the first encounter with the other is fundamentally self-consolidating.

The most literal—and less reassuring—formulation of the self as consolidated in reflection by the other is, famously, that of Jacques Lacan's "mirror stage," in which the mother is not directly "reflecting back to the child his own appearance" (that is, in her own gaze and by her own facial expressions) but enabling his self-reflection: "The striking spectacle of a nursling in front of a mirror who has not yet mastered walking or even standing, but who—though held tightly by some prop, human or artificial . . . overcomes, in a flutter of jubilant activity, the constraints of his prop in order to adopt a slightly leaning-forward position and take in an instantaneous view of the image in order to fix it in his mind" ("Mirror Stage" 4). "In Lacan's view," remarks Shuli Barzilai, "the mirror is the mother of the ego. But the mother is not in the mirror" (88).[1] Rather than grounding the subject's sense of self in an exchange of gazes with a caring other, Lacan's formulation suggests that the self will always *be* other, an unattainable fantasy of coherence and efficacy whose outcome is an alienated and defensive subjectivity, "a knot of imaginary servitude [to the ideal self-image] that love must always untie anew or sever" ("Mirror Stage" 9).

Lacan elliptically acknowledges that "love" alone will not suffice to "untie a knot" whose determinations are social as well as individual: "For such a task," he admits, "we can find no promise in altruistic feelings, we who lay bare the aggressiveness that underlies the activities of the philanthropist, the idealist, the pedagogue, and even the reformer" ("Mirror Stage" 9). The novels discussed in this chapter also "lay bare" the aggressiveness of even apparently philanthropic others, revealing the ways in which socially marginalized female subjects experience a more-than-imaginary if not quite literal "servitude" to a continually enforced reflection of themselves as alienated and abject others.

Of the novels discussed in this chapter, none makes the condition of alienated mirroring more literal than *Villette*. Here, for example, Lucy describes her conscription by the flirtatious, demanding Ginevra Fanshawe to compare their reflections before an evening party at Madame Beck's pensionnat:

> Putting her arm through mine, [Ginevra] drew me to the mirror. Without resistance, remonstrance, or remark, I stood and let her self-love have its feast and triumph: curious to see how much it could swallow . . . whether any whisper of consideration for others could penetrate her heart, and moderate its vain-glorious exultation.
>
> Not at all. She turned me and herself round . . . and finally, letting go my arm, and curtseying with mock respect, she said:
>
> "I would not be you for a kingdom." (Brontë, *Villette* 179)

Ginevra's "self-love" is fed by the comparison; Lucy's self is negated. The many points of difference that Ginevra goes on to list between the two young women emphasize Lucy's purely negative material and social condition as a subject: Lucy is "*nobody's* daughter" with "*no* relations," she "*can't* call herself young" and has "*no* attractive accomplishments—*no* beauty," and "*no* living heart will [she] ever break" (179–80; my emphasis). Lucy has, indeed, no positive counterclaim to make but resists Ginevra's negations through her own negation—silence—suffering the comparison "*without* resistance, remonstrance, or remark." It is perhaps not surprising that later in the novel, Lucy momentarily fails to recognize her own reflection (in the unfamiliar context of a concert-hall), and when she does, feels "a jar of discord, a pang of regret" (262). Lucy's experience of mirrors makes literal the tremendous social pressure on each of this chapter's protagonists toward occupying, vis-à-vis dominant forms of subjectivity, an abjected state of the not-self, the self defined by its lack or absence. In the novel of formation, the protagonist usually occupies the role of the self to whom others exist in relation. Dangarembga's title—*The Book of Not*—sums up the contrary experience of each of these protagonists.

What makes this a problem of psychological alienation as well as social oppression is the extent to which the protagonists internalize these negations and come to view *themselves* as abject others, skeptical of aid or love from other people, at various moments paranoid, angry, and self-doubting. Klein describes the vicious circle produced by this psychological position: "At the bottom our strongest hatred, however, is directed against the hatred [i.e., of our own parents for their perceived failures] within ourselves. We so much dread the hatred in ourselves that we are driven to employ one of our strongest measures of defence by putting it on to other people—to project it. . . . Hatred, as we have seen, leads to our establishing frightening fiugres in our minds, and then we are apt to endow other people with unpleasant and malevolent qualities. Incidentally, such an attitude of mind has an actual effect in making other people unpleasant and suspicious toward us" (340). Elsewhere, Klein names this "attitude of mind" "projective identification." Projective identification, in Eve Sedgwick's summary, "is related to Freudian projection but more uncannily intrusive: for Freud, when I've projected my hostility onto you, I believe that *you* dislike *me;* for Klein, additionally, when I've projected my hostility *into* you, you *will* dislike me" ("Melanie Klein" 636). Indeed, the "uncanny," in the Freudian sense of inappropriately animated bodies or bodily fragments, or of objects out of place, makes striking appearances in all of these texts—in the recurring figure of the ghostly nun in *Villette;* in the repeated references to literal and metaphorical dismemberment in *The Book of Not;* in photographs that Lucy Potter takes that attempt to "reveal to me some of the things I had not seen" (Kincaid, *Lucy* 160).

As Sedgwick observes, "Klein . . . is fearfully attuned to human relations that are driven by the uncontrollable engines of ressentiment" ("Melanie Klein" 636), but in Klein's writings, affects of hostility as well as love are largely contained within familial, rather than social or political, relations. In *Lucy* and *The Book of Not,* however, the racialized context of colonialism is inextricable from all relations. Frantz Fanon's extension of Freud in *Black Skin, White Masks* (1952) responds directly to such a context with a paradigm similar to, but more politically specific than, Klein's projective identification. "In the Antilles," he asserts in *Black Skin, White Masks,* "the black schoolboy who is constantly asked to recite 'our ancestors the Gauls' identifies himself with the explorer, the civilizing colonizer, the white man who brings truth to the savages, a lily-white truth. The identification process means that the black child subjectively adopts a white man's attitude" (126–27)—an attitude of contempt or condescension that makes the black child the other in his own eyes. This psychic identification of the self as abject other (seeing oneself as the object of the "white man's" gaze) is accompanied by a physical self-dissociation as well: "In the white world, the man of color encounters difficulties in elaborating his body schema. The image of one's body is solely negating. It's an image in the third person" (90).

Brontë's, Kincaid's, and Dangarembga's protagonists, as we will see, each encounter, and try to evade, this experience of becoming "an image in the third person." They find themselves the objects of projective identification by the novel's other characters, particularly its female characters, for whom they embody the "intolerable parts" of female selves—poverty, loneliness, and powerlessness—within the regime of Victorian domestic ideology and its colonial descendants. In each case, the protagonists respond to this projective identification with their own hostile refusals. Lucy Snowe embraces a scornful isolation rather than accept the roles of discreet spinster, loyal companion, or bluestocking in which others would be smugly quick to place her. Kincaid's Lucy Potter substitutes the transgressive identity of "slut" for the handmaiden roles—as nurse, *au pair,* or exotic muse—that others imagine as natural to a young, female, West Indian emigrant. Tambu, younger and more naïve than either Lucy, works hard to transcend her embodied identity, as a black African schoolgirl barely tolerated in a white-run convent school in white-dominated Rhodesian society, by becoming an honor student and developing a mental discipline of *unhu,* a bearing of personal dignity in response to others. This bearing cannot, however, avert the violence, exploitation, and indifference she experiences. Not surprisingly, loneliness, anger, and despair suffuse these novels; and frequently, in addition to representing their characters' rejection of or lack of opportunity for, identifications, the novels reject or severely qualify readers' identifications as well.

CHARLOTTE BRONTË
THE POLITICS OF LONELINESS

The negative affects, particularly anger and loneliness, represented within Brontë's novels have often provoked negative critical responses. Her perceived anger was a basis for Victorian disapproval or dismissal, as in

Elizabeth Rigby's conclusion that *Jane Eyre* demonstrates the "tone of mind and thought which has overthrown authority and violated every code human and divine abroad, and fostered Chartism at home" (174) and Matthew Arnold's assertion about *Villette* that "the mind of the author contains nothing but hunger, rebellion, and rage" (Allott 201). In *A Room of One's Own,* Virginia Woolf also notoriously objects to Brontë's anger, suggesting that a writer such as Brontë will find that "her books will be deformed and twisted. She will write in a rage where she should write calmly" (72–73). Not only Brontë's insistent expressions of anger but also her frank portrayal of female loneliness, romantic and implicitly sexual, have aroused critical unease. Like her anger, such representations often seemed unwomanly or overly revealing to Victorian readers. After reading *Villette,* for example, W. M. Thackeray condescendingly speculated that "rather than have fame, rather than any other earthly good or mayhap heavenly one [Brontë] wants some Tomkins or another to love her and be in love with" (Allott 197). After Brontë's death, Elizabeth Gaskell's 1853 autobiography attempted to redirect Brontë's association with loneliness, depicting her not as a thwarted single woman but rather as a brave and blighted domestic angel who maintained a self-sacrificing devotion to her father as she was increasingly isolated by the successive deaths of her siblings.[2] Gaskell transformed Brontë's image from that of a lonely spinster to that of a Romantic *isolata;* later, twentieth-century feminist criticism transformed that icon, again, into a double-sided emblem of female rebellion. One side depicts self-sufficiency; the other, deprivation. For Sandra Gilbert and Susan Gubar, for example, Jane Eyre's is a journey of "astounding progress toward equality" representing an "emblem of hope" (370, 371); the later Lucy Snowe, however, is "from first to last a woman *without*—outside society, without parents or friends, without physical or mental attractions, without money or confidence or health" (400). This negative depiction has important implications for twentieth-century feminist criticism, since Brontë in this analysis becomes an object of readerly identification, "a powerful precursor for all the women who have been strengthened by the haunted and haunting honesty of her art" (440).

In a later analysis, however, Gilbert suggests that such a recuperation of Brontë's "haunted and haunting honesty" by 1970s and 1980s literary criticism may have underestimated or undervalued how far she goes in the depiction of the romantic and sexual longing and loneliness, "refus[ing] to acknowledge the rebellious sexual passion" (355) that Jane Eyre expresses. The subtitle of the most recent academic biography of Brontë, by Lyndall Gordon, "A Passionate Life," similarly captures an emphasis on a desiring rather than simply enduring Brontë. Gordon's aim is not to deny Brontë's loneliness but to reassert "the strength that turned loss to gain" (4) in both Brontë's intimate relationships and her writing, and portray Brontë as a "fiery survivor" (23) in a social context that distrusted female passion and creativity. Other twentieth- and twenty-first century critics have recuperated Brontë's representations of negative affect for analyses not specifically feminist or focused on gender. John Hughes, for example, calls *Villette* "a great novel of affective estrangement" (711) that "provokes and, as it were, disquietingly *reads* the reader by implicating him [*sic*], through his fascinations and insecurities, in an affective drama in which he finds aspects of himself" (714). Christopher Lane argues that Brontë's novels capture an ambivalence at the heart of citizenship, in a "preoccupation with hatred" that exceeds protest against any specific social limitations (such as those of Victorian gender ideology) or any possibility of the protagonist's reconciliation with those limitations (199).

Brontë's representations of anger and loneliness, then, seem by now to have been recuperated as particularly truthful, if not liberatory, in a twentieth- and twenty-first-century context, especially when they can be understood as aggressive or at least assertive—as suggested by critics' use of words like "passionate," "provok[ing]," and "hatred." But if such recuperations honor Brontë's aggression, they also scant her ambivalence about the isolation of which such aggression is sign, cause, and effect. At the center of *Villette,* for example, is Lucy's *cri de coeur:* "Is there nothing more for me in life—no true home—nothing to be dearer to me than myself, and by its paramount preciousness, to draw from me better things than I care to culture for myself only? Nothing, at whose feet I can willingly lay down the whole burden of human egotism, and gloriously take up the nobler charge of labouring and living for others?" (453). These words do not celebrate "affective estrangement" or "hatred"—those affects are real but they are ones that, as *Villette* makes clear, Lucy feels herself to have been *forced* into as a matter of sheer survival. The longing for intimacy and even interdependency—not always synonymous with "rebellious sexual passion"—that coexists with hostility and aggression in *Villette* comprehends, I will argue, not only desire, or romantic intimacy, but also identification, the experience of the self reflected and made legible in the other and the opening of the self *to* the "others" with whom Brontë identifies the "nobler charge."

In *Villette,* all such intimate relations, including identification, are suffused with and finally foreclosed by the disintegrative operations of a particularly female form of humiliation. As Thackeray's response, for example, suggests, Brontë's analysis of the social and emotional forces that prevent intimacy for herself and her protagonists runs the risk of a reduction of the author to the abject status of the single woman or the even more shameful status of an unrequitedly desirous one. Brontë's letters as well as her fiction make clear that she was all too aware of the shaming aspects, for a Victorian woman, of acknowledging loneliness. She writes to Ellen Nussey while finishing *Villette:*

> *My* reserve . . . has its foundation not in design, but in necessity—I am silent because I have literally *nothing to say.* I might indeed repeat over and over again that my life is a pale blank and often a very weary burden—and that the Future sometimes appals me—but what end could be answered by such repetition except to weary you and enervate myself?
>
> The evils that now and then wring a groan from my heart—lie in position [*sic*]—not that I am a *single* woman and likely to remain a *single* woman—but because I am a *lonely* woman and likely to be *lonely.*" (Brontë, *Selected Letters* 25 August 1852)

Defending herself against the accusation of "reserve" that Ellen Nussey has apparently leveled, Brontë re-performs rather than breaches that reserve, by insisting not only that that there is "nothing to say" but also that she has already said it—no further revelation is possible. As if anticipating a response from Ellen that would supply, as the unspoken referent of this "nothing," their shared status as single women, she insists that her difficulties belong to a "position" that refers to a general rather than a particularly matrimonial isolation. For to be "single," of course—the identity that she rejects—is specifically to be unmarried, a state whose misfortune for women in particular was receiving increased attention in mid-Victorian society.[3] The single woman was becoming a species, and as such taking on a socially recognized identity—but she was a species defined almost entirely negatively, as a problem, a surplus, a symptom of personal failure.

The humiliation of being single, and its relation to loneliness, forms a central theme of *Shirley,* the novel that immediately precedes *Villette.* Much of the novel is devoted to Caroline Helstone's depression in the face of her lack of occupation and the prospective deprivation and humiliation of joining the "very unhappy race" (Brontë, *Shirley* 192) of "old maids." But the humiliations of being a spinster, vividly illustrated by the bitter Miss Mann and the "very ugly" (196) Miss Ainslie, are surpassed by the shame of exposing a wish for romantic love, as Caroline fears that she has done. She "despise[s] herself" (236) for such revealing actions as having asked Robert Moore for a lock of his hair. "A lover masculine [who is] disappointed," the narrator explains, "can speak and urge explanation; a lover feminine can say nothing: if she did, the result would be shame and anguish, inward remorse for self-treachery. Nature would brand such demonstration as a rebellion against her instincts, and would vindictively relay it afterwards by the thunderbolt of self-contempt smiting suddenly in secret" (128). That a woman should not be the first to declare her love was a nineteenth-century truism, and certainly responses to her own work could only have reinforced Brontë's conviction of the "shame and anguish" courted by any such speaking.

In contemporary Anglo-American culture, the stigma attached to feminine displays of sexual interest, and the absoluteness of the spinster/wife divide, have greatly diminished (though not entirely disappeared). At the same time, the number and kind of subjects for whom being single implies a kind of failure seem only to have expanded. In article about the status of singleness in current queer culture and theory, Michael Cobb echoes Brontë's distinction between "single" and "lonely": "Now, instead of simply thinking 'single,' I've been *thinking* 'lonely' because I want a notion of sexlessness to be attached to singleness. . . . In fact, I want to suspend questions of sex and sexuality altogether . . . to start asking other questions about what it means to be alone, to be in solitude, and whether or not that is now permitted when the world wants people to feel desperate, lonely, and ready for toxic forms of sociality. Cobb draws on Hannah Arendt to suggest that "the feeling of loneliness produces sensations of desperation that open one up to the cruel ideologies of totalitarianism—ideologies that produce compelling ideas, full of persuasive power, that have logics that are much too consistent, much too able to misread the circumstances of the world, providing, instead, a paranoid 'sixth sense' through which the strong idea can order the world, regardless" (447).[4] While *Villette* is not a primarily a political critique, Brontë does represent Catholicism as something like a totalitarian ideology and Madame Beck as increasingly iron-fisted in her imposition of order; at her lowest point of "desperation" Lucy seeks solace, against all her prejudices and training, in the confessional. For both Brontë and Cobb, then, while the concept "lonely" may function less narrowly and less shamingly than the concept "single," it does not resolve the threat to the self posed by a social context that does not facilitate intimate relations for all its subjects.

Brontë finds in "lonely" a description of her position that is less humiliating—in her case, less contemptuously gendered, narrowly sexualized, and weighted with socially conscripting identities (such as that of the spinster) and drastic solutions (such as emigration, undertaken by Brontë's friend Mary Taylor)—than the description "single." Further, loneliness connects Lucy and Brontë to an elevated aesthetic tradition; it is the condition of Wordsworth's Lucy Gray, who "dwelt among untrodden ways" and also of Matthew Arnold's "mortal millions [who] live alone"; a condition both mourned and exalted in masculine poetics.[5] In choosing "lonely" over "single" to describe her state, Brontë rejects identification with a socially stigmatized role for one both more rarefied and more potentially universal, from which she might still be able to depict with some frankness her protagonists' need for intimacy and the social blockages to its fulfillment.

Villette, however, continually threatens to undo this distinction, revealing almost compulsively the extent to which Lucy Snowe's apparently personal and private condition of being "a lonely woman" is already, and cruelly, constructed by her publicly recognized and shaming condition as a *single* woman in the most comprehensive sense—a woman lacking in familial protection or romantic companionship and, embodying these lacks, something close to a nonself. *Villette* is notoriously grim and lacking in palliatives. In *Shirley,* Brontë, after leading Caroline Helstone deeply into the despair and shame of singleness and loneliness, relieves her of both conditions, providing her in rapid succession with an intimate friendship, a mother, and a husband.[6] In *Villette,* by contrast, Lucy fails to escape, and must rather learn to coexist with, the shame of the "divergence between [her life] and the intimate sphere that is alleged to be simple personhood" (Berlant and Warner 553). She must come to terms with the loneliness that makes inevitable her singleness (how can she, with no family or position, attract a mate?); the singleness that becomes the crux of her loneliness (how can she, as a single woman, experience intimacy?); and the humiliation that shapes her experience and her representation of both by blocking her affective bonds, including bonds of identification, with other subjects.

Like many narratives of formation, *Villette* begins in its protagonist's childhood, but only to establish its lack. Lucy lacks even the defined, if deprived, status of an orphan, like Jane Eyre or Pip. We encounter her only as as a visitor from a home never described. Her non-home is that of her godmother, Mrs. Bretton, who, with her son, Graham Bretton, "bore . . . the name of their birthplace—Bretton of Bretton: whether by coincidence, or because some remote ancestor had been a personage of sufficient importance to leave his name to his neighborhood, I know not" (Brontë, *Villette* 1). This problem of nomenclature introduces, on the novel's first page, an unproductive hypothetical detail about characters whose ancestry is of no importance to the story, establishing from the outset an emphasis on lack—of knowledge, of history, of narrative connection—not only within the novel but in the reader's relation to it. The excess of the Bretton name, its dual reference to patrilineage and autochthony, also serves to reinforce Lucy's contrasting absence of connection to family or place, a point further emphasized by the equally hyperbolic surname of the Brettons' other child visitor, Polly Home. Polly, too, is temporarily displaced, but she will go on to accumulate new names, and homes, at an impressive rate; the "Polly Home" of the first chapters becomes Paulina Mary Home de Bassompiere Bretton, the "little Countess," in the novel's third volume. Finally, marrying Graham, Paulina comes home—and brings Home—to the Brettons. Her changes of name and the movements they accompany reinforce a contrast with Lucy's absence of familial or geographical roots.

From a psychoanalytic point of view, in which the family, as the earliest scene of nurture, is where identification first occurs, this blank of Lucy's childhood not only anticipates but also precipitates her later experiences of loss, unstable selfhood, and failed intimacy. In "Mourning and Melancholia," Freud connects melancholia, as a pathological condition, with the loss of an object that is not grieved but rather is disavowed by the unacknowledged incorporation of aspects of the lost object into the self. Lucy Snowe's circumstances suggest that she has experienced early and significant loss, and it appears "ungrieved" to the point that the founding experience of loss *itself* is lost to—cannot be represented within—her narrative. The causes of her apparently parentless state are referred to only briefly, by teasing ellipsis and metaphor, in the novel's early chapters, before being banished entirely from the narrative:

> On quitting Bretton . . . I betook myself home, having been absent six months. It will be conjectured that I was of course glad to return to the bosom of my kindred. Well! the amiable conjecture does no harm, and may therefore be safely left uncontradicted. . . . I will permit the reader to picture me, for the next eight years, as a bark slumbering through halcyon weather. . . . However, it cannot be concealed that . . . there must have been a wreck at last. . . . In fine, the ship was lost, the crew perished.
>
> As far as I recollect, I complained to no one about these troubles. . . . Of Mrs. Bretton I had long lost sight. Impediments, raised by others, had, years ago, come in the way of our intercourse, and cut it off. (Brontë, *Villette* 42)

Lucy's sarcasm suggests that, whatever family members constituted this "bosom," she has certainly lost, if not her parents, the love and nurture that family is supposed to provide. Upon the death of her subsequent employer, Miss Marchmont, Lucy daringly emigrates to 'Labassecour' (Brontë's fictionalization of Belgium) and talks her way into a position at Madame Beck's school, but once there she "shrinks into [her] sloth as a nursery governess. . . . The negation of severe suffering was the nearest approach to happiness I expected to know" (94). It requires the actions of another (Madame Beck) to precipitate Lucy into action, and these actions are represented not as caring but as hostile: "At that moment she did not wear a woman's aspect, but rather a man's. Power of a particular kind strongly limned itself in all her traits, and that power was not *my* kind of power: neither sympathy, nor congeniality, nor submission, were the emotions it awakened. I stood—not soothed, not won, nor overwhelmed. It seems as if a challenge of strength between opposing gifts was given, and I suddenly felt all the dishonour of my diffidence" (95). In a slightly different narrative, Madame Beck could be, even if formidable, a mother figure: She is what Lucy becomes—the owner of a school; and she gives Lucy her start in this career. But Lucy as narrator disavows any identification with, or even gratitude toward, the older woman, as an object of emulation or a mentor, and Brontë as author represents Madame Beck as increasingly grotesque, developing from "a charitable woman, [who] did a great deal of good" (88) at the novel's opening to a scheming harpy at its end, not above drugging Lucy into submission.

If Lucy's early life is lost to her, our singular narrator, it must be lost to the reader as well, since whatever "residues of the lost object," or "succession of phantasies" we might attribute to Lucy or to any fictional unconscious, there is nowhere that readers can recover them. We may posit, certainly, that Lucy did not benefit from the ideal Kleinian mother whose "capacity for love has developed in such a way that she can make a strong identification both with her child, and with a wise mother of her own whom she keeps in mind" (Klein 319), but Lucy herself never invokes the name of "mother." Just as Lucy the character initially appears to lack psychological grounding for relations of identification, Lucy the narrator works hard to complicate a reader's potential identification with her, or even understanding of her circumstances. Much as Lucy's unreliability and hostility as a narrator has been critically canvassed, it remains difficult to over-emphasize how thoroughly dislocation, misrecognition, and failures of identification in all senses saturate the narrative. Consider, for example, an early interaction, between Lucy and one Mrs. Barrett, once Lucy's nurse and now housekeeper at a "grand mansion." When Lucy, unemployed, seeks her advice, she has apparently little to offer:

> The housekeeper was slowly propounding some difficulties, while she prepared orange-rind for marmalade, when a child ran past the window and came bounding into the room. It was a pretty child, and as it danced, laughing, up to me—for we were not strangers (nor, indeed, was its mother—a young married daughter of the house—a stranger)—I took it on my knee. Different as were our social positions now, this child's mother and I had been schoolfellows, when I was a girl of ten and she a young lady of sixteen; and I remembered her—good-looking, but dull—in a lower class than mine.
>
> I was admiring the boy's handsome dark eyes, when the mother, young Mrs. Leigh, entered. What a beautiful and kind-looking woman was the good-natured and comely, but unintellectual girl become! Wifehood and maternity had changed her thus, as I have since seen them change others even less promising than she. Me she had forgotten. I was changed too; though not, I fear, for the better. I made no attempt to recall myself to her memory: why should I? She came for her son to accompany her in a walk, and behind her followed a nurse carrying an infant. I only mention the incident because, in addressing the nurse, Mrs. Leigh spoke French (very bad French, by the way, and with an incorrigibly bad accent, again forcibly reminding me of our schooldays); and I found the woman was a foreigner. . . . When the whole party were withdrawn, Mrs. Barrett remarked that her young lady had brought that foreign nurse home with her two years ago, on her return from a Continental excursion; that she was treated almost as well as a governess, and had nothing to do but walk out with the baby and chatter French with Master Charles; "and," added Mrs. Barrett, "she says there are many Englishwomen in foreign families as well-placed as she."
>
> I stored up this piece of information. (Brontë, *Villette* 53–54)

In what seems an arbitrary, if not downright hostile, distribution of narrative emphasis, readers learn the contents of Mrs. Barrett's marmalade but not what difficulties she "propounds," just as we learn that Lucy once had a nurse, a friend, and a different social standing, but no more about the family to whom that nurse must have been attached, the cause of the change in standing, or the failure of Lucy's former friends to come to her aid. Orange rind aside, the narrative here favors abstraction even as it seems to offer detail. Speech is characterized—Mrs. Barrett speaks slowly,

Mrs. Leigh inelegantly—but not directly represented. The only piece of dialogue that appears in quotation marks—the French nurse's remarks—belies them by being reported. The passage implies a connection between the nurse's remark and Lucy's own decision, in the next chapter, to leave England, but it is striking that she makes this decision not as a result of aid or advice offered by any character in this scene, but rather as the result of a series of chances whose contingency is emphasized: Lucy "only mentions the incident" of Mrs. Leigh's entrance because it reveals, accidentally, that the nurse is a "foreigner," prompting Mrs. Barrett to remark on the situation of similarly-placed Englishwomen, but not, apparently, directly to recommend such a course.

Lucy's description of her relationship to Mrs. Leigh and her child is given in peculiarly tortured syntax: "We were not strangers (nor indeed was her mother a stranger)" conveys positive information (the two women know each other) negatively, and the information is then re-negated when we are told that "Me she had forgotten," a phrasing that places Lucy in the syntactical and logical position of the sentence's subject and yet contrives to return her to the objective case. This (non)-encounter with an old schoolfriend adumbrates the novel's many later scenes of mis- or non-recognition. Sometimes Lucy recognizes while not being recognized, as in her identification of the louche pursuers of her first night in Labassecour with the two bullying professors for whom she later writes an essay on "Human Justice," as well as in her recognition of the "Dr. John" of Villette as both the "true young English gentleman" (Brontë, *Villette* 78) of that same night and the "Graham Bretton" of her youth. Sometimes she fails to recognize others, such as, initially, Paulina Home, in Labassecour; Ginevra Fanshawe's suitor, Alfred de Hamal, in disguise as a nun; even herself, in the mirror in an unfamiliar dress.

Such failures of recognition—literal forms of non-identification—are not surprising, given the disconcerting tendency of *Villette*'s characters to be unrecognizable even to the reader from one moment to the next. Madame Beck's transformation from commanding professional to desperate housewife, mentioned above, is one instance; the baffling oscillation in the representation of John Graham Bretton is another. Brontë acceded to her publisher's objection that there was a "defect [in] the want of perfect harmony between Graham's boyhood and manhood; the angular abruptness of his change of sentiment toward Miss Fanshawe" (Brontë, *Selected Letters* 3 November 1852). Lucy (perhaps as a result of this response from George Smith) highlights this inconsistency. First she apologizes for the "modification" that her opinion of "Dr. John" seems to undergo by saying "I give the feeling as at the time I felt it" (Brontë, *Villette* 239–40); then she ascribes "a seeming contradiction in the two views which have been given of Graham Bretton" to "the public and the private—the out-door and the in-door view" (247). Such mutability might be viewed as conveying Lucy's changing relationship to the characters, as underscoring the extent to which the narrative is controlled by her deeply subjective point of view. But rather than encourage readerly identification, as does the subjective narration of *Jane Eyre,* this oscillating point of view may disrupt it, by reminding the reader that these characters are fictive constructs, that a character called "Dr. John" is the same as one called "Graham Bretton" only inasmuch as, and when, Lucy says so, and that Lucy's—or Brontë's—motivations for such changes may escape readerly comprehension.

In its sometimes baffling subjective point of view, *Villette* not only challenges readerly identification but also avoids the expression of social critique. In *Shirley,* Caroline Helstone ponders at some length the social question of employment for young women and "old maids." Although she docilely concedes that "nobody in particular is to blame . . . and I cannot tell . . . how [things] are to be altered for the better," she nevertheless concludes, in a peroration of over two pages, that "single women should have more to do—better chances of interesting and profitable occupation than they possess now" (377). Lucy more thoroughly refuses to take on the sociological burden of the "Woman Question." When she breaks down after being left alone, over the school vacation, in charge of a disabled boarder, she insists that her situation "is no living being's fault" and that the blame lies with "a great abstraction on whose wide shoulders I like to lay the mountains of blame they were sculptured to bear . . . Fate" (Brontë, *Villette* 232). When M. Paul harangues her on the subject of "women of intellect . . . a luckless accident, a thing for which there was neither place nor use in creation, wanted neither as wife nor worker," she steadfastly repeats: "Cela ne me regarde pas: je ne m'en soucie pas [that's nothing to do with me; I don't care about that]" (445). In both cases, the narrative raises the possibility of placing Lucy's trials in the context of social relations—her employer/employee relation with Madame Beck, the larger question of women's position—only to dismiss it. Yielding to it, perhaps, would require Lucy to identify herself with the role of the "luckless accident"—a dependent single woman—in front of men whose fixed and conventional ideas of feminine perfection would not allow them to imagine solutions, either personal or social, to her troubles. It would thus do the same for Brontë in front of her readers, who were often—as publishers and reviewers as well as readers—indicatively male, and of whose discomfort and potential condescension she was never unaware.[7]

Nevertheless Lucy's narrative repeatedly, if indirectly, demonstrates that it is her social context that eliminates opportunities for constructive identification with others and instead threatens her with coercive misidentifications. When the snobbish Ginevra Fanshawe repeatedly asks "Who *are* you, Miss Snowe?" the answers she expects are not, of course, psychological—Ginevra, her own mind "chaotic as a rag-bag" (Brontë, *Villette* 111), disclaims any interest in depth of character. She simply wants to classify, and class, her unclassifiable companion: "You used to call yourself a nursery-governess . . . and now Madame Beck treats you with more courtesy than she treats the Parisienne, St. Pierre; and that proud chit, my cousin [i.e., Paulina de Bassompiere], makes you her bosom friend!" (383). Lucy rebuffs Ginevra's attempts not only to identify her socially but also to offer herself for another kind of identification. When she refuses to walk arm-in-arm with Ginevra because "when she took my arm, she always leaned upon me her whole weight, and as I was not a gentleman, or her lover, I did not like it," Ginevra responds: "There, again! . . . I thought, by offering to take your arm, to intimate approbation of your dress and general appearance: I meant it as a compliment" (384). This exchange can be read for a cross-gendering of Lucy, in her relation to Ginevra, that harks back to their performance in the school play, where Lucy, in skirts and a mustache, plays the "fop" to Ginevra's ingenue. Focusing on identification rather than desire, however, what I see here is Lucy's refusal of Ginevra's insistence that she acknowledge a likeness based on "approbation": Ginevra's projections, "proving . . . her incapacity to conceive how any person not bolstered up by birth or wealth, not supported by some consciousness of name or connection, could maintain an attitude of reasonable integrity" (385), only weigh Lucy down.

Other characters share this insistent desire to identify Lucy with some pre-existing type. Dr. John views her as a sisterly chaperone of both his first infatuation (Ginevra) and his settled love (Paulina). This misreading is more painful than Ginevra's, since it overlooks not only her general capacity for passion but also her particular, though unexpressed, passion for him. After he calls her "quiet Lucy Snowe" and "a being inoffensive as a shadow," she "wished he would just let me alone—cease allusion to me. These epithets—these attributes I put from me . . . not with scorn, but with extreme weariness"; in sum, she observes, "he always wanted always to give me a role not mine" (Brontë, *Villette* 394, 395). Similarly, "Madame Beck esteemed me learned and blue; Miss Fanshawe, caustic, ironic, and cynical; Mr. Home, a model teacher, the essence of the sedate and discreet" (375). Everyone around Lucy, in other words, misidentifies her, eager to place her within a narrow range of female images: Paul Emmanuel goes so far as to recommend to her contemplation in Labassecour's museum the four pious scenes from "La vie d'une femme," comprising a church-going young girl, praying wife, young mother, and widow. Repeatedly Lucy is assured that she can achieve social and personal recognition only by identifying with positions and images that embody what is undesirable to others (the spinster schoolteacher) or unattainable or undesirable to herself (conventionally domestic femininity, here rendered particularly dismissable in Lucy's eyes through its Catholic visual vocabulary). Paradoxically and damagingly, she can retain her sense of herself *as* a self (rather than as a stock character) only by refusing all such identifications and thus becoming almost invisible to others.

It is, as the examples above suggest, not only men in the novel but also other women seek to identify Lucy with stereotypes of failed or marginalized femininity, and their cruelty can be read as a form of projective identification. Projective identification, as summarized by Eve Sedgwick, results from a subject's "prophylactic need to split good from bad, and the aggressive expulsion of intolerable parts of oneself onto—or, in [Melanie] Klein's more graphic locution, *into*—the person who is taken as an object" (Sedgwick, "Melanie Klein" 636). For the novel's female characters Lucy embodies the "intolerable" outcomes of loneliness, impoverishment, or class decline that seem to shadow Victorian middle-class women. Madame Beck's professional success has demanded from her suppression of her own romantic desires (which, like Lucy's, are directed toward Graham Bretton and Paul Emmanuel), and she is isolated by her position at the pinnacle of an edifice of surveillance. With a consciousness of social position but no money, Ginevra as much as Lucy is forced to live by her wits. Even the privileged Paulina is reminded by her father that Lucy's fate could be hers: "If my Polly ever came to know by experience the uncertain nature of this world's goods, I should like her to act as Lucy acts: to work for herself, that she might burden neither kith nor kin" (Brontë, *Villette* 356). Lucy herself completes the circle of hostility that Klein's model anticipates; having functioned as the object of other female characters' negative projective identifications, she reciprocally dismisses them all.

In a different narrative or psychological context the projective identifications of Madame Beck, Ginevra, and Paulina might be less definitive, since they coexist with gestures of goodwill or aid toward Lucy. Madame

Beck takes her in literally from the street and promotes her professional development; Ginevra, in her own selfish way, befriends her; Paulina offers genuine companionship—"I liked her," Lucy acknowledges—and an entrée into familial comfort. But Lucy remains trapped in a nexus of *scarcity* that is social as well as psychological—for the displaced women depicted in *Villette,* there is simply not enough intimacy, any more than there is enough financial security, to go around.

At the end of the novel, Lucy does become, in one sense, someone very much like Madame Beck, a lone woman mistress of her own school. But this development is hardly presented as a triumph. Unlike Madame Beck, who is a widow with children, and deeply rooted in the religious and social life of her community; unlike Paulina; unlike even the flighty Ginevra, Lucy never passes through the conventional stages of the "vie d'une femme." Most important, she never attains the psychological "true home" for which she longs. In a geographical sense, as well, she remains excluded from what she identifies as the "true home" of her nationality and religion—England. *Villette* is not overtly an imperialist text, especially in comparison to *Jane Eyre.* In *Jane Eyre,* not only do colonized female subjects form the metaphorical, abjected "other" to Jane's liberal autonomy, but also imperial expropriation, in the form of a legacy from her uncle's interests in Madeira, enables Jane to feel that she has achieved a "true home" with Rochester because she is financially autonomous as well. In *Villette,* by contrast, Paul Emmanuel's imperialist mission to Antigua to supervise an estate has the effect of destroying Lucy's hopes, since it is on his return that he is shipwrecked. Yet Brontë's novel retains a nationalist, if not a colonialist, identification. Lucy's continuing attachment to England and English values is signified not only by her isolation from Labassecourien society but also by her continued rejection of Catholicism and "Continental" culture and her frequent laudatory invocation of Englishness and Protestantism as identical with freedom and truth. Indeed, her anti-Catholicism is nourished by attitudes toward the other similar to those of imperialist and colonialist ideology. As Rosemary Clark-Beattie observes: "Like many of her contemporaries, Lucy escapes her insignificance within English society by fleeing to a setting where her adherence to the mores of the very culture she has fled sets her apart, in her own mind, as superior. Her identity is formed by the contradiction implicit in the phrase 'Protestant in a Catholic country'" (825).

In the novel's most explicitly nationalist moment, M. Paul during a class attacks "les anglaises" with a vituperation that falls "not only upon our women, but upon our greatest names and best men; sullying the shield of Britannia, and dabbling the union-jack in the mud." Enraged, Lucy erupts, "Vive l'Angleterre, l'Histoire et les Héros! À bas la France, la Fiction et les Faquins [Long live England, history, and heroes! Down with France, fiction, and ruffians!]" (Brontë, *Villette* 429). This exchange is not only risible ("I suppose [the students] thought me mad," Lucy acknowledges) but is also represented as more personal than political in its motivation: the reader understands M. Paul's attack to be one of the manifestations of his jealousy of the relationship between Lucy and Graham Bretton. Inasmuch as Graham is emphatically represented as a perfect English gentleman, Lucy's attraction to him and M. Paul's jealousy of it might themselves be read as signs of national value. And her response here, echoing her mockery in the previous chapter of M. Paul's "very inefficient" translation of "un drame de Williams Shackspire" (415), reveals her continued contempt for her adopted culture. Lucy's exile serves less to liberate her from English culture than to put a distance between that culture and the "conditions of denial and privation" that she has actually experienced there. The ocean that separates her from M. Paul (through death) and from England (by geography) allows both the "true home" of domestic ideology and the homeland of English nationality to remain lost and idealized objects of identification. As we will see in the next section, the retention of this capacity for idealization is one of the most significant differences between the English Lucy Snowe and her West Indian descendant, Lucy Potter.

JAMAICA KINCAID

THE POLITICS OF APPROPRIATION

Jamaica Kincaid cites Charlotte Brontë as one of her favorite novelists, and a number of critics have analyzed the relationship between Kincaid's and Brontë's novels, which is typically characterized as one of revision. Susan Lanser, for example, writes that "Even as the narrator seems to honor the paradigmatic female voice of white nineteenth-century British fiction . . . a major project of *Annie John* is to reverse the racism of Brontë's novel by re-presenting British characters and values through Antiguan eyes" (215). Kincaid herself claims *Jane Eyre,* rather than *Villette,* as *Lucy*'s precursor: "The great influences on [Lucy Potter's] life are Genesis and Revelation and, strangely enough, *Jane Eyre.* . . . Lucy is a very moralistic person and she's very judgmental. Her view of the world is very much shaped by a nineteenth-century view, filtered through the mist of colony and mother country" (Vorda 22).[8] Indeed, Brontë is present in *Lucy* only inferentially, when Lucy mentions "Emily, Charlotte, and Jane" as "the names of the authoresses whose books I loved" (Kincaid, *Lucy* 149); other writers and artists—Wordsworth, Milton, Gauguin, Simone de Beauvoir—are more explicitly referenced. Nevertheless, echoes small and large between *Lucy* and *Villette* abound, and Lucy Snowe embodies that "moralist . . . judgmental . . . nineteenth-century view" that forms part of Lucy Potter's complex colonial heritage. Kincaid's effort in *Lucy,* I will suggest, is not so much to "reverse" the proto- or implicitly imperialist narrative of *Villette* as it is to reinhabit it, to move it forward, to "write what [Brontë] would write were she in my place, or if I were she, yet living my life" (Schwartz, *Ruined by Reading* 67). In the full knowledge of the history of "foul deed[s]" that separates them, Kincaid in *Lucy* tacitly invokes what Susan Bernstein terms a "dissonant identification," which "captures the value of affective engagement as a strategy for approaching, for self-consciously apprehending, traumatic knowledge" (158–59). Kincaid's dissonant identification with Brontë's Victorian protagonist apprehends the postcolonial subject's "traumatic knowledge" of a colonial inheritance through reappropriation and refiguration that stop well short of reclaiming or reversing the effects of that burden.

For Kincaid, dissonant identification is expressed frequently, necessarily, through reappropriation. In an interview, Moira Ferguson asks Kincaid whether she "would position [herself] in the Caribbean writing tradition." In response, Kincaid invokes Tsitsi Dangarembga:

> Well, that's a very funny question. I speak as someone from the British Caribbean. What tradition is that from? That is from English tradition. You know, most people, especially people from my generation, had an education that was sort of an English public-school education. We got the height of empire. They were trying to erase any knowledge of another history, another possibility . . . I was reading a book by a woman from Zimbabwe and it said that it was truly an African novel that doesn't owe any debt to English writing. And that is not true at all. The book reminds me of Jane Austen in its humor and its kind of irony and its mannerisms. . . . The tradition of novels is not an African form, as far as I can tell. But what is so wrong with that? This woman has written a novel that draws on Jane Austen. Jane Austen and her people would not hesitate for one second if they found something in Zimbabwe that they liked. They would just take it. And so she could take Jane Austen. . . . [*Nervous Conditions*] is a fabulous book, borrowed from Jane

> Austen, and who cares? It is a fabulous book. Take. It's okay. (Ferguson, "A Lot of Memory" 168)[9]

This is a slightly startling comparison. While Dangarembga is frequently ironic, she is hardly writing Austenian social comedy. But to startle is part of Kincaid's aim: intertextuality, identification, and influence in her hands are appropriative, aggressive, unsettling. What colonial conquest took from colonized people was (at least initially) not narrative forms but labor and the raw materials of wealth; the language and literatures of the "English tradition," contrarily, as Kincaid suggests, were imposed. For Kincaid, however, these facts do not mean that narrative forms are not available for taking or that the trajectories of appropriation can never be altered.

Elsewhere, Kincaid is less insouciant about the complexities involved in "tak[ing]" the narratives of colonial power, in forms of identification that are so deeply linked to cultural and historical loss. The injunction to "take" Austen is made literal in repeated references to stealing books in Kincaid's writing. Annie John, for example, steals library books and hides them under her house (Kincaid, *Annie John* 55). In their hiding place Annie's books share room with her precious collection of marbles, tokens of unladylike play that she also conceals from her mother:

> My mother now crawled under the house and began a furious and incredible search for my marbles . . . tearing apart my neat pile of books, which, if she had opened any one of them, would have revealed to her, stamped on the title page, these words: "Public Library, Antigua." Of course, that would have been a whole other story, and I can't say which would have been worse, the stolen books or playing marbles. (66)

What these two apparently unlike objects—books and marbles—have in common is that they embody pleasures and skills initially offered by representatives of the regimes of power (colonial and maternal) to which the young Annie hardly realizes her subjection; when, however, she attempts to make those pleasures and skills her own—to take them—she discovers they were never hers to keep, and that keeping them by force or stealth entails the danger of discovery and punishment.

In more recent narratives Kincaid links this desire to possess texts as a reader with the desire to produce texts as a writer. In an interview with Frank Birbalsingh and in the memoir *My Brother* (1997), Kincaid similarly recalls her mother searching out and burning all her books, because

Kincaid had neglected domestic and chores and childcare while reading. Kincaid's reading here figures as a double theft: her (undiscovered) theft of books from agents of a colonial regime; and her theft of labor (chores undone) from a mother who also serves, in her commitment to domestic ideology, as such an agent. That her mother responds with a third robbery, (re)taking from Kincaid what is (not) hers, compounds the inextricability of textuality and theft. Recalling the event later, Kincaid claims it as an authorial origin story: "Books were the only things I knew and loved, and I did not know what would replace them. I didn't know what else to love. It was a significant moment. I'd quite possibly spend the rest of my life trying to write the books that were taken away from me then" (Birbalsingh 144). *Lucy* can be read as part of that project, emphasizing dissonant identifications that take the form of reappropriations of Victorian and colonialist narratives, particularly *Villette.*

Lucy Potter's initial situation in many respects resembles Lucy Snowe's: the emigration of both is motivated by material deprivation and enabled by their perceived suitability, as young, powerless women, to perform the labor of childcare, in potentially exploitative circumstances, in their host countries. As Lucy Snowe is always a visitor or employee in the homes of others, so at the beginning of Lucy Potter's narrative, in *Lucy,* we learn that the family she works for calls her "the Visitor. They said I seemed not to be a part of things, as if I didn't live in their house with them, as if they weren't like a family to me, as if I were just passing through" (13). Lucy's employers are not, of course "like a family" to her, and she is "part of things" only on the thinnest of suffrances. With a surely willed obtuseness, her employer Mariah (who shares a given name with Lucy Snowe's employer, Modeste Maria Beck) and her husband, Lewis, read her responses as though they could only signify individual affect. After she recounts a dream about Lewis in which she falls "down a hole, at the bottom of which were some silver and blue snakes," Mariah laughs and says "Dr. Freud for Visitor" (14, 15). Not recognizing the reference, Lucy does intuit their failure to acknowledge her intended meaning: "I had meant by telling them my dream that I had taken them in, because only people who were very important to me had ever shown up in my dreams" (15). But though Lucy has been "taken . . . in," in the sense of being offered shelter, by her employers, and she believes herself to have "taken them in" in the sense of beginning to care about them, both parties have been "taken in" in the sense of being fooled, for their lack of mutual understanding—particularly the employers' inability to imagine the concrete details of Lucy's experience—will be continually revealed.

As Lucy Snowe is circumspect about the "*impediments*, raised by others, [that] had years ago, come in the way of our intercourse" that initially prevent her from turning to her godmother, Mrs. Bretton, for help (Brontë, *Villette* 42), so Lucy Potter does not comment on the self-delusion that allows her employers to redescribe employer–employee relations as peer or family relations and puzzle over her assertion of distance. Evie Shockley calls the suspended state of "passing through" that Brontë's and Kincaid's Lucys share—their loss of ordinary social connection and their insistence on an independence that others are unwilling to recognize or grant—"gothic homelessness . . . the state of the individual who is unwilling and/or unable to achieve or maintain performances of ideologically privileged norms and, as a result, comes to be located socially outside or on the margins of domestic space and the communities privileged by domestic ideology" (49–50). For Shockley, the Lucys are united in their marginality and their repudiation of existing feminine roles.[10]

At the same time, in two crucial ways, one relating to personal and one to public history, the situation of the two Lucys is different. Lucy Potter, unlike Lucy Snowe, is not motherless: the references she makes to her mother throughout her narrative make it clear that she has had only too much mothering:

> My mother . . . spoke to me in a language anyone female could understand. And I was undeniably that—female. Oh, it was a laugh, for I had spent so much time saying I did not want to be like my mother that I missed the whole story: I was not like my mother—I was my mother. And I could see now why, to the few feeble attempts I made to draw a line between us, her reply always was "You can run away, but you cannot escape the fact that I am your mother, my blood runs in you, I carried you for nine months inside me." How else was I to take such a statement but as a sentence for life in a prison whose bars were stronger than any iron imaginable? (Kincaid, *Lucy* 90–91)

As Klein proposes, less vividly, "Some mothers . . . exploit [the maternal] relationship for the gratification of their own desires, *i.e.* their possessiveness and the satisfaction of having somebody dependent on them. Such mothers want their children to cling to them, and they hate them to grow up and to acquire individualities of their own" (318). In the absence of a mother, Lucy Snowe can idealize the maternal charge of "labouring and living for others" (Brontë, *Villette* 453). Lucy Potter has a more vivid sense of the price of that relation: "I said [in a letter to my mother] that she had acted like a saint, but that since I was living in this real world I had really wanted just a mother" (Kincaid, *Lucy* 127). Like Virginia Woolf, Lucy imagines escaping her own identification with the angel of the house only through the angel's total destruction: "She should not have married my father," she tells the compatriot who comes to convey news of her father's death: "She should not have had children. She should not have thrown away her intelligence. She should not have paid so little attention to mine. She should not have listened to someone like you. I am not like her at all" (123).

Lucy Potter's relationship with her mother cannot be separated from its colonial context, with its strong impress of British Victorian culture. This is the second important difference between the two Lucys: though both are exiles, one is the citizen of what was, in the nineteenth century, the world's largest imperial power, the other of one of the "small places" colonized by that power.[11] For Lucy Snowe, Victorian culture is present time; for Lucy Potter, its persistent ideological traces represent the fraught articulation with modernity that imperial conquest imposes on colonized societies—at once insisting on the inevitability of "modernization" and yet stalling its subjects in the moment of colonization. The economic imperative that Lucy Potter feels to leave her home is the direct result of the colonial conquest that remains marginal in Lucy Snowe's narrative. As a result, in Kincaid's *Lucy,* a "true home" remains unavailable even as an object of fantasy. A moment of nationalist assertion comparable to Lucy Snowe's occurs in *Lucy* when, at "fourteen or so," Lucy Potter "stand[s] up in school choir practice and say[s] that I did not wish to sing 'Rule, Britannia! Britannia, rule the waves; Britons never, never shall be slaves,' that I was not a Briton and that until not too long ago I would have been a slave" (135). Like Lucy Snowe's outburst, Lucy Potter's occurs in a classroom, in the context of explicitly nationalist pedagogy; also as in Lucy Snowe's case, the political implications of the protagonist's resistance are de-emphasized. The young Lucy Potter's immediate concerns are aesthetic: "If only we had been ruled by the French: they were prettier, much happier in appearance, so much more the kind of people I would have enjoyed being around" (136). The result of her outburst, too, is deflating: "My choir mistress only wondered if all their efforts to civilize me over the years would come to nothing in the end" (135).

Lucy Potter thus rejects the imperialist nationality with which Lucy Snowe identifies ("Vive l'Angleterre!"/"I was not a Briton") and embraces the one that Lucy Snowe deplores ("À bas la France"/"If only we had been ruled by the French"). The relation between the two moments of protest, however, is not simply one of reversal: Lucy Potter's eruption is not proto- but anti-nationalist. Her rejection of the "foul deed" (Kincaid, *Lucy* 135) of English conquest necessarily involves a rejection not just of "Britannia" but also of her own just-post-colonial homeland, marked as it is by Victorian cultural norms imposed at the moment of conquest and not entirely superseded by decolonization. Unlike Lucy Snowe, Lucy Potter is alienated at the outset from even the most attenuated or abstract of attachments to her mother country: "An ocean stood between me and the place I came from," she reflects, "but would it have made a difference if it had been a teacup of water? I could not go back" (9–10). Although she outgrows her initial impulse to exchange one colonial regime for another—"I understand the situation better now; I understand that . . . my pen pal [on a French-ruled island] and I were in the same boat"—she "still think[s] those words [*liberté, egalité, fraternité*] have a better ring to them" (136). Lucy's fantasy is not of an aboriginally "free" homeland but of worse and better colonial regimes.

As *Lucy* begins, Lucy has just arrived to work as an au pair in an unnamed U.S. city (very much like New York) from an unnamed West Indian island (very much like Kincaid's homeland, Antigua). Everything about her new situation—the weather, the food, her homesickness—initially surprises and disappoints Lucy. "In books I had read," she reflects:

> —from time to time, when the plot called for it—someone would suffer from homesickness. A person would leave a not very nice situation and go somewhere else, somewhere a lot better, and then long to go back where it was not very nice. How impatient I would become with such a person, for I would feel that I was in a not very nice situation myself, and how I wanted to go somewhere else. But now I, too, felt that I wanted to be back where I came from. (Kincaid, *Lucy* 6)

Lucy here records two unexpected experiences: homesickness and the discovery of an unlooked-for home in a fictional tradition—the "books [she has] read"—she had believed to be inadequate to her unique, non-fictional experience. Previously she has not identified with the characters she has read about in these abstractly summarized books; now, retrospectively, she begins to see the possibilities of such identification.

Lucy's initial comparison of her feelings to the feelings described in "books I had read" is the first of many such comparisons that she makes of present experience to proleptic textual representation. The accumulation of these comparisons emphasizes what may not be apparent in any single example alone: their inextricability from Lucy's status as a colonial subject, whose compulsory education (at the evocatively-named "Queen Victoria Girls' School" [Kincaid, *Lucy* 18]) has emphasized the aesthetic, geographic, and even meteorological norms of the English colonial power at the expense of local ones: "At ten years of age I had to learn by heart a long poem about some flowers I would not see in real life until I was nineteen" (30); "In one of the few films I had seen in my life so far, some people on a train . . . settled into their compartments" (31); "I had read of this lake in geography books" (35); "her blue eyes (which I would have found beautiful even if I hadn't read millions of books in which blue eyes were always accompanied by the word 'beautiful'), grew dim" (39); "as a child in school, I had learned how the earth tilts away from the sun and how that causes the different seasons" (85–86). The details of Lucy's education work to replace her knowledge and experience of her own locality with a European, and particularly English, literature, history, and geography, interpellating her as a subject estranged from two cultures: a dominant but inaccessible colonial one and an accessible but devalued local one.[12] Lucy's experience of learning and reciting "Daffodils" as something she "had to" do, from which she immediately begins to dissociate herself, contrasts with Tambu's embrace of her opportunity to recite Browning's verses; Lucy, unlike Tambu, seems aware of these hegemonic implications almost from the start. There is much less distance between the older narrating and younger experiencing voices in *Lucy* than there is in *Nervous Conditions.*

Lucy's experiences of readerly identification must always be moments of repudiation, disidentification, or dissident identification as well. Lucy Snowe, as we have seen, is silent about her name and familial origins. Lucy Josephine Potter, however, is bitterly aware of the origins of every part of hers; the effects of imperial history are difficult to evade, and Lucy Potter, unlike Lucy Snowe, does not represent herself as mysteriously *sui generis.* "Josephine" honors an uncle whom his family believed to be "rich, from money he had made in sugar in Cuba," but whose death reveals him as a bankrupt who "had been living in an old tomb in the Anglican churchyard"—a revenant of English conquest. Lucy's surname, Potter, "must have come from the Englishman who owned my ancestors when they were slaves" (Kincaid, *Lucy* 149). Growing up, she repudiates these names, with their colonialist history: "In my own mind, I called myself other names [than Lucy]: Emily, Charlotte, Jane. They were the names of the authoresses whose books I loved. I eventually settled on the name Enid, after the authoress Enid Blyton, because that name seemed the most unusual of all the names I thought of" (149–50). These female authors, read outside of school, offer Lucy a sense of self apart from the official prescriptions of country, school, and family.

At the same time, however, the names Emily, Charlotte, and Jane are part of, rather than alternative to, the colonial history that Lucy rejects; in particular, as the names of women who wrote in the idiom of domestic realism, their names are freighted with the resonance of Victorian domestic ideology. Lucy's use of the noun "authoresses" to describe the Brontës and Austen serves as a reminder of this anachronism and marks the distance of the older narrator from her childish preferences. Nothing in Kincaid's fiction, with its depictions of what Ian Smith calls "the symbolic intersection of colonial territorialization and the writer's embattled relationship to her mother" (804), encourages the reader to view women or female authors as inherently more liberating objects of identification than men or male authors. Indeed, Lucy remembers that her mother became "a ball of fury" when she voiced her preference for the name Enid, which she takes from Enid Blyton: "A woman with whom my father had had a child and who had tried to kill my mother and me through obeah was named Enid. . . . I felt ashamed of the mistake I had made. Even to hurt my mother I would not have wanted the same name as the woman who had tried to kill my mother and me" (Kincaid, *Lucy* 150). The fury of Lucy's mother not only underlines the possibility of literally murderous relations between women, but also asserts a personal meaning where the reader might anticipate a political one: as an overtly racist writer and the representative of imperial power, Enid Blyton could be described, metaphorically, as a "woman who had tried to kill my mother and me." The proper names of proper English women are not reliable signposts for Lucy's own development as a colonial subject.

Nevertheless, in repossessing apparently colonial names and identifications—across nationality, across gender (when she later identifies her name with Milton's Lucifer), and athwart relations of exploitation—Lucy insists on the ability of an individual to interpret and appropriate even the signifiers of oppression on their own terms. On a small scale, these cooptations exemplify Kincaid's writerly advice: "Take. It's okay." Lucy has no choice about the colonialist pedagogy that has enforced her knowledge of the English literary canon; but she can choose to identify herself with an icon of masculine rebellion (Lucifer) rather than one of feminine renunciation, such as Wordsworth's Lucy Gray—or, for that matter, the suffering Lucy Snowe. Repossessing these names, Lucy revises the Victorian norms of duty, renunciation, and sexual chastity that they represent, that are exported and maintained by colonial history and colonial education, and that in *Lucy* are represented as maternally transmitted and enforced.[13] Despite her relative frankness about loneliness and longing, Brontë in *Villette* remains largely loyal to these norms. Kincaid, through Lucy, rejects them with some fury. While her mother has brought her up to be "clean, virginal, beyond reproach" (Kincaid, *Lucy* 97), Lucy writes her a letter in which "I . . . gave a brief description of my personal life, offering each detail as evidence that my upbringing had been a failure and that, in fact, life as a slut was quite enjoyable, thank you very much" (128). When she becomes involved with a photographer named, with an echo of Lucy Snowe's most important relationship, Paul, she describes her sexual enjoyment in detail to the other mother-figure in her life, Mariah (113). As Gary Holcomb writes, "Among the aims of Lucy's slut identity is to welcome dominant society's condemnation for the slut's body to release [her] from dominant society's narrow authorization of how a young black woman of the servant and immigrant class may use her body" (307). This sexual pleasure—and the fact that Lucy has found a mother-figure who is not shocked by her recounting of it—seem like triumphant ripostes to the ideology of feminine purity embodied in and reproduced by the foremothers in Lucy's life: her own mother; Brontë and the other nineteenth-century women authors Kincaid reads; and the fictional English Lucys whose name she shares. As Kincaid says in one interview, "I really do believe that whatever is a source of shame—if you are not responsible for it, such as the color of your skin or your sexuality—you should just wear it as a badge" (Garner). In embracing the term "slut," she seems to refuse Lucy Snowe's burden of shame.

In the novel, however, Lucy's pleasure is short-lived; her relationships with men named Paul are (like Lucy Snowe's) limited by the tendency of those men to view women as objects of dominance or possession. Her boyfriend Paul's role is doubled in Lucy's life by a connection with another Paul—the painter Gaugin. On a museum visit encouraged by Mariah, Lucy "immediately identified with the yearnings of this man," despite her awareness of what separates them: "He had the perfume of the hero about him. I was not a man; I was a young woman from the fringes of the world, and when I left my home I had wrapped around my shoulders the mantle of a servant" (Kincaid, *Lucy* 95). Once again, Lucy is able to identify with images of rebellion across gender, history, and ideology. But her relationship with her boyfriend Paul reminds her of the limitations of such attempts at dissonant identification. An ominous note sounds early in their relationship, when he takes her on a drive to "an old mansion in ruins, formerly the home of a man who had made a great deal of money in the part of the world that I was from, in the sugar industry. I did not know this man, but if he hadn't been already dead I would have wished him so" (129). Soon enough, Paul reveals that in his eyes she is the object—exotic muse and model—rather than the subject of those yearnings she identified with in Paul Gauguin: "[Paul] . . . gave me a photograph he had taken of me standing over a boiling pot of food. In the picture I was naked from the waist up; a piece of cloth, wrapped around me, covered me from the waist down. That was the moment he got the idea he possessed me in a certain way, and that was the moment I grew tired of him" (155). Both boyfriend-Paul and his implicit namesake Gauguin recall *Villette*'s M. Paul, who wants to see Lucy Snowe as the one of the panels of "la vie d'une femme," the domestic angel; Lucy Potter's Paul sees in her the image of one of Paul Gauguin's Tahitian women represented as sexually available to European men. The two masculine views, the domestic sexually repressive and the transnational sexually libertine, converge on the same possession of the feminine object, suggesting that the transgression represented by Lucy's assumed identity of "slut" is not, in itself, enough to reverse the gaze or install Lucy in the position of the subject.

Both *Villette* and *Lucy* end ambiguously, with the protagonist isolated and mourning, on the one hand, but having established the authority to tell her tale, on the other. In *Villette,* all three of these elements are expressed indirectly. Brontë implies rather than describes the loss at sea of M. Paul by invoking "a thousand weepers." "There is enough said," Lucy concludes, "Trouble no quiet, kind heart; leave sunny imaginations hope" (Brontë, *Villette* 617). An audience and therefore an author are suggested by the address to "sunny imaginations"; audience and author are also invoked by Lucy's final word, "Farewell" (618). But Lucy Snowe is not explicitly depicted as *writing,* or even as narrating orally to anyone in particular. Indeed, whenever Lucy Snowe engages in creative expression—when she performs in M. Paul's play; when, at his behest, she writes an essay on "Human Justice"—she represents herself as doing so under duress and with reluctance. Any sense of Lucy Snowe (as distinct from Brontë) as an author remains only implicit.

Kincaid, however, holds out more possibility: unlike Brontë, she projects a future for her protagonist not just as a viewer or subject but as the creator of representational art. Lucy's creative activities are facilitated not by the men in her life but by her visits to a museum to which Mariah, seeing her interest, gives her a membership. Lucy's interest in photography expands on and revises Lucy Snowe's relation to painting. Lucy Snowe, in a defense of realism that is obviously also a defense of Brontë's own methods, objects to paintings that are "not a whit like nature," finding satisfaction only in "fragments of truth here and there which satisfied the conscience, and gleams of light that cheered the vision. Nature's power here broke through in a mountain snow-storm . . . an expression in this portrait proved clear insight into character" (Brontë, *Villette* 249). Lucy Potter, as she becomes interested in photography, rejects Mariah's travel albums, posed depictions of a happiness falsified by the crumbling of Mariah's marriage, and instead takes quotidian pictures of "the children eating toasted marshmallows; a picture of them with their bottoms facing the camera . . . a picture of Mariah in the middle of an elaborate preparation of chicken and vegetables cooked slowly in red wine" (Kincaid, *Lucy* 120–21). While it's hard to imagine Lucy Potter admiring a painted "mountain snow-storm" (as irrelevant to her national imaginary as Wordsworth's daffodils), or Lucy Snowe amused by a photograph of children's "bottoms," in their different contexts both Lucys are champions of realist representation—what Lucy Potter describes as "photographs of ordinary people in a countryside doing ordinary things, but for a reason that was not at all clear to me the people and the things they were doing looked extraordinary—as if these people and these things had not existed before" (115).

The difference, however, is that Lucy Potter begins to create such representations, while Lucy Snowe remains a viewer. In *Lucy*'s concluding paragraph, this contrast is extended into the realm of written narrative:

> Then I saw the [blank] book Mariah had given me. It was on the night table next to my bed. . . . At the top of the page I wrote my full name: Lucy Josephine Potter. . . . I could write down only this: "I wish I could love someone so much that I would die from it." And then as I looked at this sentence a great wave of shame came over me and I wept and wept so much that the tears fell on the page and caused all the words to become one great big blur. (163–64)

Lucy's words here are as much haunted as liberated. They are haunted by the relations of global labor that have brought her to the United States and precipitated Mariah's gift; by the colonial history that produced those relations, encoded in her three names; and by the loneliness and shame, shared with Lucy Snowe, over her unfulfilled longing for intimacy. ("I wish I could love someone so much that I would die from it" echoes Lucy Snowe's desire to "take up the nobler charge of labouring and living for others.") This impression of haunted writing, the retrospective lure of literary identification, complicates Kincaid's injunction to "Take. It's okay," by acknowledging that fictional forms are freighted with histories that cannot be erased even by the appropriations of dissonant identification or disidentification. Nevertheless, they propel Kincaid's Lucy into a future in which she can be imagined as the subject, rather than the object, of narrative representation.

TSITSI DANGAREMBGA

THE LONELINESS OF POLITICS

Like *Nervous Conditions,* Dangarembga's sequel, *The Book of Not,* begins strikingly with a familial loss—not the offstage death of a brother, but the vivid dismemberment of a sister: "Up, up, up, the leg spun. A piece of person, up there in the sky. Earth and acrid vapors coated my tongue. . . . In the darkness, Netsai's leg arced up. Something was required of me! I was her sister, her elder sister. I was, by position, required to perform the act that would protect her. How miserable I was, for nothing lay in my power" (3). Netsai, who is fighting for the *chimurenga,* the African resistance to white minority rule in Rhodesia, has stepped on a land mine. The scene is one of literal collapse: Tambu's mother falls to the ground in horror at her daughter's injury, and her uncle Babamukuru lies beaten almost to death by the rebels in the civil war now raging. Having been brought to the scene of this *morari* (a gathering aimed to inspire political fervor) by her mother, Tambu is not indifferent, as she was at her brother's death, but horrifically powerless. She can identify fully neither with the bloodlust roused in the villagers by oppression and resistance, nor with the dominant position of her white peers at school, from whom she must hide her connection to such events.

Like Lucy Potter, she is also haunted by her identification with her mother, whom, at sixteen, she sees as "nothing" (Dangarembga, *Book of Not* 31)—and yet whose embodiment of impoverished, uneducated, exploited femininity is precisely what propels Tambu's dedication to escape. "You don't see the contradiction," she observes retrospectively, "when the front of your uniform has plumped out and you have been brought the three sensible elastic bras stipulated by the senior school's clothes list . . . when you yearn to say to your mother, 'I'll give you a book' so that she can sit first her grade seven and then her form two and then her O-Level certificate. . . . No, you don't see the contradiction of being astonished at being oneself so plenipotentiary and begging God to make you not like your mother" (11). Under these intolerable conditions of both physical and psychic contradiction, of external and internal civil war, Tambu frequently "forced [her]self into an emptiness; and yes, it is better where there is nothing so there is nothing to tell" (19). The beginning of the narrative thus repudiates the condition of narratibility—an ironic echo of George Eliot's dictum that "the happiest women, like the happiest nations, have no history" (*MoF* 385). Over the course of the novel, this enforced "emptiness" will destroy all of Tambu's opportunities for identification and intimacy; her retrospective narrative anatomizes closely the ways in which this social situation results from the racist condition of minority white domination. In adopting the genre of the school story, through the relations of the students and teachers at the elite Young Ladies' Convent of the Sacred Heart, *The Book of Not* recapitulates both the intensity and the setting of *Villette* (as well as the setting of Enid Blyton's formulaic series) while asserting the historical specificity of Tambu's suffering under English colonial rule.

This opening scene indicates the novel's distance from *Nervous Conditions:* in the threat and presence of violence; Tambu's despairing conviction that "nothing lay in [her] power"; and most important her growing estrangement from those around her, a social world arrayed in oppositional pairs—"African" and white schoolgirls; resistance forces and accommodationist elites; family of origin and family of aspiration. Tambu scorns the poverty of her parental family of origin and fears their close involvement with the rebellion; the upward mobility of her uncle's family, to which she aspires, is threatened not only by the violence directed at her uncle but also by her own increasing incapacity to maintain the role of perfect schoolgirl and obedient daughter that he demands. Tambu's relationship to her peers at the Sacred Heart Convent exhibits a similar double bind, for her relationships with her fellow "African" students are fraught with intimacy and rivalry, and those with the white majority of the students with distance and racism. As Rosanne Kennedy writes, this is a novel of "unbecoming—of the loss of identity, feeling, and attachments. Despite her concentrated efforts to exercise agency over her life, Tambu is repeatedly thwarted: by the psychic damage she sustains as a result of internalizing a Eurocentric view of her African 'inferiority,' by her mother's respect for tradition, and by the violent events she witnesses during the war" (89). In fact, Tambu's stubborn, if sometimes self-defeating, efforts to bear herself as a human subject in relation to other human subjects suggest that she never fully internalizes that view of herself as an inferior self, an object for others. Nevertheless, as a result of her internalization of, and attempts to navigate, these oppositions, the dominant affect of *The Book of Not* recalls and amplifies that of *Villette*—a pervasive and corrosive shame. Like Brontë's novel, but in the physically as well as psychically violent twentieth-century context of colonialism and anti-colonial resistance, *The Book of Not* narrates the psychic costs of socially structured failures of identification and intersubjective relations.

After its horrific opening, *The Book of Not* seems to revert to Tambu's upwardly mobile trajectory of *Nervous Conditions,* reflecting the resilience of its protagonist's youth and the forward-looking conventions of the narrative of formation. Babamukuru recovers; Tambu's sister survives the loss of her leg; and Tambu herself returns to school believing that she can overcome the experience of trauma. Back at Babamukuru's mission for the holidays, she reflects, sounding like the Tambu of *Nervous Conditions:*

> My possibilities were infinite in my present circumstances! This I truly believed, and was ready to face the little inconveniences to be dealt with along the way. All in all, I felt I was all right now, and so was the world. I was on a direct route to a future so bright it—or I in those tomorrows—would light up more than my community; probably, I imagined, the whole universe. . . . Taking my cue from my uncle, I was very glad to remind myself, with a degree of superior gloating over lesser individuals who did not have the ability, how you didn't enter institutions just like [Sacred Heart] by playing. My list of lesser mortals included [her father and mother] Baba and Mai, whose better qualities were, as far as I could see, not more than an envious sluggishness. (Dangarembga, *Book of Not* 82)

Tambu's optimistic project of a brightly blazing future self—"I in those tomorrows"—recalls the Lacanian infant's "jubilant" identification with the integrated self it sees reflected, ahead of its own bodily control, in the mirror, and recalls, too, Lacan's representation of this identification as a *mis*recognition. Tambu's substitution of her uncle and aunt ("I was home for the holidays. Or more precisely, I was at the place I called home, which was the mission" [80]) for her own parents likewise recalls Freud's "family romance," the fantasy of substituting for one's own, unsatisfactory, real parents more glamorous progenitors and objects of identification. By drawing attention to the fantasies undergirding Tambu's self-recognition, the retrospective narrator reveals it as a dangerous lack of recognition.

The degree of feverish exaggeration with which the retrospectively narrating Tambu represents her former self's thoughts also signals to the reader their roots in misrepresentation and fantasy. Tambu's ideal of belonging and achievement at Sacred Heart can be maintained only by hiding most of her life from others—her association with Netsai, the traumatic events of that school break—and, even more destructively, from herself. Attempting to do so, she is haunted by the image of her sister—"walking backwards over those stones of learning and concentration, hopping, going hop-hop-hopla because she had only one leg. I could see her clearly as I sat in class" (Dangarembga, *Book of Not* 28). This distraction, and the need it causes for mental retreat, conflict with Tambu's aspiration to rise above the social contexts of racism and violence by ignoring the body, by focusing steadily on the academic achievements available to her, working for a place on the school honor roll, high marks on her O levels, the school medal, and the A-level scores that will earn her a University scholarship. These academic achievements stretch out like crossbars on a bridge perilously suspended over the whirlpool of racism, poverty, and violent resistance; if she can avoid looking down or being pulled down, she can reach the bright abstraction of "those tomorrows."

But the body in its most uncanny form—fragmented—continues to haunt her. Even away from the violence of war, images of dismemberment recur as an embodiment of the fracturing of Tambu's subjectivity by racist projections. These images give a political particularity to Lacan's discussion, in "The Mirror Stage," of the "fragmented body . . . [which] is regularly manifested in dreams when the movement of an analysis reaches a certain level of aggressive disintegration of the individual. It then appears in the form of disconnected limbs or of organs exoscopically represented" (6). For Lacan's analyst and analysand this "aggressive disintegration of the individual" is the sign of a successful, if difficult, psychic challenge to the "donned armor of an alienating identity" (6) encouraged by a more or less repressive society. For Tambu, it is fragmentation itself, symbolic as well as literal, that is a sign of repression. Her white teachers and fellow students frequently express their racism through metaphorical dismemberment of African bodies. The school's headmistress, informing the black students of quotas on their admission, jokes about cutting them up: "Sister Emmanuel pulled one corner of her mouth down, then up while her eyes frosted with a cold humor. 'Whatever memoranda they send us, we aren't going to chop anyone in half, nor in any other portion. That is what I called you here to inform you'" (Dangarembga, *Book of Not* 73). In the dining hall, Tambu's white peers subject her and her classmate Ntombi to an alienating, disintegrative gaze:

> "Look at them," said Bougainvillea, gazing first at my hand as it hovered over the butter dish, and then at Ntombizethu's. . . . "They've both got such fine hands. Look at those amazing fingers! . . . It's not just those two! . . . It's all of them! . . . See!" Bougainvillea stretched out her own [hand] as if she would touch her classmate's, but did not quite. "Just look at the shape of that nail, and that crescent, it's a perfect half moon! Isn't it wonderful!" (37–38)

Bougainvillea as a character is something like *Villette*'s Ginevra Fanshawe (and like her named after a flowering plant). Like Ginevra's, her self-regard and equal lack of regard for others of others have a kind of riveting candor. Like Ginevra's gloating positioning of herself and Lucy in front of the looking-glass at Madame Beck's, Bougainvillea's insistent scrutiny offers Tambu a kind of mirror. Tambu sees herself in Bougainvillea's gaze as fragmented and objectified; the reflection that this scrutiny offers is the opposite of the reflection by the other that, whether negatively (as in Lacan's mirror stage) or positively (as in Winnicott) enables the ego-construction of the normative subject.

That such fragmentation is devastating to the young Tambu calls into question a celebration, in postmodern theory and literature, of fragmentation over a coherence that is assumed to be always false. As Lynne Layton observes, "In postmodern work that lauds indeterminacy, fragmentation is essentialized, universalized, and celebrated in a way that seems not to acknowledge what it feels like to experience it. As in the Lacanian frame, here, too, fragments do not derive from specific relational interactions or specific historical circumstances. But Lacanian theory situates the subject firmly within a patriarchal family structure, whereas the work on the play of fragments suggests that nothing constrains gender performances" (124). On the contrary, Layton insists, "fragmentation arises historically, from public and private developmental traumas" (139). Tambu's response to her situation indeed illustrates both Layton's perception that fragmentation itself is often the product of trauma and Lacan's insight that the attachment to wholeness is dangerous in itself. Tambu is placed in an impossible position, and efforts to resist the fragmenting gaze lead her to an equally problematic identification: "Tracey was looking into her milk mug with embarrassment. . . . [I] decided this was a good way to distance myself from what was going on and imitated [her] concentration" (Dangarembga, *Book of Not* 38). Tambu cannot reject the gaze entirely but can only identify with the less overtly racist white girl in the scene, who later will be awarded the school trophy that Tambu should have won.

Dangarembga most immediately draws for her psychological schema on Frantz Fanon's theorization of a black internalization of and identification with the white racist fetishization of dark skin as a mark of otherness and abjection. Tambu resembles Fanon's "black child [who] subjectively adopts a white man's attitude" (Fanon 127) and has a "solely negating" experience of her own body (Fanon 90). In particular, she has internalized a taboo against contact between white and black skin. When her favorite (white) teacher, concerned, reaches out to touch her, "I was appalled at having let my skin and this white person's touch. . . . I started with all my muscles to pull away. I was horrified to see my hand disobedient and motionless" (Dangarembga, *Book of Not* 32). The "disobedien[ce]" of Tambu's hand might stem from an unwilled desire for the teacher's forbidden touch or an equally unwilled rebellion against the racist taboo, but what it most immediately seems to represent is Tambu's lack of control over her own person—her identification with a view of herself as not subject but object. In a passage that also focuses on the movement of the hand, Fanon suggests that the ability to control bodily movement mentally is a mark of coherent subjectivity:

> I know that if I want to smoke, I shall have to stretch out my right arm and grab a pack of cigarettes lying at the other end of the table. As for the matches, they are in the left drawer, and I shall have to move back a little. And I make all these moves, not out of habit, but by implicit knowledge. A slow construction of my self as a body in a spatial and temporal world—such seems to be the schema. It is not imposed on me; it is rather a definitive structuring of my self and the world—definitive because it creates a genuine dialectic between my body and the world. (90–91)

Here, Fanon, like Layton above, emphasizes the importance of a bodily sense of wholeness—an "implicit knowledge" that enables a "definitive structuring of my self and the world." This "schema" is not socially "imposed," and unlike the "orthopaedic" form of wholeness that for Lacan becomes the "armor of an alienating identity that will mark [the individual's] entire mental development with its rigid structure" (6), it remains "dialectic" in its relation to the other. Throughout *The Book of*

Not, however, this "definitive structuring" and the dialectical experience that it enables remain unavailable to Tambu, replaced by a white-imposed structure that intends to obliterate her. In another instance, she unwittingly ends up fighting with another mistress, Miss Plato, over a bedsheet and momentarily fails to recognize her own voice speaking (Dangarembga, *Book of Not* 56). Such moments of dissociation recall those of Lucy Snowe, also adrift in a community of girls and women in which she is a national and cultural outsider, regarded with suspicion or indifference. In Tambu's case, however, such depersonalization is a direct result of the violent racism of colonialist dispossession—she is displaced within her own homeland and within her own skin.

The problem is not just that Tambu's body continually eludes her control, but even more that its control is skillfully, lethally disassembled by and in view of her white classmates and teachers. Many occasions draw attention to bodily realities, of mutilation, hunger, and excretory functions that, for Tambu, reinforce a view of herself and her black classmates as less than fully civilized—embodied to the point of bestiality or monstrousness. On one occasion, torn between a desire not to be late and a need to move her bowels, she makes the fateful decision to use a more convenient white girls' bathroom. Discovered by the matron, she exits the stall in humiliation, "without sufficient care of my nether regions, which felt messily moist and sticky," and is then reprimanded for having failed, in her haste, to flush the toilet: "I who, unlike a lot of the other girls in my dormitory, had sat on flushing toilets at an early age [was] now being humiliated in this fashion!" (Dangarembga, *Book of Not* 67). The reader familiar with Tambu's early history, in *Nervous Conditions,* might here remember her first encounter with a flush toilet, on arriving at Babamukuru's house: "I had not used a panelled toilet before so it was necessary to experiment. I climbed on to the seat and squatted, first facing the cistern and then, more comfortably, facing away from it" (79). In this earlier context, still surrounded by family and optimistic about the future, Tambu registers some embarrassment at her lack of sophistication, but more confidence in her ability to adapt (and she is given enough privacy to do so). In *The Book of Not,* by contrast, Tambu experiences a shame that causes her to disavow her relationship to those "other girls in [her] dormitory"—that is, to earlier versions of her own self. This disavowal also recalls Tambu's attempt to distance herself through pity from Ntombi, whose father is "responsible for the toilets" at a school. As Kathryn Stockton observes, "Freud . . . spelled out the 'civilized' assumption that moral and economic progress together require one to leave one's attachment to the bottom behind" (68). Here, the abjection of Tambu, who embraces such assumptions and would like to "leave . . . the bottom behind," is enforced through the insistent public identification of her with those "nether regions": her experience literalizes the metaphor of being treated like shit. Such treatment, in the school as in the society at large, enables a numerical white minority to project the *status* of minority—that is, abject—subjectivity onto and *into* the majority black population.

Striving after academic achievement, Tambu attempts to solve the problem of her identification with the fragmented or filthy body by reducing the amount of space occupied by her "person" to almost nothing. She cannot, however, get away from the body—her own memories of Netsai's amputated leg; her embodiment as black and female; her classmates' and instructors' objectification of her and reduction of her to bodily fragments and processes. In any case, she is always doomed to lose, because where their metaphoric reduction of the African students fails, the nuns and white students can resort to exercises of direct power. When Tambu receives the best O-level results in the school, the school trophy for this achievement goes instead to the white student, Tracey, who comes second, on the patently specious grounds that "'This young lady . . . is also a champion swimmer'" (Dangarembga, *Book of Not* 155). Rather than take in fully the implications of this injustice, Tambu blames herself: "There *must* have been a mistake in the results, otherwise, as my uncle had pointed out concerning the report Sister Emmanuel once wrote, the headmistress would not have done it. . . . How afraid I was that in fact I was worth nothing" (157). Like Kincaid's Lucy, the younger Tambu was an eager reader of Enid Blyton's school stories. Her experience at Sacred Heart drives her, reluctantly, closer and closer to confronting the difference between the jolly world of Blyton's Mallory Towers and Saint Claire's and the one that she, as an "African student," is forced to occupy.

In the last quarter of the book, the narrative tempo accelerates, at one point leaping over years before refocusing on daily life. When an increasingly disturbed Tambu does poorly on her A-levels, her angry uncle reveals that it was her mother who betrayed him to the rebels at the *morari*. Tambu, who vows "never to talk to [her mother] Mai again" (Dangarembga, *Book of Not* 192), is now thoroughly dispossessed, her dreams of bright tomorrows banished, and undertakes a series of temporary jobs (194). The arrival of Independence (in 1979, though Dangarembga does not note the date), and the subsequent departure of many white Rhodesians, abruptly open a place in the university to Tambu despite her exam results, and finally—possibly through the intervention of her white former classmate, Tracey, now an account executive—she becomes a copywriter at an advertising agency.

At this point, post-Independence, narrative time slows and the narrative seems to repeat itself. Tambu's experience working at the largely white firm of Steers, D'Arcy, and MacPedius and living in a nearby women's hostel recapitulates her experience at Sacred Heart, producing the same failures of identification and intimacy, daily experiences of racism, inter- and intraracial rivalry, and exploitation. Just as the black "nannies," or meal-servers, at Sacred Heart, "when they set a jug or plate before Ntombi or me . . . smack it down with a jut of the chin and spills, as though slapping a hard, crushing thing down on obnoxious crawling objects" (Dangarembga, *Book of Not* 46), so the "tea boy" at Steers "pass[es] up the office handing out mugs," only to "snarl[] at me in Shona. 'I'm not your boy, I'm not your servant, he!'" (219). Just as Tracey accepted, while at Sacred Heart, the medal that should have gone to Tambu, so now "the new Tracey, in the new Zimbabwe, advertising executive for Afro-Shine, a local product by young entrepreneurs in baggy suits" (216), patronizes and bosses Tambu and colludes with a white copywriter, Dick, to let him take the credit for very successful copy written for the Afro-Shine campaign by Tambu. This appropriation finally causes her to resign. She returns to the hostel to find that, just as Sister Emmanuel once threatened to expel her (89), so her landlady is evicting her: "'If you're that unhappy here . . . um . . . ' she decided not to risk specification and continued ' . . . my dear, I'm sure you could find somewhere else that suits you'" (244). The white landlady does not "risk specification" because she consistently confuses Tambu with another black resident, Isabel. Tambu's narrative thus ends with her loss not just of external and contingent supports—her job, her home—but also of central features of identity by which the subject usually hopes to make herself known: her own thoughts, her own name. Racism and white domination mean that Tambu's self has been formed not through positive forms of identification—not even through the reappropriation of dissonant identifications achieved by Brontë's or Kincaid's Lucy—but by the vicious misidentifications of others, which she has internalized: as a result, she is almost literally, at the end of the novel, unrecognizable as a subject.

She is as unrecognizable to herself as to others: "I could not go back to the homestead where Netsai hopped unspeakably on a single limb, and where Mai would laugh at me daily. I had forgotten all the promises made to myself and providence while I was young concerning carrying forward with me the good and human, the *unhu* of my life. . . . So this evening I walked emptily to the room I would soon vacate, wondering what future there was for me, a new Zimbabwean" (Dangarembga, *Book of Not* 246). As the stress on emptiness indicates, this lack of recognition is ominous. Tambu's self-characterization here as "a new Zimbabwean" seems more ironic than hopeful, since it is the term she also used to characterize Tracey, with whom her relationship has not changed from the "old" Zimbabwe. Like Lucy Snowe and Lucy Potter, Tambu is an exile; unlike them, she is an exile in her own land, cut off from both the consolatory fantasy of a prior national identity (such as Lucy Snowe nourishes) or the emancipatory possibilities of leaving a prior nationality behind, of an elsewhere that will allow her to begin anew.

Dismemberment still haunts her, in the vision of Netsai, "hop[ping] unspeakably on a single limb." Unspeakability or "the curse on passing observations" (Dangarembga, *Book of Not* 23) is something that Tambu frequently notes as a sapping feature of the "new Zimbabwe": "People thronged the streets [at Independence] rejoicing so thoroughly that there was no place for remembering the acts their hands and their feet, and their teeth, and the fingers, boots, and mouths of their children committed. So we never remembered and grieved together as women sorrow in groups many years after a birth" (196). Here, failure to remember is figuratively joined to the trope of dismemberment, through the attribution of the *chimurenga*'s violence to body parts, rather than persons. Failure to remember is indeed, as Dangarembga represents it, a kind of historical dismemberment, a disjoining of the present moment from the body of history.

The unsettled question is whether Netsai's haunting single limb is a synecdoche for the disintegration of the self, or, on the contrary, for its persistence: she has, after all, survived. The very fact of Tambu's narration, emerging from her own persistently whole body, and her ability to continue wondering about the future might also be taken as signs of hope for reversing these conditions of unspeakability and dismemberment.[14] Kennedy acknowledges that the novel ends "bleakly" but finds some hope in the "release from her melancholic pattern of repetition" indicated by Tambu's resignation of her position and renewed concern for *unhu,* or the practice of mutual recognition, in which Kennedy reads a "belated recognition that [Tambu's] desire for success and recognition is implicated in the same hierarchical structures of colonialism that have damaged her" (102). Nevertheless, the novel ends on notes of loss and irresolution, and the question of whether the "melancholic pattern of repetition" in which Tambu finds herself trapped is individual or amenable to individual, rather than societal, reform remains up in the air.

The narrative of *The Book of Not* demonstrates the destructive effects of the failure of identification in its fullest operation—as the basis for mutual recognition. The novel's relationship to its audience, as well as its construction of its characters, demonstrates some of these effects as well. Speaking of the novel's effect on readers, Dangarembga says:

> One of the points that came up in a reading [in Leeds] was what a painful read *The Book of Not* can be. One has to see that whole world unfolding as Tambudzai herself experiences it, and yet the reader also stands outside it so one can see the damage that is being wrought. My mother said the same thing. She said she got to one part of the book and had to put it away for several weeks before she went back to it. But interestingly, people do go back. I am aware that it is not a comfortable read, as perhaps *Nervous Conditions* was. And I was aware that people would wonder why it wasn't so comfortable [laughs] but these things happen. (Rooney 62)

What makes the book less "comfortable" to read than *Nervous Conditions* is not only the presence of both inter- and intraracial conflict but also the greater distance between Tambu's consciousness of the experiences she relates and the reader's analysis of those experiences. Readers' identification with the protagonist is mediated by the desire to repel Tambu's own intimacy with depersonalization. Dangarembga suggests that this knowledge is as painful to represent as to read: "I do find it very difficult—especially in *The Book of Not* where the racism that Tambudzai experiences impacts very negatively on her—and she does not find a way of fighting it. It was very difficult for me to enter into that circumstance in the way that I needed to in order to make Tambudzai's reactions credible. . . . One element was the whole process of having to understand Tambudzai's psyche, to understand how minds can be so totally colonised. That really was a big process for me: I gritted my teeth and went through it" (Rooney 58). For author as well as for readers, identification with a self that has been "totally colonised" by the *mis*identifications of racism registers as painful and threatening.

Nevertheless, as Dangarembga observes, "people do go back," even if occasionally they have to grit their teeth. Stark evocations of the unmaking produced by racist and colonialist histories run through Dangarembga's work: her first published short story, "The Letter" (1985) is about a South African woman who is arrested because she cannot bear to part with the incriminating letter she has received from her husband, a political dissident in hiding; Dangarembga's play *She No Longer Weeps* (1987) concludes with its Zimbabwean protagonist, defeated by patriarchal oppression, about to go to jail for killing her ex-lover. Yet in interviews, Dangarembga speaks less about anger than about the power of narrative representation of all kinds: "I am conscious of the fact that, because I have been so very deeply affected by narratives—whether poetry, prose or film—that there have been certain turning points in my life created by these narratives. I am aware of the impact that narratives can have on people, and am very conscious that I need to guide the work so it has a positive impact" (Rooney 59).

It is hard to find statements of such directly didactic intent in the comments of Brontë or Kincaid on their work. Brontë asserts, perhaps disingenuously, that she "cannot write books handling the topics of the day. . . . Nor can I write a book for its moral" (*Selected Letters* 30 October 1852). Kincaid emphasizes personal expression and embraces anger; Judith Halberstam includes Kincaid in a heterogeneous but suggestive list of "antisocial writers, artists and texts" whose "dyke anger, anticolonial despair, racial rage, counterhegemonic violence, punk pugilism" comprise an "antisocial turn" in contemporary literature ("Politics of Negativity" 824).[15] As I hope I have demonstrated, however, representations of an at least partly "counterhegemonic" anger and despair have nineteenth-century antecedents, and their representation, whether then or now, is not necessarily "anti-social." The paradox of these novels' address is that, although they depict the more-than-marginalization—the rendering of self into abject other—of their protagonists, for their readers, these protagonists are inevitably not marginal but central. Certainly the anger or despair of Brontë, Kincaid, and Dangarembga has sometimes discomfited or driven away readers. But when we do read, we are invited, perhaps even impressed, into a situation in which, as readers, we have the power to offer the recognition that the other characters have withdrawn. These novels leave no doubt that such recognition is, for the subject, a matter of life and death, and thus a profoundly social concern.

FOUR

Coming Out

VIRGINIA WOOLF, RADCLYFFE HALL, AND JEANETTE WINTERSON

A NEW KIND of subject—the subject of sexuality—became possible for fictional discourse at the beginning of the twentieth century. This is true in two senses: In one sense, the subject, or topic, of sexual behavior began appearing more openly in English fiction in the last several decades of the nineteenth century (in, for example, the work of Thomas Hardy and some of the "New Women" novelists), and sexual discourse was a significant aspect of the innovation of some Modernist novelists, such as D. H. Lawrence and James Joyce. In another sense, a new subject of narrative appeared, one whose history was defined primarily by his or her relation to this newly significant aspect of selfhood: sexuality. As the examples of Lawrence and Joyce suggest, the subject of sexuality could be a heterosexual one, but its emergence was preceded and accompanied by the increasing exposure, in Freudian psychology and in the sexology of Krafft-Ebing and Havelock Ellis, of same-sex practices and narratives. In Michel Foucault's well-known formulation, "The nineteenth-century homosexual became a personage, a past, a case history, and a childhood. . . . The sodomite had been a temporary aberration; the homosexual was now a species." This "personage," whose birth Foucault dates to 1870, with the publication of "Westphal's famous article . . . on 'contrary sexual sensations'" (43), does not enter as protagonist into the novel of formation until some decades into the twentieth century, when the scandal of (hetero)sexual representation has already become familiar. By the end of the twentieth century, the "coming-out" novel has become a familiar subcategory of the novel of formation.

The coming-out novel is defined not only by the protagonist's growing realization that, as a sexual subject, she or he does not conform to normative expectations of heterosexual feeling or behavior—that he or she is, in current terms, queer—but also, and equally importantly, by the *communication* of this realization to some other person (who may, but does not have to, be an object of erotic desire). Each of the three novels discussed in this chapter—Virginia Woolf's *The Voyage Out* (1915), Radclyffe Hall's *The Well of Loneliness* (1928), and Jeanette Winterson's *Oranges Are Not the Only Fruit* (1985)—represents a different moment in the representation of such communication: from indirection and inconclusion (as in Woolf's novel); to loudly announced unspeakability (in Hall's); to parodic play with traditions of indirection and announcement (in Winterson's). In any form, some gesture of communication of the subject's sexual narrative is the crucial "out" of coming-out narrative. The complete phrase, of course, is "coming out of the closet"; and what has most consistently defined a closet *as* a closet is its doubled relationship to privacy and revelation, the absence of others *within* the closet and the pressure of their presence just on the other side of the door. "Coming out," then, places the protagonist in a new ethical relation to some other(s) in the narrative—a relation of making oneself *known* to the other that allows for the possibility, not previously available, of recognition.[1] An author's staging of such a moment of communication and recognition may, in turn, trigger an equivalent wish, or even demand, in the relationship between queer reader and potentially queer author: that an author make herself *known*, as a sexual subject, to her readers. In this relationship too, the wish is, such knowledge may produce recognition; for even if the reader herself remain unknown to an author, her knowledge of the author's sexuality can make possible the queer reader's identification, and that identification, indirectly, confers recognition—the affirmation of the self in the other.

In this chapter, I trace the lines of filiation and resistance among three authors who have, with varying degrees of explicitness, portrayed queer sexual subjects, and also the ways in which these authors are cast in or negotiate their roles as queer objects of readerly identification. The three authors are linked by cultural and intertextual relations. Woolf and Hall were prominent contemporaries, recipients of the same literary prize (the Prix Femina Vie Heureuse); Woolf was prepared to testify on Hall's behalf at the trial for obscenity of *The Well of Loneliness,* though she was caustic about its literary qualities. Woolf's *Orlando* appeared in the same year as

Hall's novel, and critics have juxtaposed the two novels to contrast their authors' relations to Modernism and to the representation of queer sexuality. Finally, Winterson's polemical essay collection *Art Objects* (1997) emphasizes her identification with Woolf (and indicates her disdain for Hall) as an heir to the Modernist tradition and rejects the significance of shared queer subjectivity.

The word "queer" is applicable to these novels in two linked but not identical senses. The first is the conventional sense of "queer" as "strange, odd, peculiar, or eccentric"; this sense is particularly emphasized by the narrative strategies of *The Voyage Out* and *Oranges Are Not the Only Fruit.* According to a more recent sense, established in the 1980s by both queer activism and queer theory, that which is queer "challenge[s] or deconstruct[s] traditional ideas of sexuality and gender, esp[ecially] the acceptance of heterosexuality as normative and the perception of a rigid dichotomy of male and female traits,"[2] a project of overt importance in both *The Well of Loneliness* and *Oranges Are Not the Only Fruit.* In each case, queerness of form and the representation of queer subjectivity are linked, but not always in straightforward or in the same ways. Virginia Woolf's concern in *The Voyage Out* to queer, or render eccentric, conventions of readerly identification is in tension with her interest in representing a queer subjectivity; contrarily, in *The Well of Loneliness,* Hall calls upon conventions of identification to normalize the representation of queer subjectivity. *Oranges Are Not the Only Fruit,* I will suggest, pursues both these projects—the queering (eccentricity) of representation, and the representation of the (sexually) queer—simultaneously.

It can be argued that the simultaneity of these two reverberations of "queer" is endemic to Modernist literature itself. Heather Love, for example, suggests that:

> *Queer modernism* has an air of inevitability about it. Since the term *queer* is so closely linked to the concept of the margin, the prominence of exile and alienation in even dominant modernism resonates with the outsider glamour of *queer.* In addition, since the classic period of aesthetic modernism coincides with the emergence of modern sexual identities, there is a historical fit between the two terms. . . . But perhaps what makes *queer* and *modernism* such a good fit is that the indeterminacy of *queer* seems to match the indeterminacy, expansiveness, and drift of the literary—particularly the experimental, oblique version most closely associated with modernist textual production. ("Modernism at Night" 745)

Even *within* the work of a High Modernist such as Woolf, however, queerness of form ("experimental, oblique") and queerness of content ("the emergence of modern sexual identities") can operate in tension as well as in tandem, and those tensions are exacerbated in the representation of modern sexual identities in general.

The schematic distinction that I make here, between a queerness of form and one of content, partly corresponds to the twentieth-century division, in English and American literature, between high Modernist aesthetics and more popular or middlebrow forms of realist representation. This bifurcation iteslf gives rise to, and depends upon, a host of parallel and mutually reinforcing binary oppositions—traditional/experimental, form/content, high/low, aesthetic/political—that define competing forms of literary value. Woolf has often been represented as an exemplar of High Modernist aestheticism, while Hall, contrarily, has been remembered as the author of an aesthetically deficient, formally non-innovative polemic.[3] These distinctions have more recently been contested, as feminist critics have focused on Woolf's explicitly polemical writings (such as *A Room of One's Own* and *Three Guineas*), reinterpreting her aesthetic experimentalism within the context of her oppositional politics, while some new readings of *The Well of Loneliness* have resituated it in relationship to Modernist aesthetics. Nevertheless, schematically, the careers of Woolf and Hall might stand for the continuingly uneasy, if not competitive, relationship between two modes of representation—the middlebrow and the highbrow, one for which perception and experience coalesce around a singular and coherent subject, which relies on conventions of readerly identification (as in *The Well of Loneliness*), and one for which subjectivity is fragmentary and mutable, which employs techniques that disrupt identification with a singular subject (as in the work of both Woolf and, to some degree, Winterson).

Within postmodern fictional theory and practice, there is a similar conflict over whether the representation of protagonists with identities peripheral to the Anglo-American canon of the novel of formation—for example, as in *Oranges,* a provincial, working-class, lesbian protagonist—can draw upon conventions of identification, or whether such traditional forms of representation are inherently constraining and misrepresent the insurgency of such protagonists. *Oranges Are Not the Only Fruit,* with a first-person coming-of-age narrative interrupted by interpolated and invented fairy-tales, performs a bravura oscillation between these two poles. However, Winterson's fiction has continued to move away from realist conventions of representation, and her writing has become less and less encouraging of readerly identifications—developments that have disturbed some readers and that suggest the tension between the two continuing projects, for the fictional representation of consciousness, of queering representation and of representing the queer.

VOYAGING OUT OF THE VICTORIAN NOVEL

An unscientific survey (of friends and colleagues) suggests that *The Voyage Out* (1915) is a novel remembered indistinctly and at a long remove, even by readers familiar with Woolf and with women's novels of formation. Woolf's first novel seems stuck, somehow, not only in its author's youth but also its readers' and protagonist's. This state of chronological arrest is not the necessary fate of novels of formation—not, for example, of *The Mill on the Floss,* or even of *David Copperfield,* which unlike *The Voyage Out* supplement their protagonists' juvenile experience with more mature points of focalization. This association of the novel with early reading reiterates the very fear that *The Voyage Out* expresses—a writer's fear of being left behind, not liberated but trapped by literary tradition, doomed to repeat a recursive narrative structured by Victorian ideologies of gender and sexuality and by the realist narrative practices of combined plenitude (material) and evasion (psychological) that, in Woolf's view, had ossified around them. *The Voyage Out* expresses, even as it works to overcome, a fear of being unable to plot, or even fully to desire, an escape from a long, late, murmurous adolescence of Victorian culture into a clamorous (and dubious) maturity of Modernism. But the novel's trajectory, I will argue, is not reducible to the failed outward voyage—ending abruptly in death—of its protagonist, Rachel Vinrace. *The Voyage Out* both is, and is not, Rachel's story, as it is, and is not, a Victorian novel; it both rehearses and attempts to interrupt readers' habits of identification with what Gayatri Spivak, speaking of *Jane Eyre,* famously calls "the psychobiography of the militant female subject . . . the mesmerizing focus of the 'subject-constitution' of the female individualist" (897). In doing so, like the other novels considered in this chapter, it both solicits and deflects readerly identification; both longs and has little patience for that exchange of recognition; gestures toward, but cannot fully imagine, the readerly relation that might take its place.

The Voyage Out at first seems familiar as an heir to the tradition of the narrative of female formation such as those of Brontë and Eliot. Rachel Vinrace is a motherless girl, brought up with Victorian scrupulosity by paternal aunts in the London suburb of Richmond and discovering, on the threshold of adulthood, a modest resistance to the gender constraints of her milieu. Through the mentorship of her more sophisticated maternal aunt, Helen Ambrose, she is awakened to new possibilities of identification and desire in both the people that she meets and the novels that she reads; she emerges through this process into her own romance narrative as she becomes engaged to a young writer, Terence Hewet, while on holiday with the Ambroses in the fictitious South American village of Santa Marina. At this promising juncture, she develops a feverish illness and dies. This interruption itself is not entirely untypical in the nineteenth-century narrative of formation—death also interrupts the romance plots of Maggie Tulliver and Lucy Snowe, for example. For Woolf, however, I shall argue, this narrative suspension aims more fully to distance the novel both from the identification of *The Voyage Out* with the nineteenth-century novel of female formation and from identification—of reader and author with protagonist—as a convention of the novel of formation. Further, while the death of Rachel and the foreclosure of her romance do not—any more than do the deaths of Maggie Tulliver and M. Paul Emmanuel—enable the ascendancy of a lesbian counter-romance, a shift of narrative attention at the conclusion, to the sexually ambiguous character St. John Hirst, does allow the novel's elliptical references to and ostentatious silences about sexuality to reverberate with a certain queer intensity.

Critics have frequently observed the strength and ambivalence of Woolf's connection to her Victorian literary and cultural heritage.[4] The century inhabited by the authors whom Woolf grouped together as the "four great women novelists"—Jane Austen, Charlotte Brontë, Emily Brontë, and George Eliot—offered Woolf her most immediate set of objects of literary identification; but like her actual Victorian parents—her eminent literary father, her beautiful mother—this literary parentage was overwhelming as well as generative. Gillian Beer, for example, observes, "The Victorians are not simply represented in Virginia Woolf. They are internalized, inseparable, as well as held at arm's length. . . . Woolf did not simply reject the Victorians and their concerns, or renounce them. Instead she persistingly rewrote them" (93–94). Indeed, particular Victorian concerns and repeated literary formulations persist for Woolf throughout her career. In a late memoir, for example, she describes her training in what she calls "the Victorian manner," which "is useful—it has its beauty, for it is founded upon restraint, sympathy, unselfishness—all civilised qualities. It is helpful in making something seemly and human out of raw odds and ends. But the Victorian manner is perhaps—I am not sure—a disadvantage in writing" (*Moments of Being* [hereafter *MB*] 129). Woolf's ambivalence here recalls a moment in *The Voyage Out,* written a quarter-century before, when Rachel describes her upbringing to Terence Hewet: "Here [her aunts] are at Richmond at this very moment building things up. They're all wrong, perhaps, but there's a sort of beauty in it. It's so unconscious, so modest. And yet they feel things. . . . That was what I felt when I lived with them. It was very real" (246). This persistently divided note in Woolf's response to a heritage that is "all wrong, perhaps, but [with] a sort of beauty in it" similarly marks her critical writing, in the 1920s, about Victorian women novelists. That reponse suggests her ambivalence about her own identification, as a reader and writer, with her literary precursors, and about what she represents as the overidentification of many Victorian realist novelists with their characters.

For example, while Woolf credits Eliot's early novels with evincing "the large mature mind spreading itself with a luxurious sense of freedom in the world of her 'remotest past'" (*Collected Essays* [hereafter *CE*] 1: 199) she finds even in these works "traces of that troubled spirit, that exacting and questioning and baffled presence who was George Eliot herself." This "presence" infects Eliot's female protagonists, Woolf argues, so that they "bring out the worst of her, lead her into difficult places, make her self-conscious, didactic, and occasionally vulgar" (201–2). Like critics before and after her, Woolf found Eliot overidentified with her heroines: "Her self-consciousness is always marked when her heroines say what she herself would have said" (202). If Eliot's "large mature mind" is unfortunately narrowed by the "troubled spirit" that infects her protagonists, Charlotte Brontë's difficulty is apparently the reverse, as Woolf finds her emotionally compelling but philosophically narrow: "[In reading *Jane Eyre*] the writer has us by the hand, forces us along her road, makes us see what she sees, never leaves us for a moment or allows us to forget her," but she "does not attempt to solve the problems of human life; she is even unaware that such problems exist; all her force, and it is the more tremendous for being constricted, goes into the assertion, 'I love,' 'I hate,' 'I suffer'" (*CE* 1: 186, 187). In both cases, what troubles Woolf is the appearance of a marked "I"—not just an author-function, but a wounded, assertive ego—within what ought to be the separate world of the fictional text; the "I" both indicates the author's identification with her own character and solicits the reader's.

Woolf's distrust of such authorial presence and its solicitation of readerly identification is not confined to her discussion of women authors; she finds such self-consciousness also present in male writers, particularly working-class ones such as George Gissing and D. H. Lawrence.[5] Again,

Woolf's ostensible objection is not that Brontë's and Eliot's novels draw attention to matters of gender, or Gissing's and Lawrence's to class relations—she understands these structures to be fundamental to both the social and the literary text. The problem, for Woolf, is that such forms of representation may draw attention to the troublesome feelings and experience of an implied author as an extra-textual consciousness, exhibiting the author's identification with the character and encouraging the reader's identification with that author. "At the end of [*Jane Eyre*] we are steeped through and through with the genius, the vehemence, the indignation of Charlotte Brontë. Remarkable faces, figures of strong outline and gnarled feature have flashed upon us in passing; but it is through her eyes that we have seen them. Once she is gone, we seek for them in vain" (Woolf, *CE* 1: 186). Such a fiction, according to Woolf, is liable to diminishment when the reader is not immediately within the spell of its powerful identifications; furthermore, such identifications paradoxically have the effect of arrogating too much power to the charismatic figure of the author. In "Character in Fiction," Woolf asserts that readers must "insist that writers shall come down off their plinths and pedestals" (*CE* 4: 436); as Susan Stanford Friedman points out in her discussion of *The Voyage Out* as a precursor to Woolf's *Common Reader* essays, "Woolf's 'common reader' [. . .] always maintains a certain distance from what is read" ("Pedagogical Scenes" 121). Allowing or encouraging literary identification undermines the possibility of such distance.

Feminist critics, troubled by Woolf's apparent discomfort with protofeminist indignation and anger, land sometimes in the paradoxical position of working to distance her from her own distance from feminist anger. Jane Marcus, for example, redirects Woolf's critique of Brontë to make it explicitly feminist rather than *ad feminam,* asserting that "Woolf's anger [in her criticism of Brontë] is directed at Haworth parsonage, not at Brontë" (*Art and Anger* 32). In *A Room of One's Own,* it is true, Woolf connects Brontë's "indignation," which she considers aesthetically deforming, with her material circumstances, wondering "what might have happened if Charlotte Brontë had possessed say three hundred a year" (73). But it is not precisely the fault of "Haworth parsonage" that Brontë had no independent means, and her straitened emotional and financial circumstances could sometimes provoke Woolf's sarcasm at what seems to be Brontë's expense: "Always to be a governess and always in love is a serious limitation in a world which is full, after all, of people who are neither one nor the other" (186). Elsewhere, Marcus asserts that Woolf "will not supply us with characters with whom we may egotistically identify. This would be weakness on her part, encouragement of self-indulgence on the part of the reader"; and she characterizes this choice as specifically "a feminist attack on the ego as *male* false consciousness" ("Thinking Back" 9; my emphasis). I am suggesting, contrarily, that Woolf sees both male and female writers, and male and female readers, as subject to the temptations of "egotistic[al] identif[ication]."

Jane de Gay takes a different tack, acknowledging Woolf's ambivalence but locating its origin outside Woolf, in paternal(istic) influence: "Three of the female writers who feature prominently in [*A Room of One's Own*] had already been discussed at length by [Leslie] Stephen [whose] admiration of Austen for accepting the narrow confines of a woman's life, and his qualified sympathies for Brontë [. . .] and Eliot [. . .] can all be seen to have an impact on Woolf's ambivalent valuation of her female precursors in *Room,* even as she claims them for a female tradition" (14). But to displace Woolf's ambivalence in this way is, paradoxically, both to reattach her to the two powerful influences (her father and her female precursors) from which she was working to distance herself, and—by emending her as she emends Brontë and Eliot—to replicate her wish that female precursors might have offered themselves as more appropriate, more liberating objects of authorial identification.

Such myriad temptations of literary identification function as both theme and structure of *The Voyage Out.* Though this novel has attracted less scholarly attention than her later, more assertively Modernist works, feminist critics in particular have been interested in its representations of reading and its role in Woolf's development as a critic.[6] Friedman, for example, has described *The Voyage Out* as a "parable of reading" (117) that works to replace "the kind of female reader of books and people who is most likely to be victimized," represented by Rachel, with the "resilient, resisting, and dialogic reader [that Woolf] calls 'the common reader'" (116–17).[7] Gay suggests that the novel marks the transformation of Woolf the reader to Woolf as novelist: "The process of writing *The Voyage Out* . . . can be seen as a period of transition [for Woolf] from reading books by earlier authors to writing her own" (19). Such readings frequently point to a tension between their own narrative of Woolf's development as an author and Woolf's foreclosure of Rachel Vinrace's development as a protagonist, often characterizing the novel as either about, or enacting, narrative failure. Friedman suggests that the novel is "founded on a basic contradiction [because] it simultaneously narrates a failed *Bildung* for its protagonist and inscribes a successful *Bildung* for its author" ("Spatialization" 107); for Geoffrey Castle, it participates in allied feminist and Modernist critiques of the Bildung tradition because it is "quite patently a story of development that features a protagonist who does not develop—at least in the sense implied by classical Bildung" (216–17). Locating a similar tension, my own argument characterizes it in terms of Woolf's relations of identification with, and disavowal of, the Victorian novel of female formation. Revisiting recognizable but submerged elements of the female-formation plots of Eliot and Charlotte Brontë, Woolf pays homage to, even as she gently critiques, this Victorian heritage. But the brief flowering and the abrupt termination of Rachel as a romantic and a reading subject, like Woolf's well known later assertion that "killing the Angel in the House is part of the occupation of a woman writer" *Death of the Moth* [hereafter *DM*] 238), expresses a more directly murderous fantasy, a symbolic destruction of Woolf's literary matrilineage.

The Voyage Out engages with this inheritance not only at the levels of plot (in the death of Rachel Vinrace) and representation (in the novel's many parodically rendered scenes of reading) but also in its narrative syntax, in the hyperbolic profusion of literary allusion that both acknowledges and mocks the seduction of literary identification. As Beverly Schlack observes, in *The Voyage Out* "even the minor characters . . . are drawn with allusive brushstrokes. Their character is often derived *primarily* from their expressed literary preferences" (2; emphasis in original).[8] Conscious displays of literary allusion by both male and female characters, however, are revealed as largely empty gestures, attempts to invoke an identification with past powers that instead reveal an underlying impotence. This literary past is patriarchally defined but not exclusively masculine. Jane Austen, praised by the pompous Richard Dalloway as "the greatest female writer we possess" because "she does not attempt to write like a man" (Woolf, *Voyage Out* [hereafter *VO*] 64), and Sappho, admired by the sexually ambiguous young scholar St. John Hirst, both make sustained appearances. Amid the profusion of literary reference, there are two names of women writers whose absence is as notable as their importance to Woolf: George Eliot and Charlotte Brontë. I will argue below that Eliot and Brontë are the novel's unacknowledged interlocutors and objects of authorial identification; Woolf revisits and redirects key scenes and themes of *Middlemarch, The Mill on the Floss,* and *Jane Eyre* in order to both to challenge the readerly identifications on which these novels draw and to demonstrate her own passage beyond identification with these authors.

Woolf implicitly introduces the thematics of literary identification in the very first scene of *The Voyage Out,* in which Rachel's aunt and uncle,

Helen and Ridley Ambrose, stride through London on their way to embark for South America on Rachel's father's ship. As they walk, Helen weeps at the thought of parting for many months from her children, while Ridley, a classicist, occupies himself with reciting aloud verses from Macaulay's *Lays of Ancient Rome:* "Lars Porsena of Clusium / By the nine Gods he swore / . . . That the Great House of Tarquin / Should suffer wrong no more" (Woolf, *VO* 5). They both display "eccentricity" (3, 4); but juxtaposed with Helen's maternal grief, Ridley's delight in this nationalist jingle (like Mr. Ramsay's recitations of "The Charge of the Light Brigade" in *To the Lighthouse*) has a particularly bathetic quality, especially to the extent that it juxtaposes the wronged "House of Tarquin" and the more prosaically situated family of Helen and Ridley, who are facing not exile, but an extended holiday. As Schlack suggests, "Ridley obviously identifies with Macaulay's robust, virile imitations of the *Iliad* manner. But an admiration that borders on identification may indicate something of a bully lurking beneath the would-be hero" (8). (Perhaps more of a baby than a bully; later, Helen sees his stride change and guesses that he "was either a Viking or a stricken Nelson" [Woolf, *VO* 6], like a child at play; and it is Rachel's father Willoughby whom Helen suspects of "nameless atrocities with regard to his daughter, as indeed she had always suspected him of bullying his wife" [20]). Because one of the wrongs visited upon the "House of Tarquin" is the rape of Lucrece and her subsequent suicide, Ridley's recitation foreshadows, albeit with exaggeration, Rachel's incipient sexual experiences, in all of which she experiences or observes some degree of coercion—a kiss forced on her by Richard Dalloway; the disturbing vision of two hotel guests entangled in an embrace (155–56); Rachel's own engagement to Terence Hewet, and her subsequent, if not precisely resulting, death.

These performances of gendered literary identification suggest the potentially parodic imitation of the kind that, as Judith Butler has influentially argued, reveals the foundationally performative nature of heterosexual roles. But Helen's gendered performance also reveals the potential limitations of such parody, for her behavior seems less to disrupt gender conventions than to allow her to flourish within them. Ridley and Helen, despite their eccentricity, stake out conventional gender roles, including distinctions between masculine intellect and feminine embodiment, masculine activity and feminine passivity, masculine poet or maker and the female muse or model. While Ridley orates, demonstrating his scholarly knowledge of classical allusion, Helen—"Tall, large-eyed, draped in purple shawls . . . romantic and beautiful" (Woolf, *VO* 9)—*embodies* a classical allusion. She, too, is hardly innocent of self-aggrandizement; her Niobe-like grief over her entirely voluntary departure from her children appears both exaggerated and willful. As Patricia Juliana Smith points out, "Why [Helen's] presence on this journey takes priority over her maternal duties is [. . .] unclear, and while her grief is ascribed to this separation, little subsequent reference is made to the children or to her concern for them" (130). Commenting on an earlier version of the same scene in her reconstruction of the composition of *The Voyage Out,* Louise DeSalvo calls Helen "an irresponsible and infantile parent" who deludes herself by thinking "that she cannot return to her children [rather] than . . . realizing that she will not because she does not want to" (37). These critics perhaps understate the evidence for Helen's concern about her children; she brightens when asked about them (Woolf, *VO* 17, 57); is eager for news of them (95); and enjoys thinking about childrearing (12). And since Woolf was childless herself and accustomed to the upper-class child-rearing norms of early-twentieth-century England, we may not be justified in extrapolating her evaluations of maternal behavior and attachment from our contemporary expectations; there is no evidence that any other characters in the novel think that Helen is shirking "maternal duties" or is "irresponsible" or "infantile." In fact, in her representation of Helen here as elsewhere, Woolf's narrative attitude seems (designedly) impossible to fix. Sometimes the narrative is focalized through Helen, but sometimes she is represented from a distance; she seems at times incisive and inviting as a character, at others too cool for comfort. The slipperiness, from the opening scene, of the narrative stance and of the character herself, serves immediate notice that the novel will be more intent on dislocating than on encouraging readerly impulses to identification.

Ridley Ambrose's allusiveness enacts, in minimalist form, what I have been calling literary identification—he projects his self-conception through these scraps of highly stylized textual representation. Certainly his behavior—comforting himself with what are essentially nursery rhymes, identifying with nursery heroes—is childish; nevertheless his authority (to demand, for example, a fully furnished study on board Willoughby Ambrose's ship; to bestow his company on, or more frequently withhold it from, his womenfolk; to direct the flow of domestic dinner conversation) is never challenged. This pattern in the representation of masculine literary allusion and identification—in which it is revealed as expressing impotence rather than power but nevertheless facilitates male social authority and interconnectedness—prevails throughout the novel. For example, the first shipboard dinner (which immediately follows the opening scene) is dominated by an exchange between Ridley Ambrose and Mr. Pepper (an amateur scholar and old friend of both Willoughby Vinrace and, as it turns out, Ridley Ambrose):

> "You knew Jenkinson, didn't you, Ambrose?" asked Mr Pepper across the table.
>
> "Jenkinson of Peterhouse?"
>
> "He's dead," said Mr. Pepper.
>
> "—Ah, dear!—I knew him—ages ago," said Ridley. "He was the hero of the punt accident, do you remember? A queer card. Married a young woman out of a tobacconist's and lived in the Fens—never heard what became of him."
>
> "Drink—drugs," said Mr Pepper with sinister conciseness. "He left a commentary. Hopeless muddle, I'm told." (Woolf, *VO* 10)

Later, Mr. Pepper observes of a different Jenkinson—this one "of Cats"—that "'This year he has had the misfortune to lose his wife. . . . There's an unmarried daughter who keeps house for him, I believe, but it's never the same, not at his age.' Both men nodded sagely as they carved their apples" (11). The men's dismissive references to nameless wives and daughters, as well as their obliviousness to the presence of Rachel, the actual "unmarried [and motherless] daughter" with whom they are sitting, emphasize the casual misogyny of such male bonding. In a later scene, when an Englishwoman remarks coquettishly, "'You men! where would you be if it weren't for the women!'" Ridley responds "grimly" "'Read the *Symposium*'" (224). But as Ridley's "grimly" suggests, male homosociality, at least for this older generation, is as much a matter of rivalrous *schadenfreude* as of erotic attachment or even friendship, and the comic multiplication of Jenkinsons, like the rapid-fire exchange of proper names more generally, suggests their fundamental interchangeability. Ridley Ambrose's identification with the second Jenkinson's failure—"'I confess I sympathize,' said Ridley with a melancholy sigh. 'I have a weakness for people who can't begin'" (11)—also emphasizes impotence rather than power. In the narrative structure of male homosociality identified by Eve Sedgwick, the "ruined carcase of a woman" often functions as "just the right lubricant for an adjustment in differentials of power" between men (*Between Men* 76). *The Voyage Out* is surprisingly full of female "ruin[s]" and "carcase[s]," from Rachel's dead mother, to Jenkinsons's dead wife, to the prostitute who is expelled from the tourist hotel in Santa Marina, to Rachel herself at the novel's end, but for this older generation of men, at least, homosocial power seems to be waning rather than waxing. In one sense, this is not surprising: The texts that Sedgwick discusses, and thus their reproduction of homosocial structure, are all by men; in her representations of masculine dialogue, Woolf turns the tables by demonstrating the female author's power to mock and to diminish such homosocial exchange.

As instantiated by the novel's eldest male generation—Pepper, Ridley Ambrose, and perhaps the scholar Hughling Elliott, whom they encounter at Santa Marina—the homosocial world of literary allusion is not only moribund but also—perhaps because—disembodied. It seems directed not only to the marginalization of women but also to the suppression of any realized emotional or erotic connection among men. For the younger men in the novel, however, literary allusion carries a charge of both hostility and desire across heterosexual and homosocial relations. Encountering the erotic and intellectual blank slate of Rachel, the novel's male characters are drawn to leave both a textual and a sexual impress on her. Pepper, as we learn, has given her copies of all his scholarly monographs. The conventional politician Richard Dalloway, who has hitched a ride on board the ship with his wife, Clarissa, promises to send Rachel a copy of a work of Edmund Burke. After pondering this question—"'Which shall it be, I wonder?' He noted something in his pocket-book'")—he unexpectedly pounces: "Holding her tight, he kissed her passionately" (Woolf, *VO* 80). This experience both awakens Rachel's sexual curiosity and also causes her to have nightmares of confinement and pursuit. The young scholar St. John Hirst promises in his turn to send her Gibbon, at the same time demeaning her sexual inexperience: "'I suppose you've led an absurd life until now—you've just walked in a crocodile, I suppose, with your hair down your back" (172). St. John's erotic insecurity and ambiguity (he is represented overtly as misogynist and unattractive to women, implicitly as homosexual) have a similar effect on Rachel to Dalloway's erotic domination, making her weep and "shiver[] with anger and excitement."

Hirst's friend Hewet is the exception; he promises Rachel, "*I* shan't lend you books" (239), and thus, perhaps inevitably, becomes her sexual object choice. But textual banter also mediates the relationship between Hirst and Hewet, who is deserting his friend and their shared Cambridge environment in his engagement to Rachel. Hewet confesses that he has lost a book of Wordsworth's poems that he has borrowed from Hirst, to which Hirst, after letting him fret for a few moments, responds, "'It is here'" and "point[s] to his breast"; Helen Ambrose remarks to Hewet after this exchange, "'I should think you were always losing things'" (159). On the one hand, Helen seems to mark indirectly the coming loss of Hirst and

Hewet's exclusive relationship, which will be triangulated by Rachel; on the other, the book is not lost but passes from heart to heart between Hirst and Hewet. For the younger generation literary allusion seems to mediate relations of desire potentially less imbricated with relations of domination than those of the previous, male-dominated generation.

In fact, women in *The Voyage Out* share the habit of literary allusion. However, here as in Jamaica Kincaid's *Lucy,* simply replacing masculine texts and proper names with feminine ones does not in itself dissolve the relations of domination that these literary identifications facilitate. First, the feminine use of literary allusion can be as empty and manipulative as the masculine, a possibility illustrated most conspicuously in the character of Clarissa Dalloway. Clarissa is both submissive to her husband, professing to feel for him "what my mother and women of her generation felt for Christ" (Woolf, *VO* 53), and at the same time sexually predatory like her husband. As a character she embodies what Luce Irigaray calls the "hom(m)osexual" economy of an apparently heterosexual order, whose "logic is the logic of masculine sameness. This sameness that is proliferated everywhere and on everyone is the sameness of phallic identity. Within this logic women are reduced to the position of a mere semblance of difference" (Grosz 342). Clarissa Dalloway's seduction borrows the male power-form of literary allusion, revoiced as a kind of charming, inconsequential feminine chatter. She entrances Ridley Ambrose with the assertion that she'd "give ten years of her life to know Greek" and then disappears when he has offered to tutor her. She promises Rachel to "insist on your playing [the piano] to me tomorrow" (Woolf, *VO* 48) and then interrupts her practice seductively:

> She pressed Rachel's shoulder.
> "Um-m-m—" she went on quoting—
> "'Unrest which men miscall delight'—
> " . . . When one's young and attractive—I'm going to say it!—*everything's* at one's feet." (60)

Like the male characters, Clarissa seems impelled by erotic impulses toward Rachel channeled through displays of literary superiority. When the Dalloways disembark, Clarissa kisses Rachel and "murmur[s] to her 'I *do* like you,'" as she gives her a copy of *Persuasion* (83). But the new narrative of female solidarity and perhaps of lesbian desire that Woolf adumbrates at the end of *A Room of One's Own*—"sometimes women do like women" (86)—is unlikely to be written by or about Rachel or Clarissa.

The younger woman is the elder's sexual rival, and the elder fails to protect Rachel from her husband's sexual exploitation.

Helen Ambrose's motives toward Rachel are more actively benign, and her negotiations with a masculine social order more directed toward independence and self-respect, but she too is complicit with that social order. As we saw at the novel's opening, for example, she allows and indeed encourages Ridley's self-dramatizing identification with the role of devoted and unworldly scholar, and compensates with her own (as devoted mother). She is a social pragmatist who encourages Rachel to "take things as they are . . . if you want friendship with men" (Woolf, *VO* 87). Her pedagogical approach to Rachel is certainly less coercive than that of the other characters who bestow on Rachel texts that reflect only their *own* identifications and desires, whereas Helen "would have been the first to disclaim any influence, or indeed any belief that influence was within her power" (137). Nevertheless, her reticence proves almost as unhelpful as the others' aggression.

Within the novel, then, feminine relations routed through textuality are not free of dynamics of erotic and intellectual aggression; a male-oriented web of intertextuality cannot simply be replaced by a female-oriented one. To the extent that moments in *The Voyage Out* recall and redirect scenes and characters in *Middlemarch, The Mill on the Floss,* and finally *Jane Eyre,* Woolf suggests that the same is true for her as an author: Replacing the names of Plato, Gibbon, and Burke with Austen, Eliot, and Brontë as objects of literary identification does not simply liberate Woolf as a novelist, since their legacy—like Helen's mentorship of Rachel—is an ambiguous one.

The shipboard dinner-party already mentioned revisits, and subtly revises, a similarly placed scene in *Middlemarch.* If, as other critics have suggested, Ridley Ambrose, with his intellectual distraction and kindly inattention toward his niece, suggests Leslie Stephen as his biographical original, he also recalls a fictional model, another inconsequent male guardian of a naïve young woman—Dorothea Brooke's uncle, as he appears, for example, at the dinner party at which Dorothea meets Casaubon:

> "Sir Humphry Davy?" said Mr Brooke, over the soup, in his easy smiling way, taking up Sir James Chettam's remark that he was studying Davy's *Agricultural Chemistry.* "Well, now, Sir Humphry Davy: I dined with him years ago at Cartwright's, and Wordsworth was there too—the poet Wordsworth, you know. Now there was something singular. I

> was at Cambridge when Wordsworth was there, and I never met him—and I dined with him twenty years afterwards at Cartwright's." (Eliot, *Middlemarch* 14)

Like the second Jenkinson in *The Voyage Out,* who had "accumulations enough to fill a barn," Mr Brooke has accumulated "documents" (17); and Mr. Casaubon, to whom Brooke's musings are addressed, has filled "a formidable range of volumes" with notes (21). Like the dinner in *The Voyage Out,* Eliot's also comically represents male homosocial exchange as the "accumulation" of empty tokens. Brooke is happily unaware of his own irrelevance (though it will later be underlined by his failure as a parliamentary candidate), but Casaubon, like Ridley Ambrose, seems uneasily conscious of his intellectual sterility: "I live too much with the dead," he remarks (15).

Ridley Ambrose's futility is underlined later in *The Voyage Out,* when Rachel finds her uncle sitting in his study in a chair "which became more and more deeply encircled by books, which lay open on the floor, and could only be crossed by a careful process of stepping, so delicate that his visitors generally stopped and addressed him from the outskirts" (Woolf, *VO* 191). "'You should read Balzac,'" he tells her. "'Then we come to Wordsworth and Coleridge. Pope, Johnson, Addison, Wordsworth, Shelley, Keats. One thing leads to another. . . . But what's the use of reading if you don't read Greek?' . . . He then wanted to know what people did at dances. . . . On bestowing a kiss she was allowed to go." She leaves "lost in wonder at her uncle, and his books, . . . and his queer, utterly inexplicable, but apparently satisfactory view of life" (192). Again Ridley Ambrose recalls Leslie Stephen, as Woolf describes him, "Slowly he would realise my presence. Rising he would go to the shelves, put the book [she was returning] back and very kindly ask me what had I made of it? Perhaps I was reading Johnson. For some time we would talk and then, feeling soothed, stimulated, full of love for this unworldly, very distinguished, lonely man, I would go down to the drawing room again and hear George [Duckworth]'s patter" (*MB* 136). Again, at the same time, he recalls Brooke's fictional futilities—"I remember when we were all reading Adam Smith. *There* is a book, now. . . . But some say, history moves in circles" (Eliot, *Middlemarch* 15). "More and more deeply encircled by books"; "One thing leads to another," "history moves in circles"; these phrases echo too the circular project of Casaubon's Key to All Mythologies, attempting "to show . . . that all the mythical systems or erratic mythical fragments in the world were corruptions of a tradition originally revealed" (20). At the same time, Ridley's dismissal of all non-classical literature recalls Dorothea Brooke's burning desire to learn Greek and Latin, and perhaps even a little Hebrew. That desire, however, is not shared by Rachel. On the one hand, Ridley's projects and phrases, with their echoes of Casaubon, suggest that all of literary tradition and even history is a gentleman's club in which Rachel (and Woolf) will never be able to find points of identification; nothing, it seems, will ever lead to *them.* On the other hand, they suggest that the club is moribund, a regime of power that has outlived its ideas and is now simply going around in circles. Greek is not, perhaps, the coming *lingua franca;* significantly, at the end of *A Room of One's Own,* it is a laboratory, not a library, that Chloe and Olivia share.

Woolf parts company with Eliot in suggesting more emphatically that power, and empowering relations of identification, in fact may now pass to women. In an essay, Woolf suggests that "the Victorian age . . . was the age of the professional man" (qtd. in S. Ellis 12). In her address "Professions for Women," she seems to believe that, despite the "many phantoms and obstacles" still present, the twentieth century will be the age of the professional woman as well: "The whole position, as I see it—here in this hall surrounded by women practising for the first time in history I know not how many different professions—is one of extraordinary interest and importance" (*DM* 241, 242). Although a schoolteacher and textbook writer, Miss Allan (whom everyone agrees in admiring), is the only prominent professional woman in *The Voyage Out,* Woolf frequently highlights a nascent professional*ism* in Helen and Rachel as well. At the dinner party, both women "being after the fashion of their sex, highly trained in promoting men's talk without listening to it, [are able to] think—about the education of children, about the use of fog sirens in an opera—without betraying [themselves]." These professional interests—in children's education on Helen's part, in music on Rachel's (she is a talented pianist), recur throughout the novel: Helen briskly dismisses, as from a position of expertise, Clarissa Dalloway's "idiotic theories about the way to bring up children" (Woolf, *VO* 88) and observes that "if [girls] were properly educated I don't see why they shouldn't be much the same as men" (104); Rachel at the hotel dance is matter-of-fact in her assumption of expertise as she improvises dance music, "sure of her melody [and] mark[ing] the rhythm boldly so as to simplify the way" (185). She asserts to the otherwise intimidating St. John Hirst that she "play[s] the piano very well . . . better, I expect, than anyone in this room" (171); and takes Hewett's "[walking] stick and [draws] figures in the thin white dust to explain how Bach wrote his fugues" (253). Terence believes that "he liked the impersonality which [music] produced in her" (339), but in fact he seems unnerved by her lack of attentiveness to him, as he persists in interrupting her practice with a series of needling comments on "Woman."

Woolf perhaps shares his ambivalence, since for both Rachel and Helen the expression of these interests and skills remains amateur: Helen exercises her own "theories" by taking over Rachel's education, with mixed results, and Rachel's most successful public performance occurs when she plays for the dancers at the hotel. Her musical abilities, in the end, come to no greater fruition than Dorothea Brooke's architectural drawings. Nevertheless, in her emphasis on the capacity of Helen and Rachel for more detached and impersonal forms of investment, Woolf rejects Eliot's contrasting emphasis on Dorothea's emotional and self-sacrificing motivations: "All her eagerness for acquirement lay within that full current of sympathetic motive in which her ideas and impulses were habitually swept along. She did not want to deck herself with knowledge—to wear it loose from the nerves and blood that fed her action; and if she had written a book she must have done it as Saint Theresa did, under the command of an authority that constrained her conscience" (Eliot, *Middlemarch* 70–71). Eliot's emphasis on self-sacrifice and an orientation toward others as the only ethical justification for feminine "eagerness for acquirement" brings a matrilineal textual legacy only too closely in line with the more directly maternal model of angelic domesticity that Woolf violently rejects.[9]

Similarly, Woolf differentiates Rachel from Dorothea Brooke in her relationship to patriarchal text itself, especially in its sometimes incongruous transformation from signifier of homosocial exchange to token of heterosexual seduction. Rachel tells Helen, "'I've got all [Mr. Pepper's] pamphlets. . . . Little pamphlets. Little yellow books.' It did not appear that she had read them" (Woolf, *VO* 15). The narrative hints that the bachelor Pepper might be in love with Rachel: He has, apparently, presented her with these books; he chooses to stay for a time with the Ambroses and Rachel in Santa Marina, despite their efforts to dissuade him; and when he does in fact leave, Helen retains "an uneasy suspicion . . . that William [Pepper] was hiding a wound" (101). Rachel's disdain for Pepper's monographs contrasts strongly with Dorothea Brooke's response to Casaubon's pamphlets: "They were pamphlets about the Early Church. . . . When [Mr. Brooke] re-entered the library, he found Dorothea seated and already deep in one of the pamphlets which had some marginal manuscript of Mr. Casaubon's,—taking it in as eagerly as she might have taken in the scent of a fresh bouquet after a dry, hot, dreary walk" (Eliot, *Middlemarch* 31).

Rachel's indifference not only distinguishes her from Dorothea but also distinguishes Woolf's relationship to her protagonist from Eliot's. Woolf and Eliot both emphasize the lack of education from which their protagonists suffer as women. Rachel's dilettante education, provided "by kindly doctors and gentle old professors [who] had taught her the rudiments of about ten different branches of knowledge" echoes Dorothea's acquaintance with "ladies'-school literature" (21) and a "toy-box history of the world adapted to young ladies" (70), but their creators represent their relationships to these limitations quite differently. Despite her lack of education, Dorothea drinks ecclesiastical pamphlets in like water and is capable of "becom[ing] engaged in conversation with Mr Casaubon about the Vaudois clergy" (20), while Rachel, according to Woolf, "would believe practically anything she was told, invent reasons for anything she said" (*VO* 31). By comparison with Eliot, Woolf takes an amused and detached attitude toward her protagonist, determined not to exalt her above the likely result of the conditions that have formed her. She declines, in doing so, to identify with her heroine or to encourage the reader's identification with her.

Indeed, Rachel is unusual as the protagonist of a novel of formation—by comparison, for example, with Maggie Tulliver—in her initial lack of interest in imaginative literature or capacity to identify with fictional heroines. Unlike the adults around her, with their constant literary allusions and rapt textual pursuits, Rachel displays a disdain for and discomfort with literature that are catholic in reach and comic in effect, encompassing Austen, whom she finds "so like a tight plait"; William Cowper, whose letters are "rather dull" (Woolf, *VO* 59); and Gibbon, whose prose she describes as "go[ing] round, round, round like a roll of oilcloth" (226), recalling Ridley Ambrose's futile circles. Even Emily Brontë's *Wuthering Heights,* whose "half-savage, and hardy, and free" (126) Romantic antiheroine might seem to offer the undersocialized Rachel a more appealing object of literary identification, appears only as a volume to be "slid out of the armchair" (59), along with Cowper, so that Clarissa Dalloway—whose living glamour Rachel finds vastly more enticing—can sit down. Again, this representation disrupts conventional links of identification among author, reader, and character in the novel of formation: these authors are all among Woolf's own favorites, and the reader is not allowed to identify with Rachel as a reading heroine.

In the second half of the book, however, when Rachel moves in with the Ambroses at Santa Marina, she abruptly becomes a more conventional reading heroine. With the well-meaning aim of "show[ing] her niece . . . how to live, or as she put it, how to be a reasonable person" (Woolf, *VO* 89), Helen provides a room "in which she could play [piano], read, think, defy the world, a fortress as well as a sanctuary" (136). Helen both offers herself as a potential object of identification, and creates a context in which Rachel can experience literary identifications. But Helen, as I have suggested previously, is herself an ambiguous model, since her own life reveals the difficulty of drawing a line between complicity with and successful negotiation of a male-dominated social world. Geoffrey Castle suggests that "By deciding to mentor Rachel, [Helen] dramatizes the paradoxical position of many female educators at the turn of the century, for she acts both as an intimate friend and as an emissary of the liberal humanist tradition dominated by men" (222). The ambiguities or paradoxes of her position are nicely captured by her ideas about what Rachel should read: "When Mrs. Ambrose would have suggested Defoe, Maupassant, or some spacious chronicle of family life, Rachel chose modern books, books in shiny yellow covers . . . which were tokens in her aunt's eyes of harsh wrangling and disputes about facts which had no such importance as the moderns claimed for them. But she did not interfere" (Woolf, *VO* 137). Woolf usually refers to this character as "Helen"; here, she becomes "Mrs. Ambrose," as though to emphasize her role as an agent of the reproduction of a social norm ("family life"). At the same time, however, her deliberate policy of non-interference suggests a faith in the triumph of a discursive rationality ("Talk was the medicine she trusted to" [137]) whose extension to female subjects (e.g., by John Stuart Mill) was an ideal of Victorian feminism. Similarly, though the proper names she cites here are those of male authors, they are adduced as examples of the genre of domestic realism ("spacious chronicle[s] of family life") equally if not more associated with women, suggesting that a humanist literary heritage cannot be claimed solely by either men or women.

If Helen Ambrose is an ambiguous model of female formation, Rachel is equally an ambivalent subject. Given everyone's tendency to treat her as a blank slate on which to project their own identifications and desires, it is not surprising that Rachel resists feminine as well as masculine mentorship, rejecting her aunt's curriculum for one that she herself devises. Unfortunately, the "shiny yellow covers" of sensational New Woman narratives will prove no more mentally nourishing than Pepper's scholarly "little yellow pamphlets." The codes of professional detachment and impersonality that guide Rachel in her piano study fail her here, and she falls with a vengeance into the posture of the reading girl. Her reading includes "Ibsen . . . succeeded by a novel such as Helen detested, whose purpose was to distribute the guilt for a woman's fall on the right shoulders." These narratives are neither "spacious" nor familial: they are narrowly focused on the female subject, with whom Rachel eagerly identifies:

> "What I want to know," she said aloud, "is this: What is the truth? What's the truth of it all?" She was speaking partly as herself, and partly as the heroine of the play she had just read. The landscape outside, because she had seen nothing but print for the space of two hours, now appeared amazingly solid and clear, but . . . for the moment she herself was the most vivid thing in it—an heroic statue in the middle of the foreground, dominating the view. Ibsen's plays always left her in that condition. (Woolf, *VO* 137)

Looking in the wrong place for the "truth," Rachel instead encounters identification as interpellation; she is "hailed" into the character of the tragic heroine of the courtship plot. In "Character in Fiction," Woolf urges readers to "insist that writers shall come down off their plinths and pedestals" (*CE* 4: 436). Rachel's overidentification of herself with Ibsen's heroine, reifying both herself and the character as "an heroic statue . . . dominating the view," associates her with the aggressive, phallic landscape of "plinths and pedestals"; she has surrendered herself to the text rather than entering into dialogue with it. Indeed, everything about her reading, as Woolf describes it, monumentalizes text: "[she read] with the curious literalness of one to whom written sentences are unfamiliar . . . handling words as though they were made of wood, separately of great importance, and possessed of shapes like tables and chairs" (*VO* 138). Friedman describes Rachel's "recognition of the materiality of language" as "anticipating Woolf's later modernism" ("Pedagogical Scenes"110); but less happily, Rachel's way of reading links her to the post-traumatic madness of another under-educated, over-literal, and doomed Woolfian reader—Septimus Warren Smith in *Mrs. Dalloway.* Septimus Warren Smith, to whose hearing "the word 'time' split its husk; poured its riches over him; and from his lips fell like shells . . . hard, white, imperishable words" (Woolf, *Mrs. Dalloway* 105), loses his sanity and ultimately his life because he feels driven to fight to "save an England which consisted almost entirely of Shakespeare's plays and [his teacher] Miss Isabel Pole in a green dress walking in a square" (Woolf, *Mrs. Dalloway* 130). Not only Septimus's reverential reading attitude but also the latent image of a pole in a square echo Rachel's "heroic statue" and the "plinths and pedestals" that Woolf wishes to banish in "Character in Fiction." As Friedman observes, Rachel "could not maintain a critical distance in negotiating the intertextual association between books and life. . . . It is not only the power of ideology that engulfs Rachel, but also her habit of complete identification with what she reads" ("Pedagogical Scenes" 120–21). If the intellectual sparring of the men and chatter of Clarissa empty signifiers of meaning other than the variations of mastery represented by their possession and exchange, Rachel's identificatory reading here goes to the other extreme: she cannot detach herself enough from the words she reads either to master or to resist their signification.

Rachel's resistance to her mentors' advice about reading thus ironically leads her—like Maggie Tulliver—into precisely the old-fashioned courtship plot, with its weight of gender ideology, that she is attempting to avoid. In fact, it is, ominously, while Rachel is reading the novel about "a woman's fall" that the note of invitation arrives from Terence Hewet to the picnic at which he and Rachel meet. After Rachel and Terence become engaged, notes again serve as messages of gender ideology: Terence admonishes Rachel that he "ought to be writing his book, and you ought to be answering these [notes of congratulation]" (Woolf, *VO* 344). Terence, despite his best intentions—and his unconventional ambitions for his own novel, which is to be about "'Silence . . . the things people don't say'" (249)—seems eager to write Rachel ever more firmly into the conventional romance plot. At the same time Rachel has rebounded from her own immersion in the narratives of that plot, judging the congratulatory notes "'sheer nonsense!'" along with other texts: "'Think of novels and plays and histories—' Perched on the table, she stirred the red and yellow volumes contemptuously" (340). Like Maggie, however, she is unaware that she has already been written—and has read herself—into that fictional plot. Though Rachel dies of a fever, not in a flood, her illness has many associations with drowning, and thus with Maggie's end; when ill she feels herself in her fever to be in a "deep pool of sticky water, which eventually closed over her head. She saw nothing and heard nothing but a faint booming sound, which was the sound of the sea rolling over her head" (398). In attempting to elude the conventional female plot, she finally, like Maggie, falls into its *mise-en-abîme*.

As with the earlier juxtaposition of Rachel and Dorothea Brooke that Woolf implicitly makes, here a contrast between Maggie Tulliver's covertly referenced death and Rachel's emphasizes Woolf's distance from the emotional situation of sympathetic identification invoked at Eliot's conclusion. Maggie's voyage through the floodwaters is both heroic and revealing "of almost miraculous, divinely protected effort" (Eliot, *MoF* 654). She goes to her death with "eyes of intense life looking out from a weary, beaten face" (654), having retained or regained the love of three men, and in the embrace of her brother, the one she has loved the longest. Although this ending thwarts readerly expectation by killing off its protagonist, its presentation works to heighten rather than to disrupt our identification with Maggie, ministering to an inverted wish-fulfillment structure: "They'll be sorry when I'm gone!" It also, by pairing off Maggie and Tom in death and enabling the future marriage of Lucy and Stephen, multiplies as much as it fractures the conventional romance conclusion. As Rachel Blau DuPlessis suggests, "the flood [in *The Mill on the Floss*] briefly destroys the oedipal nexus of gender. But when the waters recede, the landscape has not changed all that much" (19). By contrast, in *The Voyage Out,* Rachel's death is puzzling, anticlimactic, and forecloses identification. Unlike Maggie's eyes, Rachel's exhibit only "a slight look of fatigue or perplexity" as she dies (Woolf, *VO* 411). The novel continues for another chapter following her death, during which many of the novel's most sympathetic characters—Terence Hewet, St. John Hirst, the motherly Mrs. Thornbury, the aristocratic Mrs. Flushing—evince sincere grief, but others are concerned with assigning or evading blame. Mr. Flushing, who with his wife organizes the trip up the river that might have led to Rachel's illness, insists that "She probably ran [other] risks a dozen times a day" (419), and the conventional Arthur Warrington offers an epitaph that puts everyone—particularly women and the native inhabitants—back in their places: "They should have known better. You can't expect Englishwomen to stand roughing it as the natives do who've been acclimatized" (421). As the holiday-makers prepare to leave, many revert to their own concerns: Hirst "without any sense of disloyalty to Terence and Rachel . . . ceased to think about either of them" (436); even the guilt-ridden Mrs. Flushing succumbs to the lure of the final evening's "wonderful" tropical storm (436). Though beauty as well as banality reasserts itself, the overriding sense at the conclusion is of the dispersion rather than the convergence of human relations.

These returns to and revisions of covertly but specifically referenced scenes and attitudes from Eliot's narratives of formation reveal Woolf's negotiations with her own authorial identifications. They contribute to the shaping of *The Voyage Out* by what DuPlessis calls "writing beyond the ending"—"the invention of strategies [by twentieth-century women writers] that sever the narrative from formerly conventional structures of fiction and consciousness about women" (x). I have suggested above that such strategies, when they occur in conjunction with non-conventional representations of sexuality, can themselves be thought of as queer. Now, however, I want to suggest the possibilities for a queer reading of *The Voyage Out* in the second, more current sense. These possibilities are not straightforward, and they are shaped both by Woolf's resistance to any direct textual representation of sexuality and by her desire to undermine, or at least not to reinforce, conventions of representing subjectivity that would encourage literary identification.

Undertaking a queer reading of *The Voyage Out* illustrates the more general difficulty of reading queer sexuality in Woolf, or of taking her as an object of queer readerly or critical identification. Woolf, as Brenda Silver has demonstrated, has been an iconic twentieth-century figure, in popular as well as in high or academic culture. Silver's "premise [is] that Virginia Woolf's elevation to transgressive cultural icon and the contradictory, often vehement, responses provoked by it reside in her location on the borders between high culture and popular culture, art and politics, masculinity and femininity, head and body, intellect and sexuality, heterosexuality and homosexuality, word and picture, beauty and horror" (11). At least since the publication of Nigel Nicholson's *Portrait of a Marriage* (1973), Woolf has been available in popular culture as a lesbian icon, a representation augmented in the last fifteen or so years by the appearance of Sally Potter's film adaptation of *Orlando* (1992), Michael Cunningham's novel *The Hours* (1998), and the film of the same name (2002).[10] At the same time, academic feminist and queer studies of Woolf have emphasized that she "first learned to say 'we' as a woman" (J. Marcus, "Thinking Back" 83) and that her "deepest emotional bonds were to women" (Lilienfeld 37); biographical studies such as Karyn Sproles's *Desiring Women: The Partnership of Virginia Woolf and Vita Sackville-West* have explored her same-sex emotional and erotic bonds. Eileen Barrett observes that "Visitors to the Lesbian and Gay Reading Room of the new [in 1997] San Francisco Public Library will see Virginia Woolf among the names of other famous lovers of their sex inscribed in the ceiling mural. Clearly, Virginia Woolf is one of the twentieth century's best-known lesbians" (3).

But there is nothing "clear" about Woolf's status as "one of the twentieth century's best-known lesbians." Assertions of the primacy and even exclusivity of Woolf's same-sex attachments require a degree of selective inference, denying her attachment to and admiration for many structures of heterosexuality, including her own marriage. The diaries as well as the novels offer dithyrambs to married intimacy: "Rather under the weather, I say, I snuggled in to the core of my life, which is this complete comfort with L[eonard], & there found everything so satisfactory and calm that I revived myself, and got a fresh start; feeling entirely immune. The immense success of our life, is I think, that our treasure is hid away; or rather in such common things that nothing can touch it"; "But my God—how satisfactory after, I think 12 years, to have any human being to whom one can speak as directly as I to L.!" (*Diaries* 3: 30, 49). Naming Woolf as lesbian is an act of construction as much as discovery. Toni McNaron writes of her relation to Woolf as reader and critic, "I, as the lesbian I am, will go on reading Virginia Woolf, as the lesbian she was, for as long as I go on reading at all" (20). Her formulation captures the bi-directionality of readerly identification, the way it creates the objects of identification from which it then takes inspiration. Syntactically, McNaron's readerly identity ("the lesbian I am") precedes and at least partly generates a personal writerly identity for Woolf ("as the lesbian") that inspires McNaron's own writerly identity.

This difficulty applies to readings of the novels as well as the life. Queer readings of Woolf's texts are complicated by the fact that her representations of any kind of sexuality are characterized by indirection. In representing sexuality, she uses figures of paralepsis (naming sexual themes as unwritable), prolepsis (projecting a future in which they might become writable) and ellipsis (drawing attention to omissions of sexual themes), as well as metaphor and allusion. It is impossible to determine to what extent Woolf's indirection in representing sexuality is a result of conscious self-censorship in response to social norms; to what extent it points to a more fully internalized (Victorian) sexual reticence; and to what extent it reflects a more autonomous aesthetic interest in de-emphasizing traditional romantic narrative. Looking back, Woolf rues the "suavity . . . politeness . . . sidelong approach" of her *Common Reader* articles, for which she "blame[s] . . . my tea-table training" but also suggests that "this surface manner allows one to say a great many things which would be inaudible if one marched straight up and spoke out" (*MB* 129).[11] This ambivalent summary suggests that Woolf's "sidelong approach" was simultaneously a burdensome heritage and a generative aspect of her elliptical style, and this combination seems to me to apply to her representation of sexuality as well.

The Voyage Out exemplifies the ways in which this "sidelong approach" poses difficulties for a reading of the novel that attempts either to locate within it a narrative of queer identification or to read any of its major characters as objects of such identification. Critical analyses of *The Voyage Out* as a proto-lesbian narrative often emphasize either the narrative's failure or insufficiency or, in more generous readings, its representation of failure or insufficiency. Thus Louise DeSalvo, whose reconstruction of the novel's composition led to the publication of its earlier incarnation, *Melymbrosia* (1982), concludes that the successive revisions of that work that resulted in *The Voyage Out* demonstrate, particularly in regard to the novel's representation of sexuality, a "problem of authenticity—the tendency on Woolf's part to be less overt, less open, and less honest with each successive revision of a novel" (72).[12] For Deborah Hunn, contrarily, the reticence of the novel's portrayal of potential lesbian subjectivity comments on, rather than instantiates, failure: "Miss Allan senses there is something wrong with Rachel and would like to help, but is constrained by her years of social conditioning. . . . Miss Allan the schoolteacher can't put Swinburne or Sappho into her text. . . . Without access to this 'difference of view' Rachel cannot break free from her entrapment within a story" of conventional heterosexual romance (64).

Patricia Juliana Smith provides the strongest reading of lesbian possibility in *The Voyage Out,* concentrating on the character of Helen Ambrose and her relationship to Rachel. But even her affirmative reading invokes failure, since she suggests that read *without* reference to "a variety of homoerotic possibilities" the novel will "present itself as a hopelessly incoherent—if beautiful—literary failure" (128). Smith interprets Helen Ambrose and Rachel Vinrace as figures who undergo "lesbian panic . . . the disruptive action or reaction that occurs when a character—or, conceivably, an author—is either unable or unwilling to confront or reveal her own lesbianism or lesbian desire" (129); she suggests that Helen Ambrose maintains "a façade of matronly privilege and propriety that allows her hidden inclinations to pass undetected" and that "textual evidence of Helen's lesbianism . . . is concealed quite literally 'between the lines' of *The Voyage Out* by means of tacit allusion or indirect representation" (131). She points also to the "telling . . . silences that surround many of Helen's conversations, particularly those with the homosexual St. John Hirst" (131); to a scene following Rachel and Terence's agreement to marry in which Helen falls upon Rachel with "savage and erotic violence" (134); and to Rachel's "panic-ridden encounters" (140) with two other women characters, Evelyn Murgatroyd and Miss Allan.

Yet ingenious and in many ways persuasive as Smith's readings are, her attention to Woolf's ellipses still has the paradoxical effect of silencing Woolf, of implying that the novel that she actually published is best read as a cover for, or incomplete realization of, one that she did not. Since "Helen Ambrose," for example, has *only* a "literal," that is, textual, existence, and that only within Woolf's lines, "between [those] lines" is surely the one place that we cannot "literally" find "textual evidence" of "Helen's lesbianism"—indeed, the only "evidence" for Helen's lesbianism is subtextual (as a matter of inference) or extra-textual (as the product of a readerly projection of an object of identification). Similarly, while an extensive swirl of coded allusion surrounds St. John Hirst—he is uncomfortable with and often dismissive of women, reads Swinburne and Sappho, responds defensively to a mention of Wilde, and confides in Helen a "history of his life," that the reader is told involves "matters which are generally only alluded to between men and women when doctors are present, or in the shadow of death" (Woolf, *VO* 181)—to denominate him "*the* homosexual" is to transform allusion into assertion, and knowingness into knowledge, in a way that Woolf herself refuses to do.[13] Smith's declarative interpretive strategies make the narrative more susceptible to a queer readerly identification, but they do so partly by minimizing its formal queerness—by stabilizing the uncertainty, indeterminacy, and ambiguity that form aspects of Woolf's effort to de-emphasize identification as a fallback reading strategy—even for readers, such as queer readers, for whom such opportunities for identification hardly had the status, in 1915, of outworn conventions.

That is not to say, however, that we cannot feel reverberations of queer subjectivity in *The Voyage Out*. If, as I argue, it strains interpretation to speak declaratively of the sexuality of Helen Ambrose or of St. John Hirst, nevertheless the multidirectional libidinal currents and the emphatic silences, aposiopeses, and queer allusions to which Smith points remain striking.[14] Two brief examples of the ostentatiously elliptical representations of sexuality—both clearly hetero- and implicitly homosexual—that attach to both Helen and Hirst will suffice here. First, in a letter (to a male friend), Helen Ambrose writes: "'Until I explained it, [Rachel] did not know how children were born. Her ignorance upon other matters as important' (here Mrs. Ambrose's letter may not be quoted) . . . 'was complete'" (Woolf, *VO* 105). The suppression of Helen's dilation to *her* reader on "other matters" of course recapitulates, for the novel's reader, the very ignorance that Helen deplores. Similarly, when Hirst, at a dance, confides in Helen "the history of his life" mentioned above, we are told that "even in this ballroom [these matters] had to be discussed in a whisper, lest one of the pouter pigeon ladies or resplendent merchants should overhear them, and proceed to demand that they leave the place. When they had come to an end . . . Hirst rose, exclaiming, 'So there's no reason whatever for all this mystery!'" (181–82). This ironic exclamation—the only direct speech in the paragraph—underlines the fact that the narrative has reproduced rather than cleared up "all this mystery." Woolf clearly anticipates an authorial reader who will recognize that the position of "pouter pigeon [lady] or resplendent [merchant]" represents sexual conventionality and is not one with which she or he is being asked to identify; but presumably only some readers—we might think of them as sub-authorial readers (in the sense of a subgenre, or subset)—will identify with the coded aspects of homosexual style represented by Hirst and project that the "mystery" may be related to same-sex desire.[15]

Given his ambiguous sexual status and association with the novel's most elliptical forms of representation, it also seems important that St. John Hirst closes the novel. This final turn completes Woolf's series of authorial identifications with and revisions of precursor texts, since a bachelor St. John—the missionary St. John Rivers—also concludes *Jane Eyre.* His epistolary invocation of his own coming death is quoted by Jane: "Amen; even so, come Lord Jesus!" Like the biblical epitaph of Maggie and Tom at the end of *The Mill on the Floss,* "In their death they were not divided," Brontë's conclusion gives the last word to Christianity and thus to an eschatological religious narrative, with its implication of a trajectory beyond the individual life. St. John's apostrophe is matched in the novel by Jane's frequent, if cursory, acknowledgments of divine aid. In *The Voyage Out,* by contrast, unbelief is explicitly asserted. When St. John Hirst attends a church service, he has Swinburne's Sapphic ode hidden in his Bible—an overt displacement of a marriage-oriented Christian order by a homosocially organized pagan one. Rachel DuPlessis suggests that in coming to approve the love of Rachel and Terence, St. John Hirst "undergoes a gratifying, though amazing, conversion to the possibility of equality between men and women in spiritual love," and argues that his character sheds a "nimbus from Platonized Christianity [. . .] over the love plot" (53). But as a religious referent, St. John Hirst's name is made ironic by his declared lack of belief (161). Rather, I see nimbus of queerness—the Plato of the *Symposium,* invoked in the text—rather than Neoplatonism radiating from St. John.

Like St. John Rivers, Hirst gestures toward a narrative larger than that of the development of the self. In his case, however, it is in the direction not of the divine apotheosis of that individual but rather of the *dissolution* of individuality and humanity into a kind of post-impressionist aesthetic patterning. Unlike St. John Rivers, St. John Hirst is represented not by assertion but in listening repose as the novel's characters recede from him in time and space:

> All these voices [of the hotel guests] sounded gratefully in St. John's ears as he lay half-asleep, and yet vividly conscious of everything around him. Across his eyes passed a procession of objects, black and indistinct, the figures of people picking up their books, their cards, their balls of wool, their work-baskets, and passing him one after another on their way to bed. (Woolf, *VO* 437)

This ending recalls the novel's beginning, in which Helen and Ridley Ambrose "strode," tall and eccentrically dressed, among "small, agitated figures . . . decorated with fountain pens, and burdened with dispatch-boxes" (3). There, the emphasis was on the way in which the Ambroses stood out among these less distinct characters; at the end, however, the characters who stood out in the narrative as "heroic statues" have been dislodged, and with them both avenues of readerly identification and some of Woolf's authorial identifications with previous narratives. The dispersion of consciousness, the presence of others, strike Hirst not distractingly but "gratefully." An evocative queerness—of both structure and characters—remains. Judith Halberstam posits the existence of "alternative temporalities" created by queer subjects: "Queer subcultures produce alternative temporalities by allowing their participants to believe that their futures can be imagined according to logics that lie outside of those paradigmatic markers of life experience—namely birth, marriage, reproduction, and death" (*Queer Time* 2). *The Voyage Out* at least partly imagines "alternative temporalities" for its characters not by eluding but by scrambling the representation of these "paradigmatic markers of life." The tensions visible in this effort—between singular and labile consciousness, between encouragement and dispersal of the reader's identifications, between the symmetries of the heterosexual romance plot and the disruptive pull of queer figures and desires—will continue to structure Woolf's fiction.

WHO'S AFRAID OF STEPHEN GORDON?

In 1928, Virginia Woolf and Radclyffe Hall both published their fifth novels—Woolf's *Orlando* and Radclyffe Hall's *The Well of Loneliness.* At the time, the two authors' statures were for many purposes comparable: Hall's novel *Adam's Breed* (1926) received the 1927 James Tait Black prize as well as the Prix Femina Vie Heureuse—a double honor that she shared only with E. M. Forster—and Woolf won the Femina the following year for *To the Lighthouse.* Woolf undertook to testify on behalf of *The Well* at its trial for obscenity. (In the event, the judge disallowed testimony about the novel's literary merit; however, Woolf's willingness to appear contrasts with the evasions of other supposedly supportive authors, including George Bernard Shaw, Arnold Bennett, John Galsworthy, and Havelock Ellis [see Cline 254–56].) Although Woolf's response to *The Well* was publicly supportive, she was privately caustic—"The dulness of the book is such that any indecency may lurk there—one simply can't keep one's eyes on the page" (*Letters* 3: 556) is one typical remark. Like her reservations about the "indecency" of Joyce's *Ulysses,* her attitude here suggests a resistance to two shared features of Hall's and Joyce's otherwise quite different projects—relatively direct representation of sexuality ("indecency") and a more or less legibly polemical motivation. On my reading, these reservations indicate disavowal, a sign of Woolf's own ambivalent relationship to the representation of sexual experience and to the polemical possibilities of art.[16]

Because of these areas of overlap and difference between *Orlando* and *The Well*—their shared cultural moment, gender-bending protagonists, and wholly (Hall) or partly (Woolf) lesbian-identified authors on the one hand, and radical differences in execution and reception, on the other—critics have often paired them to analyze their differing relationships to Modernism and to representations of queer sexuality.[17] Here, however, I juxtapose *The Well* not with *Orlando* but with *The Voyage Out.* These two novels represent Woolf's and Hall's clearest engagements with the novel of formation and its subtending aesthetics of identification. Woolf, as I have argued, challenges the aesthetics of identification in *The Voyage Out* by subjecting the objects of her own authorial identifications to gentle mockery and revision and by beginning to dislodge the protagonist of the narrative of formation from her central position as the object of readerly identification. *The Voyage Out* queers the narrative of female formation; at the same time, it intimates the possibility of queer subjects of such a narrative.

The Well, by contrast, seems much less interested in challenging the inherited forms of domestic realism and the narrative of formation. Indeed, its long opening sentence—"Not very far from Upton-on-Severn—between it, in fact, and the Malvern Hills—stands the country seat of the Gordons of Bramley; well-timbered, well-cottaged, well-fenced and well-watered, having, in this latter respect, a stream that forks in exactly the right position to feed two large lakes in the grounds" (Hall 11)—could hardly declare more firmly the narrator's nostalgia for agrarian country-house society and the narratives (Helen Ambrose's "spacious chronicle of family life") it sponsors. Yet Stephen Gordon's trajectory propels her firmly out this milieu and into a future defined by exile. Similarly, if the novel's plotting depends upon the conventions of the heterosexual romance, its climax, in which Stephen engineers her own romantic rejection and embraces the task of narrating queer subjectivity, makes clear Hall's belief that she and her heroine were plotting an alternative fictional trajectory. Hall's relationship to both the topographical and the relational landscapes of the traditional novel, while often nostalgic, also conveys a clear sense of their insufficiency and the necessity for their passing. In *The Well of Loneliness,* Hall calls openly upon an aesthetics and ethics of identification to ground a new narrative of the formation of the explicitly queer subject. The novel combines conventional narrative forms and newly recognized subjects; it appeals to the reader at once on the allotropic, or other-oriented, basis of sympathy, and the auto-tropic, or self-referring, basis of identification. That this combination of techniques and motives has continued to produced widespread discomfort in readers (Woolf called it "that Well of all that's stagnant and lukewarm and neither one thing nor the other" [qtd. in Cline 255]) should not blind us to the boldness of Hall's effort to create a narrative of formation in which a queer subject would be at the center.

Hall, unlike Woolf, had no reservations about the polemic possibilities of art. In a lecture she asserted that "If propaganda is to be the theme of a novel, then the novel should always be written for a cause in which the author has implicit belief, for a cause which he feels in his very soul has need of someone to rise up and defend it" (qtd. in Souhami 279–80). She intended *The Well* to serve such a cause:

> I wished to offer my name and my literary reputation in support of the cause of the inverted. . . . I felt . . . that no one was better qualified to write the subject in fiction than an experienced novelist like myself who was actually one of the people about whom she was writing and was thus in a position to understand their spiritual, mental, and physical reactions, their joys and their sorrows, and above all their unceasing battle against a frequently cruel and nearly always thoughtless and ignorant world. (Qtd. in Souhami 157–58)

But the awkward pronoun shifts, as Hall vacillates between a third-person and a first-person stance in relation to her material, highlight the ambivalence inherent in even such an apparently forthright identification of author with subject. Tension appears between Hall the "experienced novelist," who serves less as a representative than as an observer of "the people about whom she was writing" and "*their* . . . reactions, *their* joys and *their* sorrows . . . *their* unceasing battle" (emphasis added); and the Hall who is "actually one of the" inverted, who represents these joys, sorrows, and battle from experience. This tension also marks the distinction between a narrative that will attempt to *foster sympathy with* its subject, and one that will attempt directly to *represent the consciousness of* its subject, inviting the reader's identification.

The former approach is familiar as what is sometimes called "sympathetic identification," and even more than the novel's Edwardian country-house values it accounts for its old fashioned tone, because sympathetic identification is most closely associated with the nineteenth-century novel of social reform. Its appeal is modeled in *The Well* in Stephen Gordon's sympathetic identification with a fox (Hall 126), when on a hunt after her father's death she imagines that

> The hounds were behind her instead of ahead, that the flushed, bright-eyed people were hunting her down. . . . The whole world was hunting her down with hatred . . . the world against one insignificant creature who had nowhere to turn for pity or protection. . . . Then Stephen saw something just ahead, and it moved. . . . A crawling, bedraggled streak of red fur . . . with the desperate eyes of the hopeless pursued, bright with terror . . . and the thought came to Stephen: "It's looking for God Who made it." (126)

After this moment of fellow-feeling, which requires the recognition not of shared *identities or characteristics* but of shared *experience* (she feels hounded by society), Stephen never hunts again. Stephen is not in fact vulpine, bedraggled, or immediately pursued; but as Suzanne Keen observes in a discussion of "readers' empathy," "Novels and stories featuring animals . . . provoke empathetic reactions of readers who report ready identification with nonhuman figures. This suggests that character identification and empathy felt for fictional characters requires certain traits (such as a name, a recognizable situation, and at least implicit feelings) but dispenses with other requirements associated with realistic representation" (68). This scene models and, ideally, evokes in its reader a kind of identification that is less narrative or developmental than immediate and emotional.

In both its emotional impact and its didactic intent this scene recalls one of the most famous nineteenth-century novels of reform, *Uncle Tom's Cabin:*

> [Eliza] caught [up] her child, and sprang down the steps towards [the Ohio River]. The trader caught a full glimpse of her just as she was disappearing down the bank; and throwing himself from his horse . . . he was after her like a hound after a deer. . . . Nerved with strength such as God gives only to the desperate, with one wild cry and flying leap, she vaulted sheer over the turbid current by the shore, on to the raft of ice beyond. (Stowe 65)

As Elizabeth Barnes writes, the narrative of Eliza's flight in *Uncle Tom's Cabin* offers "a glimpse of the methodological crux of sentimental fiction, where acts of sympathetic identification are performed *for,* in order to be reproduced *in,* the sympathetic reader" (94–95).[18] In both scenes, the desperation, the invocation of God and the representation of pursuit through the metaphor of the hunted animal are the rhetorical means through which the helplessness of the human subject, and the appropriate human response to such helplessness, are conveyed. But as Barnes also suggests, this performance has limitations as a means of generating sympathy, since "sympathy is made contingent upon similarity: that is, upon one's ability to perceive others as related to oneself" (92). It is not clear that most heterosexual readers of *The Well of Loneliness* were prepared, at its moment of publication, to take such a view of the "invert": even Woolf and E. M. Forster asserted (one must hope with tongue in cheek), in a letter to the *Nation and Athenaeum,* that the novel's topic "enters personally into very few lives, and is uninteresting or repellent to the majority" (qtd. in Cline 250).[19] And Hall has a further difficulty: while she obviously hopes to draw on such perceptions of similarity, she is equally and perhaps more interested in asserting the *difference* and the distinctive consciousness of her protagonist. (Eliza, by contrast, is not the protagonist of *Uncle Tom's Cabin;* our access to her consciousness is relatively limited; and what it displays is sanctioned feminine attitudes such as sexual modesty and maternal devotion.) The primary problem of her narrative is not to attain a particular material or political end (such as manumission) but to answer, on her own behalf and that of other "inverts," her questions about herself as a subject.

In fact, as suggested by Doan and Prosser's summary of the novel's reception, *The Well* has indeed been received more consistently as a narrative of formation and an object of identification than as the intervention in public discourse and mover of sympathy that Hall also intended.

> In the intervening years [between its publication and the first paperback printing in the early 1950s] . . . *The Well of Loneliness* was of course read. But . . . it was read mostly by private readers in England and America. . . . *The Well of Loneliness* seems removed . . . from the critical and cultural stage upon which it entered to a realm of private identity, and sometimes medical identity discourse. . . . *The Well of Loneliness* was read for identificatory, often conflicting identificatory, purposes. (15)

Because of Hall's emphasis on the tragedy, isolation, and shame of the "invert," however, readerly identification with Stephen Gordon has always been strongly mixed with repulsion, among both academic and popular readers. The novelist Donna Allegra, despite being "a black girl, Brooklyn-born and raised," nevertheless "saw [herself] reflected on those pages where Stephen Gordon lived" (71). For Allegra, an identification with Stephen Gordon seems relatively unthreatening, perhaps because overt differences in race, class, and nationality separate her from the fictional Stephen. A more typical response, however, is recorded by another novelist, Jane Rule, who remembers that at fifteen she "was badly frightened" by her identification with Stephen Gordon, which seemed to suggest that "I was a freak, a genetic monster, a member of a third sex, who would eventually call myself by a masculine name . . . , wear a necktie, and live in the exile of some European ghetto" (Doan and Prosser 78). And from Woolf forward, readers have responded with gestures of disavowal to the style as well as the content of Hall's representation: Terry Castle, for example, who calls *The Well* "that much-maligned yet still fiercely compelling fiction" (7), characterizes Hall's style as "hieratic, overwrought, full of melodramatic, dismal pomp" (51), a judgment whose own excess perhaps illustrates the novel's capacity for rhetorical contamination. As Love observes, "while critics have sought to disavow the legacy of *The Well,* they have not, finally, been able to let Stephen go. Rather, the vehemence of critics' rejection of her is a testimony to the shame and repulsion she continues to inspire in lesbian readers" (*Feeling Backward* 102)—and, as Love also makes clear, the nearness and fascination of those responses.[20] Critics who wish to claim value for the novel, Love argues, do so by "assimilat[ing] Stephen's narrative to a later, happier narrative of gendered existence." While Love insists that "Stephen is beyond the reach of such redemptive narratives" (119), these attempts, such as Judith Halberstam and Jay Prosser's readings of Stephen Gordon's "inversion" as an early representation of transgender identities, seem to me compelling and suggestive of the power of readerly identification to continue to transform the fictions that invite it.

Stephen Gordon thus presents an object of literary identification both unusually repellent and surprisingly protean across the history of the novel's reception. Hall herself is ambivalent about her identification with the variety of Victorian and Edwardian narrative and psychological schemata available to her in construction Stephen as a subject, and her negotiation of and with these discourses makes visible the seams of her construction of Stephen Gordon's identity from sexological, biblical, and literary texts. The very awkwardness of this construction—Hall's vacillations among models for, and rhetorical representations of, the identity of the "invert"—has made different Stephen Gordons both objectionable and available to successive, and differently situated, generations of readers and critics. Thus although Hall's project of defining and asserting her protagonist's queer subjectivity may seem opposed to Woolf's aim, in *The Voyage Out,* of undermining such unitary representations of subjectivity, *The Well of Loneliness* leaves us not so far from where *The Voyage Out* does, with a recognition that identifications may ground but cannot fix—either stabilize or mend—identities.

From the beginning, Hall underlines the connection between the conventional *non*narratability of queer sexual identity and its subject's experience of ontological lack. The combination of Stephen's biological feminine gender, her masculine social expression, and her romantic and sexual desire for women initially renders her both unspeakable and illegible, to herself as well as to others. "I'm nothing," Stephen reflects, "—yes I am, I'm Stephen—but that's being nothing" (Hall 70). The labels applied to Stephen as she grows into adolescence—"queer," "freak," "unnatural"—paradoxically emphasize her unnameability: "Could Mrs. Antrim have ignored Stephen Gordon's existence, she would almost certainly have done so. . . . What she called Stephen's 'queerness' aroused her suspicion—she was never quite clear as to what she suspected, but felt sure that it must be something outlandish" (91). Similarly, Stephen's mother, Lady Anna, on discovering Stephen's first affair with a woman, Angela Crossby, declares, "This thing that you are is a sin against creation" (200). Like all of Stephen's antagonists, she can or will name her only by a vicious circularity that refers to Stephen only to *defer* her indefinitely. The sexually experienced Angela Crossby uses a similar circumlocution—"'Can I help it if you're—what you obviously are?'" (149)—with the difference that her negation of Stephen's being depends on flaunting rather than refusing unspeakable knowledge. Even Stephen's loving and scholarly father cannot resist framing his child as unspeakable and ontologically absent. Sir Philip researches his daughter's condition in "a slim volume recently acquired. . . . The author was a German, Karl Heinrich Ulrichs, and reading, Sir Philip's eyes would grow puzzled; then groping for a pencil he would make little notes all along the immaculate margins" (26). But Sir Philip, "a coward because of his pity" (106), chooses to keep from Stephen the knowledge and vocabulary that this text introduce. When he suffers a fatal accident, his deathbed attempt to enlighten his wife only reinforces the representation of Stephen as a discursive nonentity: "Anna—it's Stephen—listen. . . . It's—Stephen—our child—she's, she's—it's Stephen—not like—" (118). Stephen remains, in Sir Philip's last words, undefined: not "like," but unlike, an "it" whose lack of identity is indicated by the presence of a copula without the predicate it demands. As Love observes, Stephen's "loneliness in the novel is not primarily a question of epistemology but one of ontology. It afflicts Stephen's being; it is deeply inscribed in her body. . . . Hall understands loneliness as a state of desolation, a deeply felt psychic and corporeal state of abandonment, refusal, and loss" ("Spoiled Identity" 499). The reader who recognizes in Stephen shared attributes is thus asked to identify with this terrifying state of non-identity, of "being nothing."

After her father's death, however, Stephen's narrative approaches a more familiar pattern in which objects of literary identification open possibilities of self-construction.[21] Entering her father's library after his death and on the eve of her own exile from Morton, Stephen discovers Krafft-Ebing's *Psychopathia Sexualis* and her father's Bible. Like the works encountered by earlier protagonists—*The Birds of Antarctica,* in Jane Eyre's uncle's library; *The Imitation of Christ,* which comes to Maggie Tulliver through Bob Jakin, and *Corinne,* given to her by Philip Wakem; the Ibsen drama by which Rachel is entranced—these works come through patriarchal (in her case literally paternal) channels; unlike those others, however, *Psychopathia Sexualis* and the Bible cannot easily be understood, in the form in which Stephen initially encounters them, as representing or encouraging opposition to or withdrawal from oppressive social regimes. Rather, they impose themselves upon Stephen with scientistic authority, in the forms of taxonomy and case history.

> As she slipped the key into the lock [of the bookcase], the action seemed curiously automatic. . . . Then she noticed that on a shelf near

> the bottom was a row of books standing behind the others; the next moment she had one of these in her hand, and was looking at the name of the author: Krafft-Ebing—she had never heard of that author before. All the same she opened the battered old book, then she looked more closely, for there on its margins were notes in her father's small, scholarly hand and she saw that her own name appeared in those notes. (Hall 204)

The result of Stephen's "curiously automatic" actions, this discovery of text, represented as a discovery of Stephen *by* text, recalls Louis Althusser's conception of interpellation, of being "hailed" by ideologies functioning on behalf of the state to reproduce "good" subjects who will work "by themselves"—that is, without the need for state repression or coercion.

Psychopathia Sexualis might seem on its face to suggest that Stephen Gordon is, on the contrary, a "bad subject," one of those who "on occasion provoke the intervention of one of the detachments of the (repressive) State apparatus" (181). A physician and psychologist frequently offering expert medical testimony in law cases, Krafft-Ebing represents both the hegemonic power of the ideological State and the coercive power of the repressive State. (Althusser points out that "the 'Law' belongs both to the [Repressive] State Apparatus and the system of the ISAs" [143*n*9]). In *Psychopathia Sexualis,* Krafft-Ebing draws on these experiences to produce a taxonomy of "deviant" sexual practices, a compilation of hundreds of cases of tabooed behavior including fetishism of various kinds, sadism and masochism, coprophilia and necrophilia, as well as a range of forms of "inversion." The individual cases are numbered and related pseudonymously; their context is pathological or criminal; and Krafft-Ebing himself generally equates the behavior he describes with physical and social deviance. His project in this sense seems to contribute to the nineteenth-century development of "technologies" of sexuality and the pathologization of sexual behavior that, as many critics have argued, contributed to the criminalization and persecution of homosexuality.[22]

At the same time, however, the negative authority of taxonomy is undermined by other aspects of Krafft-Ebing's project. The variety and narrative detail of his examples work against this taxonomic and proscriptive organization. In his introduction, Krafft-Ebing claims that his subjects are deviant because they controvert "the hidden laws of nature which are enforced by a mighty, irresistible impulse" (23). But his own taxonomic enterprise itself undermines the assertion that these "laws" are irresistible. First, there is the sheer number and detail of his cases—some five hundred overt challenges to "the hidden laws of nature." Second, the narrative form that he adopts—the case study—undermines the purely classificatory impulse of taxonomy. Thomas Laqueur claims that the case study arises in the eighteenth century as one of a number of discourses that form what he calls "the humanitarian narrative." The aim of "humanitarian narrative" is to shape the "unprecedented quantities of fact, of minute observations, about people who had before been beneath notice" (177) into links of cause and effect that would provoke readers to compassion with, and action on behalf of, suffering others. This aim also belongs, as Laqueur notes, to the form of the novel.[23] Such narratives put into play readerly impulses of sympathy and identification that can counter the estranging direction of categorization.

One of the cases in *Psychopathia Sexualis* that most reveals the features of such a "humanitarian narrative" is also the example of female homosexuality that most closely resembles Stephen's situation, in the protagonist's aristocratic status, her masculine identification, and her desire for women—the narrative of the pseudonymous Sandor. A wealthy, masculine, cross-dressing "authoress," Sandor enters into a fraudulent marriage with an apparently heterosexual woman, which she maintains for a year before being discovered. Krafft-Ebing devotes to Sandor an unusually extended and sympathetic treatment.[24] A tragic romance in miniature, Sandor's story compels Krafft-Ebing's admiration, and through him the reader's as well. He emphasizes her erudition and transcribes her words:

> [Sandor's] writings betray a wonderfully wide range of reading in classics of all languages, in citations from poets and prose writers of all lands. . . . This writing ends with the apostrophe: "Gentlemen, you learned in the law, psychologists and pathologists, do me justice! Love led me to take the step I took; all my deeds were conditioned by it. God put it in my heart. . . .
>
> Only God is just. How beautifully does Victor Hugo describe this in his *Légendes du Siècle!* How sad do Mendelssohn's words sound to me: 'Nightly in dreams I see thee'! (Krafft-Ebing 360–61)

The voice of Sandor, as Krafft-Ebing transcribes it, brings into his text a note of literary, rather than medical, authority. Sandor's words challenge the codifications of the taxonomy in which they are embedded by celebrating the emotional plenitude of Romantic representation.

As Jay Prosser points out, however, Krafft-Ebing's analysis of Sandor is taken not from direct interaction but from a written autobiography, leaving Krafft-Ebing in the role of "an unintended (or at least unspecified) reader" (146), and Stephen Gordon and ourselves as even more distant from intention or specification. Thus Krafft-Ebing does not make audible here an authentic voice of "inverted" identity, piercing through an obscuring medium of text, but rather continues a textual transmission. The complete scene of Stephen's reading is a scene of the reading of reading of reading: the reader reads Stephen's reading of her father's reading of Krafft-Ebing. For readers who know, or seek out, *Psychopathia Sexualis,* this chain might extend to include Krafft-Ebing's reading of Sandor, who reads Hugo and Mendelssohn. For these readers, the abyss will pause, if it does not end, with Hugo and Mendelssohn—that is, with the authority of literary voice—which is also the authority that Hall's novel assumes.

The revelation of Stephen's identity is thus a narrative revelation, but its authority hovers uneasily between two narrative forms: the scientific, which represents the empirical; and the fictional, which represents the affective. To these registers Hall proceeds to add that of theological discourse, which represents the absolute. Stephen is now sought out by the Bible: "Before she knew what she was doing, she had found her father's old, well-worn Bible. There she stood demanding a sign from heaven. . . . The Bible fell open near the beginning. She read 'And the Lord set a mark upon Cain'" (Hall 204). Like *Psychopathia Sexualis,* the Bible marks and classifies Stephen—not with scientific enumeration but by heavenly branding. This time, however, the moment of dispossession is clearly also a moment of genesis for Stephen, who can now predicate her own identity upon a textual identification, however unpromising ("I am like Cain").[25] And just as the history of Sandor extends Krafft-Ebing's narrative into potentially more generative plots, so too do biblical references multiply beyond, and temper, the apparent absolutism of Cain's curse. Stephen's governess and companion, Miss Puddleton—whose nickname, Puddle, suggests a fluidity that counters patriarchal rigidity—briskly announces Stephen's literary vocation: "Just because you are what you are, you may actually find that you've got an advantage. You may write with a curious double insight—write both men and women from a personal knowledge" (205). Puddle's circumlocution once again casts Stephen as the unspeakable subject. But her "you are what you are" (with its echo of Jehovah's "I am that I am") casts its tautology not as lack or but as doubling—a supersufficiency that, like Stephen herself, will transcend the binary structure of gender. "Where you go, I go, Stephen," Puddle further declares (205). With this echo of Ruth's words to Naomi, she demonstrates the power of revision, countering a biblical story of fratricide and patriarchal punishment with an equally canonical but redemptive story of female solidarity that turns exile into quest.[26]

Sonja Ruehl argues that Hall's engagement with sexology creates a Foucauldian "reverse discourse" that undermines its hegemonic power because "Hall claimed the right to speak about inversion on the grounds that she herself was an invert, not an expert" (174). Reversal, however, seems to me too thoroughgoing a characterization of Hall's negotiations with expert discourses; as I suggested above, in writing *The Well* she claims that right on the grounds of being herself not only an "invert" but also a novelist—that is, a literary expert. The trajectory for both Hall and Stephen Gordon is toward the authority not only of experience but perhaps even more important of literary discourse. As Puddle announces Stephen's early vocation as a writer, later, after she has achieved popular success as a novelist, the "learned and gentle Jew" Adolphe Blanc (modeled on the sexologist Magnus Hirschfeld) confers on her the role of spokesperson: "The doctors cannot make the ignorant think, cannot hope to bring home the sufferings of millions; only one of ourselves can someday do that" (Hall 390). Though Stephen responds to this exhortation with skeptical silence, she embraces her duty at the end of the novel, becoming "possessed" by the voices of her fellow inverts: "And now there was only one voice, one demand; her own voice into which those millions had entered" (437). As spokesperson Stephen is not just self-elected but anointed, and in both cases, it is her expertise as an author that gives meaning to her personal experience.

The Well in its last third thus becomes a narrative of artistic as well as sexual formation. In contrast to *The Voyage Out,* in which plots of artistic education (Rachel's piano-playing, Terence's novel) remain largely unnarrated and unfinished, in *The Well* Hall narrates Stephen's pursuit and achievement of literary success, as well as her disillusionment with that success and her decision to acknowledge her community with other "inverts" and write the novel that will speak for their experience. (This plot surely owes something to *Aurora Leigh*'s similar equation of popular recognition and cosmopolitan decadence and the protagonist's insistence on art as a mode of social intervention, as well as to Hall's own authorial experience.) Because this decision is linked to Stephen's choice to resign her partner, Mary, to the waiting arms of the heterosexual male who can give her marriage, children, and respectability, this ending has provoked some of the greatest readerly resistance to the novel. One anonymous reader remarks that "the ending of the novel dismayed me so that I rewrote it" (qtd. in O'Rourke 119). Jane Rule calls Hall a "canny propagandist in plotting an unhappy ending," but objects that Hall did not allow Stephen "the great blessing of [her] own life, the faithful love" of two women (Doan and Prosser 82).[27] Julie Abraham adduces *The Well* in arguing that novels conventionally referred to as "lesbian novels" reproduce the formula of the heterosexual romance plot (xix). *The Well,* she suggests, does challenge this formula to a limited degree, since it "concludes with a wedding, but it is the marriage of Stephen's lover Mary, which disrupts the novel's central relationship but leaves one lesbian [i.e. Stephen] committed to her deviance" (13).[28] This concession, however, understates the challenge that Hall poses, since the novel does not in fact conclude with a wedding: although we may assume that Mary and Martin marry, we do not see or hear of their marriage. It seems likely that if Mary had stayed, her needs for attention and protection would have hampered Stephen in her work. In fact, Stephen, like Joyce's Stephen Dedalus and Lawrence's Paul Morel, finds her triumph in turning away from, not taking her place within, the domestic plot. The space left by the departure of the love object is instead filled by the voices of the subjects with whom Stephen, after years of keeping her distance, is brought to acknowledge her identification. "They possessed her," Hall writes, "Her barren womb became fruitful[. . . .] In their madness to become articulate through her, they were tearing her to pieces, getting her under. They were everywhere now, cutting off her retreat; neither bolts nor bars would avail to save her. The walls fell down and crumbled before them[. . . .] And now there was only one voice, one demand; her own voice into which those millions had entered" (437). This is represented as a painful process, certainly, but perhaps not more so than any birth, and it offers a genuine, and genuinely queer, alternative to the closure of the marriage plot. As Stephen conceives a novel under the same impulses that produced the novel of which she herself is the protagonist, Hall suggests that literary identification can be transformative, that the unnamable subject can become the narrated subject, and that the narrated subject in turn can seize control of narrative, providing new opportunities for literary identification. In her invocation of a future of narrative to which Stephen belongs, Hall anticipates Woolf's conclusion to *A Room of One's Own* (1929): "The opportunity will come [for the woman writer] and the dead poet who was Shakespeare's sister will put on the body which she has so often laid down. Drawing her life from the lives of the unknown who were her forerunners, as her brothers did before her, she will be born" (118). The new woman writer of Woolf's utopia remains a fictional conception, "drawing her life" from a phantasmatic literary source. In *The Well,* Hall specifies this conception and assertively queers it. Despite the significant differences in the aesthetic and political investments of their authors, these conclusions share an orientation toward a narrative future that both emerges from, and transforms, the narrative past.

BOOKS BOUGHT OUT OF BOOKS

> I was in a bookshop recently when a young woman approached me.
>
> She told me she was writing an essay on my work and that of Radclyffe Hall. Could I help?
>
> "Yes," I said. "Our work has nothing in common."
>
> "I thought you were a lesbian," she said. (Winterson, *Art Objects* 103)

> What woman writer writing now can pass by *A Room of One's Own* (1929)? But for me, when I read my copy signed in purple ink, there is an extra power. Here she is and here she was, of private ancestors, the most complete. (131)

In "The Psychometry of Books," a meditation on her interest in collecting first editions, Winterson writes, "When I had no books and had to learn everything I needed off by heart, and when I had to hide what books I had, I promised myself a library filled with the best editions I could afford. I have it now. Books bought out of books" (*Art Objects* [hereafter *AO*] 131). On the one hand the notion of "books bought out of books" seems refreshingly frank in its recognition of the book as a material object subject to relations of productions and consumption that structure relations between author and reader: Winterson can buy books to read because we buy from her (she sells to us) the books she writes. Winterson's formulation cheerfully emphasizes her mastery (over books and readers) in these material relations: "I have it now." On the other hand, the assertion of these material relations elides—by the resonant absence of a single letter—an equally commanding but perhaps less easily mastered relationship: books *brought* out of books, the identifications that bind books to the traditions from which they emerge and in which they take their place. The essays in *Art Objects* work to assert both the author's mastery over, and her place within, the literary landscape of twentieth-century fiction. As they do so, the authorial name "Virginia Woolf" functions repeatedly as a metonym for Winterson's idea of literary value and proper author–reader relations; "Radclyffe Hall," invoked more briefly, is the disavowed other in both of these realms.

Winterson has claimed Virginia Woolf as not only a "private ancestor" but also a quite public one. Winterson is, with Margaret Reynolds, a series editor of a Vintage paperback edition of Woolf's novels. The structures and themes of the picaresque, time-travel, and gender-bending that run through most of her own fiction, including *Sexing the Cherry* (1989), *The Passion* (1997), and *The PowerBook* (2000), echo the Woolf of *Orlando.*[29] More generally, Winterson's interest in experimental novelistic forms that deemphasize traditional plot development and decenter the protagonist, while retaining a focus on the effects of gender and sexuality, also connect her to Woolf. *Art Objects,* which functions as an aesthetic credo, not only pays tribute to Woolf in its content, with two essays that celebrate Woolf novels (*Orlando* and *The Waves*), but also embodies that tribute in addressing questions—about the relationship between authors and readers and the contemporary significance of aesthetic value—addressed by Woolf in her aesthetic manifestos.[30] The title of the collection's concluding essay—"A Work of My Own"—suggests the directness of Winterson's identification with her precursor.

Art Objects embraces as ancestor not only Woolf but also the Modernist movement of which it takes her to be the representative; the collection includes essays on Roger Fry and Gertrude Stein, references to Joyce and T. S. Eliot, and celebrations of one aspect of Modernist aesthetics: "The Modernists were trying to return to an idea of art as a conscious place . . . a place outside of both rhetoric and cliché. . . . Poetry, poetic fiction is not an artificial language (or at least when it is, it ceases to be poetry), but it is a heightened language" (Winterson, *AO* 37). In other words, as Lyn Pykett has suggested, "*Art Objects* is, in large part, Winterson's attempt to situate herself in relation to the tradition of Modernism and to affirm her commitment to Modernism as a project of continuing relevance." This attempt, however, reveals the partiality—in both senses of the word—of Winterson's conception of Modernist practice: "Winterson fetishizes language in the way in which some of the (male) Modernist poets did. . . . Winterson's reification of language is closely linked to her implicit acceptance of the Arnoldian vision (mediated through T. S. Eliot) of poetry as the religion of the future" (57).[31] Thus although Winterson pays tribute to the Woolf who "fought for her work and fought for her sex" (Winterson, *AO* 62), she is hostile to the feminist scholarship beginning in the last third of the twentieth century that displaced an earlier view of Woolf as primarily an idiosyncratic High Modernist aesthete with a politically engaged and personally suffering Woolf. Winterson objects that there has been "so much concentration on Woolf as a feminist and as a thinker, that the unique power of her language has still not been given the close critical attention it deserves. When Woolf is read and taught, she needs to be read and taught as a poet" (*AO* 70). The reference to Radclyffe Hall begins an essay ("The Semiotics of Sex") that also attacks what Winterson views as the biographical fallacy, in this case queer readings of queer literature: "When I read Adrienne Rich or Oscar Wilde . . . the fact of their homosexuality should not be uppermost. I am not reading their work to get at their private lives, I am reading their work because I need the depth-charge it carries" (*AO* 109). The sharp distinctions that Winterson draws here lead to some dubious implications: that poetry cannot be impelled by thinking or by feminism; that the "depth-charge" of a work of literature can never be ignited, for reader or writer, by the spark of sexuality. But the stakes of the distinctions are clear enough: Winterson disclaims and disdains writerly motivations and reader responses based on identification in favor of a High Modernist and New Critical conception of the work as an autonomous achievement.

Winterson's High Modernist "poet" Woolf is, of course, as partial a construct as Jane Marcus's radical polemicist, "an 'outsider,' a feminist, socialist, artist, and worker" (*Art and Ardor* 121); both are retrospectively reshaped, as much as discovered, as objects of identification by their readers' own authorial investments. What animates this otherwise dated debate, in Winterson's case, is the provocative tension between the value that she assigns to an aesthetic of rigorous impersonality on the one hand, and on the other the representation of her own imaginative identification with those values, which is expressed in consistently personal and even libidinal language that blurs the very boundaries between "private lives" and the "depth-charge" of the work that she insists upon. Thus *Art Objects* concludes with the assertion that

> The true writer will have to build up her readership from among those who still want to read and who want more than the glories of the past nicely reproduced. I have been able to build up a readership, largely through a young, student population, who want my books on their courses and by their beds. Reading is sexy[. . . .] Judge the work not the writer seems to be what a new generation is prepared to do. It is for a new generation that I write. (192)

On their face, these closing words echo those of *A Room of One's Own,* quoted by Winterson at some length at the end of her previous chapter: "Drawing her life from the lives of the unknown who were her forerunners, as her brothers did before her, she will be born[. . . .] I maintain that she would come if we worked for her, and that so to work, even in poverty and obscurity, is worth while" (qtd. in *AO* 163–64). (They also, less directly, recall George Eliot's late-life desire to attract young readers, to which Rosemarie Bodenheimer calls attention: In relations with young worshipers such as Alexander Main, "she had achieved, she thought, what she most wanted: to become for young readers one of the most powerful voices in books which had fertilized and sustained her own lonely youth" [242]).

The ramifications of this deliberate echo of Woolf are complex. First, as Pykett points out, such an assertive authorial identification is "a high-risk strategy since it will inevitably lead most readers to unfavourable comparisons. Winterson's cheeky brio does not easily match up to the breadth of reading and deeply meditated sense of history that runs through the writings of Woolf and Eliot" (59). In addition to raising some hackles, Winterson appears to have overlooked the irony inherent in repudiating a literary practice that reproduces "the glories of the past" while celebrating the past glories of Modernism. Indeed, Modernism remains for Winterson not so much a past as an alternative contemporary moment: "I believe that had it not been for the disastrous effect on European culture of two World Wars, what we call Modernism might have proved only the start of a period in history as genuinely new" (*AO* 191). In this alternative universe, Victorian literature is still Oedipal progenitor to be slain: "The novel form is finished. That does not mean we should give up reading nineteenth-century novels, we should read them avidly and often. What we must do is give up writing them" (191). This elision of the current moment in which Winterson writes allows her to bracket the entire terrain of postmodern (a word that appears nowhere in *Art Objects*) experimentalist fiction. As Pykett observes, "By insisting so firmly on a particular version of Modernism from which she claims descent, Winterson erases a great deal of the history of writing since the period of high Modernism, and obscures the extent to which her own writings have been shaped by this 'after history'" (59), notably, in Pykett's view, by the work of Angela Carter.[32] To some degree like Woolf, Winterson's diachronic identification with precursors enables her to disavow or ignore synchronic relations with her peers, so that her own position appears to be unique.

More important, Winterson's homage does not simply reproduce but rather redirects Woolf's temper and tempo. In her conclusion, Woolf emphasizes sober, collective labor and avoids suggesting that her own authorship might already herald, if not instantiate, the arrival of the future she invokes. Radclyffe Hall's conclusion, which I have suggested anticipates Woolf's in its semi-mystical invocation of future authorship, also emphasizes labor, though agonized and individual rather than self-denying and collective. Winterson, like Hall, emphasizes the individual rather than the collective, the first-person singular over the first-person plural or third person of Woolf's passage, but her focus, unlike that of Woolf or Hall, is on erotics rather than labor, pleasure rather than suffering. The juxtaposition of "my books" with "[readers'] beds" and the assertion that "reading is sexy" overtly inserts erotic desire in the relationship between author and reader. Also unlike either precursor, Winterson moves frankly from the projection of a future "she" who "*will* have to build up her readership from those who still want to read" to her present success in doing so. Shakespeare's sister, the passage suggests, has now arrived. Here as elsewhere, Winterson's style signals assertion where Woolf's performs judiciousness and self-confidence where Woolf's hangs back. In Winterson's revision of Woolf, the "suavity . . . politeness . . . and sidelong approach" (Woolf, *MB* 129) that Woolf both distrusted and remained attached to in her own writing have been triumphantly vanquished. Where Woolf emphasized the need for the "common reader" to dislodge writers from their "plinths and pedestals," in Winterson's conclusion, readers remain the indirect object of the authorial subject's assertion: "It is for a new generation that I write" (*AO* 192).

Despite Winterson's deprecation of her contemporary context, then, the version of Woolf that emerges from Winterson's authorial identification seems to have been infiltrated by—or updated according to—some of its postmodern values: she is brasher, sexier, more visibly self-promoting. But if on the one hand Winterson seems stylistically postmodern in relation to Woolf, on the other hand, she can often seem atavistically attached to a Victorian intellectual heritage. *Art Objects* has its share of sententious pronouncement, particularly about the sacralization of art: "Against this golden calf in the wilderness where all come to buy and sell, the honest currency of art offers quite a different rate of exchange. The artist does not turn time into money, the artist turns time into energy, time into intensity, time into vision" (139). Winterson dismisses George Eliot in a phrase—"It is no use looking for the new George Eliot, and if she were to appear, what a ghastly creature she would be" (*AO* 177)—but her didactic mode can read like a caricature of Eliot's sage persona. The temper of "Imagination and Reality," the essay in which the discussion of the "honest currency of art" appears, is unironically close to that of Eliot's essay on "Debasing the Moral Currency": "The art of spoiling is within reach of the dullest faculty: the coarsest clown with a hammer in his hand might chip the nose off every statue and bust in the Vatican, and stand grinning at the effect of his work" [*Selected Essays* 438]). When deployed in Winterson's novels, however, this archaizing mode takes the livelier form of paradox and revisionism—"Very often history is a means of denying the past" (*Oranges* 93); "That walls should fall is the consequence of blowing your own trumpet" (112); "My mother had painted the white roses red and now she claimed they grew that way" (136)—reminiscent less of Eliot's moral pronouncements than of the glittering reversals of Oscar Wilde's dramas: "Really, if the lower orders don't set us a good example, what on earth is the use of them? They seem, as a class, to have absolutely no sense of moral responsibility" (*The Importance of Being Earnest* I.i). Like each of these precursors, Winterson negotiates between conceptions of aesthetic representation as on the one hand autonomous of social conditions and on the other a medium of social critique, and between poles of social or cultural outsider and insider status.

Winterson's overt identification with Woolf, then, both minimizes her revisions of Woolf and downplays pre-Modernist filiations, e.g. the mid-Victorian didacticism represented by Eliot; the late-Victorian decadence of Wilde; even the more polemic Woolf of *Three Guineas*. The two quotations from *Art Objects* that begin this section juxtapose her claiming of Woolf with another disavowal, of identification with Radclyffe Hall as a lesbian author. Winterson rejects the imputed personal identity of an author as a criterion for readerly identification—part of her general emphasis on formal and literary over biographical or political affiliations. But like her identification with Woolf, Winterson's disavowal of Hall belies some complexities. First, Winterson and Hall are not without commonalities. Both (like Woolf) write novels of formation in which they inherit but also strain against and modify the genre's realist conventions. Both draw on the imagery and philosophy of non-mainstream religious traditions: Hall was both a Catholic convert and a member of the Society for Psychical Research; Winterson was raised in the Pentecostal Christianity so memorably represented in *Oranges*. Hall's next novel after *The Well of Loneliness, The Master of the House* (1932), is a long allegorical tale whose protagonist, a Provençal carpenter named Christophe Bénédit, is a latter-day embodiment of Christ. Winterson's work, as Jago Morrison has argued, has steadily deepened its own concern with a "post-Christian" spirituality: "the subversive exploration of sexuality and the erotic, so celebrated in her early work, has been comprehensively subordinated to an interest in love, framed in the terms of the agapeic tradition" (176). Most important, like both *The Voyage Out* and *The Well of Loneliness, Oranges Are Not the Only Fruit* redirects the plot and structure of the novel of formation away from both the conventions of classic realism and the centrality of the heterosexual subject. Winterson's interlocutor, cited at the beginning of this section, may have phrased her query naively, but a comparison of *The Well* and *Oranges* depends not only on the sexuality of their authors but also on the sexual politics and literary innovation *of their works*. Just as Radclyffe Hall in the 1920s radically intervened in fictional traditions by representing the development of a defiantly, tragically queer protagonist, so Winterson in the 1980s radically intervened by presenting an insouciantly, wittily queer one. Like both *The Voyage Out* and *The Well of Loneliness, Oranges* plots new styles and directions for the novel of female formation.

Writing in the last decades of the twentieth century, however, Winterson faces accumulated challenges in refreshing or redirecting conventional motifs of the novel of formation. In creating a protagonist who resists, however inchoately, aspects of socialization into a heterosexual norm, Winterson like Woolf is wary of familiar motifs such as literary identification (the bookish protagonist's identification with earlier literary heroines) and of relying entirely on the developmental and rationalist assumptions of realist fictional narration. She makes her protagonist, Jeanette, a skewed and skeptical reader and disrupts the realist trajectory of her narrative with interpolated fairy-tales whose events and characters parallel, but do not mirror, those in Jeanette's life, offering the gender reversals, apothegms, and transformations that become even more central in Winterson's later, less realist novels. And like Woolf and Hall, Winterson both calls upon and challenges the conventions of readerly identification. For example, she gives the protagonist of *Oranges* her own first name and much of her own biographical location, inviting readerly identification with the character and/as author, but the interpolated tales, whose narrative voice cannot quite be identified with that of the novel's Jeanette, seem designed to disrupt those relations.

The young Jeanette is a version of the reading-girl protagonist, like Maggie Tulliver, whose subjectivity emerges in and through her connection to other narratives. From the beginning (also like Maggie) she misinterprets and redirects the normatively innocent materials of sanctioned (by church and school) childhood tales. Like Hall, Winterson draws on and rewrites biblical narrative, but in the spirit of establishing her protagonist's creativity rather than her martyrdom. Jeanette creates a feltboard narrative of the biblical Daniel being swallowed by rather than escaping the lions (*Oranges* 12–13); chooses for a sampler project the un-reassuring biblical text "The Summer Is Ended and We Are Not Yet Saved" (39); and gives the other children in her class nightmares by telling them about "the horrors of the demon and the fate of the damned" (43). Undeterred by the disapproval of her teachers, Mrs. Virtue and Mrs. Vole, she continues her efforts to please with "[a model of] *Street Car Named Desire* out of pipe-cleaners, an embroidered cushion cover of Bette Davis in *Now Voyager,* an oregami [*sic*] William Tell with real apple, and best of all, a potato sculpture of Henry Ford outside the Chrysler building in New York" (48). Winterson presents Jeanette's slant but revealing vision as the result not of a plan of resistance but of an originality that seems partly natural (later, Jeanette compares herself to an icon of untutored genius, William Blake) and partly encouraged by the eccentric nurture of her fanatically Evangelical mother, who teaches her to read from the Book of Deuteronomy, leaving her unfamiliar with "horsies, bunnies, and little ducks" but unusually informed about "pelicans, rock badgers, sloths, and bats. This tendency toward the exotic has brought me many problems, just as it did for William Blake" (42). It is the mystically inclined Elsie Norris who introduces Jeanette to Blake, along with *Goblin Market* and Yeats. Elsie is also fond of Swinburne; notably, in the heterogeneous stew of Jeanette's cultural references, queer-inflected artifacts or proper names (*Streetcar Named Desire,* Bette Davis, Swinburne, *Goblin Market*) appear, unmarked, alongside others that have more masculine, nationalist (William Tell) or commercial (Henry Ford) connotations, as well as alongside those that seem to emphasize projects of not only aesthetic but also spiritual transcendence of mundane identities (Blake, Yeats). At the same time, however, Blake and Yeats can be and have been equally recruited for projections of national identity; and the examples drawn from popular culture (*Streetcar,* Bette Davis, Henry Ford) suggest the influence of American commercial culture. What appears in one light to be Jeanette's individuality, her resistance to interpellation by narrow communal norms, in another exposes her to the hazard of interpellation by hegemonic forces of whose nature and origin she remains ignorant.

There are several forms of doubleness and ambivalence at work here. First, the strong stylistic realism of Jeanette's narrative—its detailed first-person representation of the child's perception of prosaic events—continually flickers with flashes of more fantastic narrative modes, indicated for example by the ostentatiously allegorical names Winterson gives Jeanette's teachers, the novel's Old Testament chapter titles, and the different forms of non-realist aesthetics signaled by proper names such as Blake, Yeats, and Bette Davis. This penetration of the narrative's realism, and its accompanying aesthetic of identification, by non-realist genres gathers steam at the end of Exodus (the novel's second chapter) with the first of a series of myth- or fairy-tale inspired interpolations. Second, as I have suggested above, Jeanette's own objects of identification can signal either resistance or interpellation. Third, this ambiguity also characterizes Jeanette's strong initial identification with her own mother. "I had been brought in to join [my mother] in a tag match against the Rest of the World" (*Oranges* 3), Jeanette observes; and initially Jeanette's nonconformist vision and heterogeneity of interests seem to be tolerated and even encouraged by her mother and the alternative motherly, or grandmotherly, figure Elsie Norris. Jeanette's characterization of her mother's combative attitude—"She had never heard of mixed feelings. There were friends and there were enemies" (3)—applies equally well to Jeanette's own narrating voice in *Oranges* (and to Winterson's throughout her writings). But as so many twentieth-century novels of female formation suggest (including *The Well, The Voyage Out,* and Jamaica Kincaid's *Lucy*), the female protagonist's early, productive identification with maternal figures is inevitably circumscribed by the interpellation of those figures within dominant gender ideologies. One of the earliest maternal betrayals that Jeanette experiences revolves around a familiar object of literary identification—*Jane Eyre.* Brontë's novel is Jeanette's "mother's favorite non-Bible book," which in reading aloud to her daughter she alters, so that at the end Jane marries St John Rivers. Later, Jeanette, "literate and curious . . . decided to read [*Jane Eyre*] for myself. . . . I found out, that dreadful day in a back corner of the library, that Jane doesn't marry St. John at all, that she goes back to Mr. Rochester. It was like the day I discovered my adoption papers while searching for a pack of playing cards. I have never since played cards, and I have never since read *Jane Eyre*" (74–75).

The library, as I have previously suggested, is a conventional location of revelation for the protagonists of novels of formation, underscoring the literary roots of that formation: it is, for example, where Dorothea Brooke, disabused of the romance of imagining herself one of Milton's daughters, throws herself into Will Ladislaw's arms; Stephen Gordon discovers her story in the sexological literature her father has concealed; and Jamaica Kincaid's Lucy finds that "a tongue has no taste" as she hides in the stacks and French-kisses a boy named Tanner. The betrayal that Jeanette discovers in the library in *Oranges* is also associated with sexuality, since it is the recuperation of Jane and Rochester's initially illegitimate passion that Jeanette's mother suppresses. The maternal betrayal revealed here is dual: Jeanette has been abandoned by her biological mother, presumably as a result of the stigma of unmarried motherhood, and she will be abandoned (first publicly castigated and finally kicked out of the house) by her adoptive mother when her lesbian sexuality becomes apparent:

> My mother stood up and said . . . that women had specific circumstances for their ministry, that the Sunday School was one of them, the Sisterhood another, but the message belonged to the men. Until this moment my life had still made some kind of sense. Now it was making no sense at all. . . . She ended by saying that having taken on a man's world in other ways I had flouted God's law and tried to do it sexually. This was no spontaneous speech. She and the pastor had talked about it already. It was her weakness for the ministry that had done it. . . . (*Oranges* 133–34)

With her reading lessons in Deuteronomy and her encouragement of Jeanette's preaching, her mother inadvertently teaches her to challenge authority, and she supports her as long as that authority is feminized (in Jeanette's elementary school) and unthreatening to the more absolute and ultimately patriarchal authority of her church and of the heterosexual norm. In first altering the end of *Jane Eyre* to favor the Christian mission, however, and then parroting the pastoral line on women's role in the ministry, Jeanette's mother reveals that her apparent independence was always limited by complicity with a masculine power structure whose values are fundamentally conservative. Although the more sympathetic Elsie Norris tries to intervene, she dies soon after. Her abandonment of Jeanette is, of course, unwitting, but there is a trace of more active culpability in her continued desire to believe in the church's good intentions. Both Jeanette's mother, in her complicity with masculinist norms, and Elsie Norris, as an alternative mother-figure whose good will cannot forestall the application of those norms, echo the role of Helen Ambrose in Rachel Vinrace's life.

Jeanette's mother understands the importance of narrative identifications and wishes to control her daughter's: she not only rewrites texts (*Jane Eyre*) and renarrates her own experience (of leadership as a churchwoman) to comply with patriarchal norms; she is also capable entirely of obliterating narratives that do not suit her. When Jeanette asks about "a yellowy picture of a pretty woman holding a cat," on a page devoted to "Old Flames" in her mother's photograph album, her mother quickly dismisses the woman as the sister of a male suitor, and "next time we looked, it had gone" (*Oranges* 36). More violently, the occasion of the initial discovery of Jeanette's affair with Melanie, she burns "all the letters, all the cards, all the jottings of my own" in the backyard. Book-burning as symbolic of the mother's attempt to disrupt her daughter's intellectual emergence (almost always associated with her sexual emergence) is something of a trope in women's novels of formation—for example, as I have discussed above, a similar event appears in Jamaica Kincaid's novels and autobiographical writings. Such obliterating opposition both signals the continued necessity for, and justifies, the Woolfian project of "killing the Angel in the House [as] part of the occupation of a woman writer" (*DM* 238). These betrayals loosen the hold of Jeanette's own identification with her mother.

Like Woolf and Woolf's female protagonists, and like Jamaica Kincaid's Lucy, Jeanette finds that slaying the maternal phantom is difficult. At the novel's end Jeanette still feels that her mother has "tied a thread around my button, to tug when she pleased" (*Oranges* 176). However, as Jeanette's dismissal of her mother as a "spiritual whore" suggests, her struggle against the dominance of convention is more vigorous and sustained than that of her forbears. Like Rachel Vinrace, Jeanette falls ill and has hallucinations, but unlike Rachel, she recovers. Jeanette also refutes Stephen Gordon's notorious moments of physical self-loathing: "She hated her body with its muscular shoulders, its small compact breasts, and its slender flanks of an athlete. All her life she must drag this body of hers like a monstrous fetter imposed on her spirit. . . . She longed to maim it, for it made her feel cruel" (Hall 186–87). Jeanette's appearance and self-presentation, by contrast, do not seem to be factors in her own image of herself or in others' responses to her. Indeed, although Jeanette notices that Melanie's "eyes were a lovely grey, like the cat Next Door" (*Oranges* 80) and comments when they make love on "her marvelous bones and the triangle of muscle in her stomach" (103), standards of or emphasis on conventions of beauty seem largely absent from her world and not associated with desire. (By contrast, Stephen Gordon's Angela is a very conventional beauty, with "amazingly blonde" hair, "very white" skin, and "eyes of rather an unusual blue that almost seemed to be tinted with purple" [Hall 131]). Jeanette's sole moment of disgust with her own appearance occurs when her mother hustles her into an "enormous . . . bright pink" mackintosh, which makes her feel "trapped" and "sick" (*Oranges* 79, 80).

Peggy Bailey notes the symbolism of Jeanette's mother "encas[ing]" her pubescent daughter in a garment of a color traditionally associated with femininity: "The image of Jeanette immobilized in her bright pink mac is the novel's final symbol, before serious conflict erupts, of the misfit she has become in Mother's world" (71). However, the mackintosh is so intrinsically repellent—not just pink but "bright pink," "enormous," plastic, and dragged out from "behind a pile of cardboard boxes that had SURPLUS written on the side, like branded sheep" (*Oranges* 79)—and obviously external to Jeanette that her dislike of it seems indicative of self-respect rather than self-loathing. Similarly, although Jeanette is crushed when Melanie takes up with a man, her response upon being patronizingly "forgiven" by him—"There was only one thing I could do; mustering all my spit, I did it" (124)—reverses Hall's themes of martyrdom. (In *The Well,* Stephen's beloved, Angela, betrays her to her husband in order to cover up her affair with another man; in Hall's novel *The Master of the House,* the Christ-like, pacifist hero is spat upon by soldiers who then crucify him.) Following Melanie, Jeanette engages in a lighthearted affair with a young woman named Katy whom she meets on the beach, as if responding to the objection made to *The Well* by Diana Souhami, one of Hall's biographers: "Radclyffe Hall was too troubled a person to write an untroubled book, but she might have acknowledged the privilege, seductions, freedom and fun that graced her daily life" (173). Like Stephen, Jeanette sustains real losses—her mother, her first love, her home, and a cultural context (for Stephen, country life; for Jeanette, the church) that has defined her—but she never represents herself as in any essential way a "troubled person." Her self-representation rather echoes the matter-of-fact tone of Woolf's declaration at the end of *A Room of One's Own* that "sometimes women do like women" (86); itself an echo of Rachel and Helen's mutual recognition that "we like each other" (Woolf, *VO* 91).

At the same time, however, like Rachel's and Stephen Gordon's, Jeanette's erotic presence remains relatively disembodied and elliptical in Winterson's representation. In representing Jeanette's first sexual encounter, with Melanie, Winterson avoids directly physical imagery and concludes with a biblical reference:

> She stroked my head for a long time, and then we hugged and it felt like drowning. Then I was frightened but couldn't stop. There was something crawling in my belly. I had an octopus inside me.
>
> And it was evening and it was morning; another day. (*Oranges* 88–89)

Here, Winterson echoes the creation story of Genesis; Hall, too, famously encapsulates her protagonist's first sexual consummation with a biblical reference: "That night they were not divided" (the reference also used by Eliot as the epitaph for Maggie and Tom Tulliver). Winterson's reference is both more ironic than Hall's—Jeanette has been leading Melanie in Bible study, and they feel, misguidedly, secure in the "family" (89) of their church—and more grandiose: Where David's words are spoken in mourning for one patriarch and his son (Saul and Jonathan), Jeanette's refers to the creation of an entire new world. Later, Jeanette describes her first sexual encounter with Katy with a paralepsis reminiscent of Woolf's teasing in *The Voyage Out:* "We stopped talking about it quickly because the dialogue was getting too embarrassing" (123). Like Woolf's evasions, Winterson's draws attention to our textual conventions for representing sex and raises the question of to whom, exactly, embarrassment over such representation belongs—to the author? characters? reader? In any case, the relative disembodiment with which Winterson represents sexuality in this novel suggests that, to return to Woolf's words, "marching up" to the direct representation of sex retains the threat of making "inaudible" a text's other voices.

Equally *sotto voce* in *Oranges* is its narrative of artistic formation. Like *The Voyage Out, Oranges* sketches a covert and unfinished plot of intellectual development, rather than the narrative of the protagonist's journey to triumph as a novelist that we find in *The Well.* The reader can deduce at the end of the novel that Jeanette has won a place at a university, though the word never appears. In the final section of the novel ("Ruth"), Winterson's fairy-tale interpolations follow two characters: a female wanderer—headed for "a beautiful city, a long way off" whose denizens "didn't sow or toil they thought about the world" (*Oranges* 131)—whose name, Winnet Stonejar, is an almost-anagram (four letters short) of Winterson's own; and a sad Arthurian knight, Sir Perceval, who is mourning the loss of Arthur and his self-chosen exile from the world of the Round Table. These mythical characters, with their quests and their losses, both reference and replace a more realist set of narratives that readers may mentally supply, of the young man (or occasionally woman) from the provinces making his or her way to the university cities: Hardy's Jude Fawley, Lawrence's Paul Morel and Ursula Brangwen, Philip Larkin's John Kemp (like Winterson a Lancastrian), Frederic Raphael's Adam Morris.[33] Just as "Winnet Stonejar" is almost, but not quite, an anagram for Jeanette Winterson, and Sir Perceval is almost, but not quite, an avatar of the novel's Jeanette (being male, and mourning the loss of the homosocial masculinity of the Round Table, while Jeanette is female, and mourns the loss of her woman-dominated church), so this final section of the novel maintains a slant relation to the aesthetics of identification that characterize these classic narratives of intellectual formation: It knows that they're there, it knows that its readers know, but it will not cast Jeanette, or allow us to identify with her, as simply the protagonist of such a narrative.[34]

It is perhaps partly the existence of this imposing literary lineage that accounts for the coyness of the novel's plot of intellectual formation; like the coming-out plot, the *kunstler* plot's freshness is imperiled by the lurking presence of convention if not cliché, pathos if not bathos. Winterson avoids these perils not only through the use of metaphor and innuendo but also by allowing the novel to end with an acknowledgment that old longings still exist for its protagonist, that the beginning of a new life offers no simple conclusion to the old one. At the end of *Sons and Lovers,* Paul Morel walks "toward the city's gold phosphorescence" away from his recently dead mother: "His fists were shut, his mouth set fast. He would not take that direction, to the darkness, to follow her. He walked towards the faintly humming, glowing town, quickly" (Lawrence 464). The closed fists and mouth suggest both the difficulty and the decisiveness of the protagonist's rejection of his maternal identification. *Oranges,* however, ends not with Jeanette's departure from home, but with her return to it, and to a mother still very much alive. She comes home on a train from a mysterious city "with a copy of *Middlemarch* under [her] pullover" (*Oranges* 162). In addition to offering another clue that Jeanette has entered a world of scholarship and of female intellectual ambition, the conjunction of *Middlemarch* and rail travel perhaps makes a sardonic nod to one of the most conventionally feminine characters in *To the Lighthouse,* Minta Doyle, who "had left the third volume of *Middlemarch* in the train and . . . never knew what happened in the end" (148).[35]

The mother, in this case, has the last word. It is Jeanette's mother, not Jeanette herself, who has become an author at the end of the novel. She has written "a long piece on devilry" for the "*Band of Hope* review" (*Oranges* 165) and has taken up shortwave radio broadcasting. The novel ends with the opening sentence of her broadcast: "This is Kindly Light calling Manchester, come in Manchester, this is Kindly Light" (176). The line is ironic, because neither Jeanette's mother nor the "light" of her Christianity have proven "kindly" to Jeanette, and it is poignant because the invitation—"come in"—is one that she has not extended to her own daughter, who has "come out" and been thrown out. At the same time, however, these powerful effects of the mother's utterance call attention to the creative hand behind them of both "Jeanette," the narrator, and Jeanette Winterson, the author: It is in her power to confer on her mother the power of the last word. The ending thus ambiguously suggests both reconciliation and continued tension, relations of identification and disavowal—between Jeanette and her mother; between the vivid intimacies of her former life ("If God is your emotional role model," she observes, "very few human relationships will match up to it" [170]) and the uncertain gains of her present one ("I knew a woman in another place. Perhaps she would save me. But what if she were asleep?"); between fiction and autobiography, between language as creation and language as entrapment ("[My mother] had begun a self-help kit for the spiritually disturbed. . . . I was glad she had a hobby, but not pleased that my particular sins were listed in the self-help kit" [174]). Even so undomestic a house-angel as Jeanette's mother seems, for the fascinated daughter, very hard to kill.

Like many novels of formation (including *The Voyage Out* and *The Well of Loneliness*), first novels, and first-person novels, *Oranges Are Not the Only Fruit* was received as autobiographical, and has many traits of autobiographical fiction—its protagonist shares not only a first name but many verifiable biographical characteristics with its author. In an essay in *Art Objects,* Winterson roundly rejects such autobiographical readings:

> Like *Orlando* and *Oranges Are Not the Only Fruit, The Autobiography of Alice B. Toklas* is fiction masquerading as a memoir. It seems that if you tell people that what they are reading is "real," they will believe you, even when they are being trailed in the wake of a highly experimental odyssey. I have never understood how anyone can read the Deuteronomy chapter of *Oranges* and not catch on to my game. . . . Like Stein, I prefer myself as a character in my own fiction, and like Stein and Woolf, what concerns me is language. . . . The most important thing about *Oranges* is not its wit nor its warmth, but its new way with words. (*AO* 53)

The "Deuteronomy" chapter of *Oranges* signals Winterson's "game" not only because of its topic, which is the malleability of history ("History should be a hammock for swinging and a game for playing, the way cats play" [93]), but also because it is one of the novel's extra-narrative interpolations, outside of, though commenting on, its plot; not narrating "real" events; written in a voice that is not identified as that of "Jeanette." Interrupting the trajectory of the first-person narrative, these interpolations, which seem to represent the novel's "experimental odyssey," also function to interrupt readerly identification with the "Jeanette" voice and narrative. Yet they don't fundamentally *dis*rupt; they may pause the narrative, but they do not alter it. A reader can follow Jeanette's story from beginning to end without reading these chapters or sections, and not suffer any loss of sense. Indeed, most critical readings of the novel (my own included) implicitly do just that, interpreting the novel as a realist narrative of formation in the same way we would without these sections, seeing them as complementing rather than diverting the first-person trajectory.[36]

In "The Semiotics of Sex," Winterson asserts that "Art must resist autobiography if it hopes to cross boundaries of class, culture . . . and . . . sexuality" (*AO* 106; ellipses in original), and her election of stylistically and sexually elliptical Woolf as a favored precursor over stylistically and sexually explicit Hall functions as a rejection of textual strategies that favor, over those that discourage, identifications, even queer ones. If readers tend to focus on the first-person immediacy of *Oranges Are Not the Only Fruit* and to minimize the boundaries between narrator and author, however, that may be less a sign of readerly credulity or disrespect than a response to the tension between Winterson's own preference for "[her]self as a character in her own fiction," which pulls in the direction of queer identificatory reading, and her interest in uses of language apart from novelistic character or plot. In *Oranges* the realist-autobiographical and the experimentalist-fantastic trajectories proceed in parallel rather than directly engaging or transforming each other. In her later novels, Winterson works more directly to disrupt readerly identification—creating protagonists who are not completely describable in human terms and who have fantastic relations to time and space. At the same time, a strongly marked first-person voice (assertive, epigrammatic, irreverent) and a concern with distinctively human relations of desire remain consistent throughout her work and continue to invite readings from a position of identification.

"You see you kind of belong to us," a reader and acquaintance, Rachel Sharp, wrote to Woolf on the publication of her biography of Roger Fry, taking polite issue with her inclusion of a scatological account of sadistic corporal punishment during the subject's schooldays, "and what you do matters enormously" (qtd. in Daugherty 4).[37] The intimate claim of reader on author, based on the projection of an ethical, emotional stance that seems to unite them, is magnified by narratives that address readers implicitly or directly on the basis of a shared and minoritized subjectivity, such as queer subjectivity. But, as Winterson's essays make particularly clear, this relationship between readers and authors involves struggle as much as collaboration. *Art Objects* asserts Winterson's control: over those authors and genres with which she will be identified (not Hall but Woolf and Stein, not autobiography but fiction); over the desire of readers who "want my books on their courses and by their beds" but must not want to "collude in the misreading of art as sexuality" (105). Yet the essays themselves reveal the paradoxical nature of such an authorial fantasy of power, for Winterson exerts over Woolf the power of definition that she resists having brought to bear on her own authorial persona: not the polemical Woolf, but the poetic Woolf; not the Woolf of the diaries but the Woolf of the novels; not the Woolf of *The Voyage Out* but the Woolf of *The Waves;* not shared sexual, but shared textual, orientations. Two of the essays in *Art Objects* are about Winterson as a collector (of modern art and of first editions), possessed by her art objects—"Book collecting is an obsession, an occupation, a disease, an addiction, a fascination, an absurdity, a fate" (119)—but also asserting possession. Woolf, Hall, and Winterson grapple with the question of how to mobilize literary identification to expand possibilities for the representation of subjectivity, including queer subjectivity, while resisting those aspects of literary identification—in their work and in its reception—that constrain them generically or personally. To some degree, these struggles over identification and appropriation are shared by all of the authors in this study—they are not peculiar to postmodernity or to narratives of identity, but rather endemic to the conventions of realist representation, and the novel of formation, in which reciprocal relations between the self and other are always what is at stake.

AFTERWORD

THE VICTORIAN NOVEL of formation, with which I began, negotiates among competing models of life story—the providential, the picaresque, and the psychoanalytic. The post-Enlightenment rise of a subject defined more by interiority—self-regulation, self-narration, and affect—than relations of external hierarchy or control, along with the growth of evolutionary narratives, reshaped the English novel. Within these modernizing psychological contexts, the subject could less plausibly be represented as an entity given entire (as by God) or as a *tabula rasa* inscribed by collision with largely external events (the associationist view). The life history of such a psychologized subject, whether historical or fictional, could not run smoothly along the well-worn tracks of providential plotting according to which, in Oscar Wilde's mocking *fin-de-siècle* summary of fiction, "The good are rewarded and the evil punished" (*Importance of Being Earnest* II.i), nor develop accretively through the concatenation of externally induced experiences, as in the picaresque.

Thus the connection between the novel of formation and the narrative of psychoanalysis that I have suggested here is not adventitious; the two share a historical context for their development. The psychomachia that Freud stages in the theater of the self, populated by "model, object, helper, opponent" (*Group Psychology* 1); the "good" and "bad" objects internalized by the Kleinian psyche; the "abiding sense of oneself as associated with, positioned in terms of, related to, a matrix of other people" (Mitchell 33) in relational theory: all of these encounters, embodied for psychoanalytic practice in the interchange between analysand and analyst, are individuated in the novel of formation in relations among characters, readers, and authors. In the historical moment at which the subject begins to acquire its autonomy, psychoanalytic formulations of identification suggests its concomitant dependency, its uneven and partial composition through the incorporation and loss of other selves and in the recognition of the self by the other. It is the conflict, partiality, and loss inherent in identification, as much as its affirmations, that have allowed post-Victorian readers and writers to continue to respond to the invitations proferred by the novel of formation.

Because narratives of formation are about, and solicit, the intimacy of identification and mutual recognition, these invitations, I have suggested, are themselves particularly intimate. But just as relations of identification can include hostile projections as well as affirming reflections, so every occasion of recognition also has the potential to be an occasion of misrecognition. This tension is apparent in Jeanette Winterson's dismissive response to the young woman in the bookstore who, mistaking Winterson's seductive authorial persona for an invitation to group solidarity, associates her with Radclyffe Hall: "Our work has nothing in common." Winterson objects to being expected to "shar[e] a bed with a dead body. [A] bed in the shape of a book" (*AO* 103), but she happily invites into *Art Objects* many dead bodies—Woolf, Stein, T. S. Eliot. In fact, identification with a dead author, like Winterson's with Woolf, the "complete," untouchable poet-ancestor, might seem more secure than a similar relation with living ones, since the dead cannot evade or contest it. But—as suggested by Winterson's attempts to reinscribe Woolf in her own image and defend her from competing interpretations—the dead do walk, animated by the inevitable multiplicity of their own representations and the representations of other readers and writers. Relations of identification and recognition can never be fixed, finished, or individually possessed.

These ambivalences of authorship (seeking recognition, fearing appropriation) and readership (identification as homage, identification as aggression) are writ large, for contemporary readers, in Winterson's provocative prose and in the representation of queer subjects, for whose identities the question of *recognition* is, more than ever, so visibly at stake. The current erosion, as well, of boundaries between private and public forums of self-representation, and new modes of circulation of authors in the public sphere (through blogs and websites, for example), apparently have the potential to make relations of identification and demands for recognition more immediate and more fraught. Fictional characters, too, subject to various forms of repurposing, remediation, and reanimation, can challenge our identifications of, and with, them. In the postmodern romps of Jasper Fforde, such as *Lost in a Book* and *The Eyre Affair,* real readers can enter into fictional worlds, mingling with a Jane Eyre who fails to marry Rochester, or a Miss Havisham who races cars.

But as I have shown, the dynamism of literary relations of identification is not a specifically postmodern development but has always been part of the genre of the novel of formation. George Eliot is as self-reflexive and intertextual as Jeanette Winterson, and her relations with her readers are just as vexed. When Eliot, in *The Mill on the Floss,* both invokes and then distances herself from other narratives of female formation; when Beauvoir continually recasts, in fiction, memoirs, letters, and essays, her representation of the development of a female intellectual; when Brontë and Dangarembga follow narratives of formation with narratives of profound alienation—all these authorial gestures combine an invitation to identification, a desire for recognition, and an effort to control the effect and direction of both. When Maggie Tulliver refuses to finish *Corinne,* when Lynne Sharon Schwartz first attempts to inhabit, and then redirects, the nineteenth-century narrative of female formation; when Lucy Potter claims to identify with Milton's Lucifer rather than Brontë's Lucy Snowe—all these gestures suggest both the attraction and the threat of readerly identification and the ways in which they continue.

That attraction is neither timeless nor inevitable. From *The Rise of the Novel* to "The Death of the Author," critics have emphasized not only the temporality but also the mortality of genres and styles of reading. Genres are historically and culturally bound: their rules of composition, the expectations that readers bring to them, the conventions by which their representations are legible—all are subject to obsolescence. Writing in the first half of the twentieth century, M. M. Bakhtin concludes a discussion of the "reaccentuation" of the novel's "images and languages" from one era to another on an optimistic note: "Great novelistic images continue to grow and develop even after the moment of their creation; they are capable of being creatively transformed in different eras, far distant from the day and hour of their birth" (422). On the other hand, as Terry Eagleton warns sternly, "Anything which is regarded as unalterably and unquestionably literature—Shakespeare, for example—can cease to be literature" (9); and any genre can cease to speak intelligibly to readers or authors. For the novel of formation, however, that moment has not yet arrived.

NOTES

INTRODUCTION

1. For contemporary conceptions of the Bildungsroman, see Moretti ch. 1; and Fraiman ch. 1. For a recent discussion of the origins of the term "Bildungsroman" that emphasizes its historical association with cosmopolitanism and modernity, see Boes. On the Bildungsroman in the European context, see, in addition to Hirsch, Bakhtin ch. 4; and Moretti. For a recent critique of the Bildungsroman tradition in a global framework, see Slaughter, particularly ch. 2.

2. For the Bildungsroman as a genre of women's literature, see, e.g., Abel, Hirsch, and Langland; and Fuderer for a bibliography through 1990. For a reevaluation of distinctions between male and female Bildgungsromane, see L. Ellis, particularly ch. 1.

3. Two prominent nineteenth-century examples of novels of formation with male protagonists—Dickens's *David Copperfield* (1849–50) and *Great Expectations* (1860–61)—are exceptions that paradoxically support such a claim: the protagonists of these two novels are, if not consistently feminized, at least frequently placed in feminized positions. Dickens's narrative voice always assumes a mixed (male and female) audience, and there is little in David or Pip's psychological trajectories of susceptibility to manipulation, social anxiety, and hopeless love that would debar identification from a conventionally feminine point of view.

4. The boundary between novels of courtship and novels of formation, particularly early in the nineteenth century, is not rigid, and *Pride and Prejudice* is, in fact, often discussed as an example of the female Bildungsroman, perhaps because of the relative many-sidedness with which Elizabeth Bennett and her relationships are represented, compared to a courtship heroine such as Pamela or Frances Burney's Evelina. Susan Fraiman, for example, takes the novel as presenting the suppression or undoing of development: Elizabeth Bennett's apparent progress toward a triumphant romantic ending is shadowed by "a darker, downward vector: the narrative that passes Elizabeth from one father to another and, in doing so, takes her from shaping judgments to being shaped by

them" (63). I am not entirely persuaded, however, that Fraiman's examples of Elizabeth's "humiliation" at the hands of patriarchy outweigh the impression left by Elizabeth's ability to compel Darcy to propose not once but twice; to continue her "lively, sportive manner of talking" to him (Austen 297) until almost the novel's last page; and to feel quite undiluted "delight" in attaining at last "all the comfort and elegance of their family party at Pemberley" (294). In other words, it seems to me to make as much sense to read *Pride and Prejudice* as a positive exemplar of the category of the novel of courtship as to read it as a negative example of the novel of formation.

5. James acknowledges the precedence of Shakespeare and of George Eliot but insists that their heroines are "typical, none the less, of a class difficult, in the individual case, to make a centre of interest" and that the "slimnesses" of their heroines are "never suffered to be sole ministers of [the work's] appeal, but have their inadequacy eked out with comic relief and underplot, as the playwrights say, when not with murders and battles and the great mutations of the world" (11).

6. Identification has been more systematically theorized as a viewer experience within psychoanalytic film theory, especially in the work of feminist film theorists such as Laura Mulvey, Mary Ann Doane, and Kaja Silverman. Such work recognizes and builds on the spectacular immediacy of the experience of visual identification as well as the centrality of the visual in Freudian and Lacanian scenes of identification—the child's vision of the parents' genitals as representing what it has or lacks or of its own autonomy figured in the mirror. As I have already suggested above, however, identification is the subject and mainspring of verbal as well as visual narrative (including verbal narratives of visual scenes).

7. For the "mock reader," see Gibson; for the "narratee" see Prince; for the "implied reader," see Iser 27–38.

8. According to Ross Chambers, reading is "transactional" in the sense that it is produced by a relationship of exchange between reader and narrative: "in that it mediates *exchanges* that produce historical change, it is transactional, too, in that this functioning is in itself dependent on an initial *contract,* an understanding between the participants in the exchange as to the purposes served by the narrative function" (8). On the basis of this transaction, narrative is not hermetic but "has the power to change human situations" (7), and its study cannot only be formal or structural but "must open eventually onto ideological and cultural analysis of these enabling agreements" (9)—an obligation to which narratological theorists have increasingly acceded since these words were written in the early 1980s.

9. See also Schweickart: "Does the text control the reader, or vice versa? For David Bleich, Norman Holland, and Stanley Fish, the reader holds controlling interest. Readers read the poems they have made. . . . At the other pole are Michael Riffaterre, Georges Poulet, and Wolfgang Iser, who acknowledge the creative role of the reader, but ultimately take the text to be the dominant force. To read, from this point of view, is to create the text according to *its* own promptings" (36).

10. The passage of time, of course (perhaps this is what Rabinowitz means by "historical situation"), also separates audience members from each other and from the author's ability to have a "firm knowledge of the actual readers who will pick up his or her book." Rabinowitz later discusses temporal "problem[s] of recovery" (33–34).

11. Spivak writes of *Frankenstein:* "Within the allegory of our reading, the place of both the English lady [i.e., Margaret Saville, the narrative's internal addressee] and the unnamable monster are left open by this great flawed text. It is satisfying for a postcolonial reader to consider this a noble resolution for a nineteenth-century novel" (909).

Comparison between two iterations of a narrative may also, of course, privilege chronological priority, the original over the adaptation. See J. Sanders 32–41 for a discussion of adaptation, originality, and plagiarism in contemporary literature.

CHAPTER ONE

1. Many readers—most of them women, many of them writers—have written about their attachment to *Little Women* and particularly to Jo March. See, e.g., the essays in Alberghene and Clark. See also Sicherman 246–47, 256–64.

2. "Cathexis" refers to "the fact that a certain amount of psychical energy is attached to an idea or to a group of ideas, to a part of the body, to an object, etc." (LaPlanche and Pontalis 62). Schwartz's "psychical energy" is directed here both to the ideas for which *Little Women* stands (authorship) and to the object that embodies them (the book itself).

3. For a reading of a "pedagogic erotics" based on identification within *Little Women,* see Kent 43–59.

4. On eighteenth- and nineteenth-century women readers, see also Badia and Phegley.

5. See Heller 94–114 for a discussion of Hazlitt's emphasis on imagination, particularly imaginative identification with fictional and dramatic characters; and 43–45 for a discussion of Coleridge's view of the pedagogical value of imaginative literature and literary identification.

6. On connections between sympathy and melodramatic spectacle in nineteenth-century literature, see Jaffe. See Warhol for a recent analysis and defense of affective reading and film-viewing in the sentimental and melodramatic tradition.

7. For a complex analysis of the "countermovement of desire within Eliot's central characters that can be seen to divert them from any orientation to others at all, and to turn them irrevocably inward instead" (117)—that is, partly, the difficulty for those characters of achieving and maintaining sympathy—see Kucich ch. 2.

8. Ablow has a different reading of the ethical situation brought about by the pain of identification that accompanies sympathy, for both characters and readers, in *The Mill on the Floss.* She suggests that "Maggie's understanding [of Lucy's and Philip's pain] is made wholly unselfish by her consciousness of having caused it. This consequence is almost unbearably painful. Yet it is also deeply ethical" (88); similarly, Eliot's "willingness to accept responsibility for Maggie's fate constitutes the ethically valuable position, binding the novelist to both the character and the reader by bonds of remorse" (3).

9. The early twentieth century also saw the popularization in English aesthetics, through the writing of Vernon Lee, of the term "empathy," from the German "Einfühlung," to describe a reader's or viewer's affective investment in a work of art. Currently, "empathy" is a term used in a variety of contexts in philosophy and psychology; for an account of its uses, see Keen ch. 1.

10. On Freud's emphasis on oral incorporation and cannibalism as an expression of and figure for certain primary identifications, and later in Lacan, see Barzilai 115–21.

11. See Mitchell pt. 1 for a discussion of the distinction between drive-related and relational origins.

12. Brooks argues for the importance of "Freud's progressive discovery of the transference, which brings into play the dynamic interaction of the teller and listener of and to stories, the dialogic relation of narrative production and interpretation." This consider-

ation, Brooks suggests, "should . . . help us complicate, and refine, versions of narrative analysis that do not take account of the relations of tellers and listeners" (50). While transference, and the figure of the analyst, fall outside the scope of my reading, I share Brooks's emphasis on the "dialogic relation of narrative production and interpretation."

13. On Freud's disavowal of literary technique, see Fuss 4–5; and Jacobus 197–204.

14. Often Freud resolves such circularities by assigning their elements to hierarchical locations within a developmental narrative, so that, for example, a confusion between identification and object-choice is "primitive": "*At the very beginning,* in the individual's primitive oral phase, object-cathexis and identification are no doubt indistinguishable from each other" (*EI* 23). See Butler for an argument that the "dispositions" are effects of an unacknowledged prior social prohibition on homosexual desire (*Gender Trouble* 57–65).

15. For discussions, with differing emphases, of the ideologically normalizing tendency and logical instability of the classical opposition between identification and desire, see (in addition to Fuss, cited above) Butler, *Gender Trouble* 35–78 and *Bodies* 93–119 and 239–40; Sedgwick, *Tendencies* 73–103; Kent 7–15 and *passim.* See Sinfield for a taxonomy of the possible combinations produced by keeping in place the binarisms of male/female, gay/straight, and identification/desire while freeing them from any necessary relation to each other.

16. See Woolf, *Death of the Moth* 176–86. For a discussion of how Woolf herself is represented within the middlebrow "Great Books" culture of the mid-twentieth-century United States, see Silver 68–78.

17. Brantlinger locates the beginning of this cultural conflict between visual and written narrative earlier, in the first couple of decades of the twentieth century, when "the cinema . . . was just coming into its own. Cultural critics of various ideological persuasions lined up to prophesy that this new technology of entertainment . . . would mean the death of reading, of literacy, and of the wholesome book-culture of the past. The activity of novel-reading, which to many diagnosticians of cultural disease had seemed so dangerous to the mental health of the reading public from the 1700s down to [Virginia Woolf's famous date] 'December, 1910,' and sometimes beyond, now seemed benign and even healthful to those who looked upon movies as toxic. Exactly the same arguments would be repeated, of course, about television" (209–10).

18. Keen reviews contemporary psychological and neurosicentific research on empathy in ch. 1, and the limited empirical studies of empathy toward others as a result of reading in ch. 3.

19. This suspicion of the ideological functioning of identification is often part of a more general suspicion of the ideological function of fictional realism. In this analysis, in Harry Shaw's summary, "realist representation is said to be naively *transparent* and malignantly *totalistic*. . . . The realist attempt to represent the complexities of a given historical moment turns out to be simply an attempt to 'naturalize' that moment, to make its working seem part of nature, not culture, to deny that it is a product of contingent historical forces" (9; emphasis in original). Readerly identification with fictional characters, ratifying the representation and "reality" of their experience, enhances the "natural[ized]" representation and thus the denial of historical agency.

20. On Brecht's dramatic theory and his opposition to Lukaçs, see Eagleton 63–72. For examples of the mistrust of identification, see Brecht 91–99. Brecht is cited as the "first Marxist theorist" to focus on the "identification effect" (89) by Balibar and Macherey; for a similar analysis applying specifically to English realist fiction, see Gagnier, 163–73, also discussed below.

21. Williams's readings of the way this "negative identification" plays out for Victorian authors are nevertheless more sympathetic than condemning. See ch. 5, on industrial novels, and 175–79 on Gissing.

22. For the mixed nineteenth-century responses to *Daniel Deronda,* see Carroll 360–447.

CHAPTER TWO

1. See Barzilai ch. 2 for an overview of the argument of this essay.

2. The novel's displacement of moral significance was evident, and distressing, to many Victorian reviewers. "What does it all come to except that human life is inexplicable, and that women who feel this find the feeling painful?" wonders the *Saturday Review*'s reviewer uncomfortably (Carroll 117); Sir Edward Bulwer-Lytton finds that "this remarkable writer does not enough weigh what is Agreeable or Disagreeable" (Carroll 121); and the popular novelist Dinah Mulock Craik asks "What good [the novel] will do?—whether it will lighten any burdened heart, help any perplexed spirit, comfort the sorrowful, succour the tempted, or help bring back the erring into the way of peace . . . ?" (Carroll 156).

3. For an exhaustive account of Eliot's allusions to *Corinne,* see Moers ch. 9. For a reading of Corinne as "a feminist text engaged with issues of subjectivity as process" see Miller 165; for a reading of Corinne as "openly celebrat[ing] the value of European book culture," see Peterson 80. Peterson also analyzes representations of the "reader protagonist" (3) in some nineteenth-century English and French novels, including *The Mill on the Floss* and *Jane Eyre.* For her discussion of reading as a "process of identification [which] constitutes a fantasy process in which readers shape, change, and adapt the text, sometimes even rewrite it, until it can meet and deal with their wishes and fears so that their fantasies may ultimately be gratified," in both real-life readers and reader-protagonists, see 29–36.

4. For a reading of *The Mill on the Floss* as more straightforwardly a revenge fantasy on Maggie's behalf, see Moers 266–67.

5. Peterson notes that in her childhood reading of illustrated religious books such as *The History of the Devil,* "Maggie's tendency is to split herself in two and to identify with each of the main characters in the picture" (190).

6. For a discussion of the brother–sister relationship as a template for nineteenth-century representations of heterosexual relations, see V. Sanders, particularly 101–3 for *The Mill on the Floss.*

7. On their first occasion alone, Maggie takes Stephen's arm, as the narrator suggests that "there is something strangely winning to most women in that offer of a firm arm" (408). Later, the "winning" effect will be reversed, as a reverie on "the beauty of a woman's arm" (441) ends with Stephen "dart[ing] towards [Maggie's] arm, and shower[ing] kisses on it" (442). For discussions of the erotic significance of the arm in the novel, see Homans, "Maggie's Arm," particularly 175–77; and Ramel.

8. The full coincidence of novelistic with romantic closure in the nineteenth-century novel—a completely achieved "marriage plot"—is surprisingly rare in the nineteenth-century novel, and its incidence diminishes as the century advances. The subdued projected union of Lucy and Stephen in *The Mill on the Floss* anticipates, for example, the completely disenchanted return of Grace Melbury to her unfaithful husband, Fitzpiers, some thirty years later, at the end of Hardy's novel *The Woodlanders* (1887). In a more

comic mode of deflation, Margaret Oliphant's *Phoebe, Junior* (1876) concludes with its heroine rejecting the interesting suitor to whom she is romantically attracted in favor of a dull but respectable young man through whom she will be able to fulfill her political, rather than romantic, ambitions.

9. In addition to Maggie and Lucy and Romola and Tessa, variations of this pattern occur with Dinah Morris and Hetty Sorel in *Adam Bede* (1859); and with Dorothea Brooke and Rosamund Vincy in *Middlemarch* (1871–72). In *Adam Bede,* Dinah's renunciations (first of worldly ambition in her preaching, then of spiritual ambition when her sect bans women preachers) enable her to take over the elements of the marriage plot—Adam's love and a reproductive future—from Hetty, whose selfish desires bring her exile and death. In *Middlemarch,* Dorothea and Rosamond both survive and marry, but Dorothea's renunciations (of her inheritance from Casaubon and of her intellectual ambitions) earn her romantic love and authorial approval, while Rosamond becomes Lydgate's vampiric "basil plant" (680). Further, Eliot maintains a difference of physical, reflective of moral, scale between the monumentalized protagonist and her infantilized counterpart: Dinah "appears above the middle height for a woman" and is first presented preaching, whereas Hetty, churning butter, has "a beauty like that of kittens, or very small downy ducks making gentle rippling noises with their soft bills, or babies just beginning to toddle and to engage in conscious mischief" (*Adam Bede* 83); similarly, Romola is Titianesque beauty, with hair "of a reddish gold colour, enriched by an unbroken small ripple, such as may be seen in the sunset clouds on grandest autumnal evenings" (*Romola* 93), first seen engaged in reading to her father, while Tessa is introduced with emphasis on her "blue baby-eyes" and "baby face" as she offers milk and bread to Tito Melema (68, 69).

10. Showalter writes, in 1980, "In the 1970s, Eliot became the most difficult and controversial figure for feminist literary criticism, the focus of a troubled anger that testifies to her lively and enduring reputation and to the cycles of projection and rejection that have been part of her critical history" (299). See also Ablow 71*n*7 for references to feminist critical responses to Eliot.

11. McLaughlin offers a straightforwardly biographical reading of the novel; Homans (*Bearing the Word* ch. 6) analyzes, from a psychoanlaytic point of view, the connections among Eliot's representations of the brother-sister relationship in *The Mill on the Floss* and the "Brother and Sister" sonnet sequence, Eliot's reading of Wordsworth, and her own sense of literary authority; Carlisle, "Autobiography as Discourse," argues that "the further the novel moves from the facts of Eliot's life, the more genuinely it becomes autobiography" (179); and Peterson suggests that while "autobiographical in spirit" (182), *The Mill on the Floss* also draws inspiration in plot and character from the writing of George Sand.

12. For a discussion of Beauvoir's ambivalence, if not naiveté, on the question of representation, see Angelfors 66.

13. For the sake of clarity and to avoid collapsing the represented with the writing subject, I will refer to the author and the first-person narrator of *Memoirs of a Dutiful Daughter* as "Beauvoir," and her protagonist, the younger self whose story she tells, as "Simone."

14. On Beauvoir's identification with Eliot, see also Showalter 299–302. For an argument that Beauvoir's adult commitment to Existentialism retrospectively shapes her representation of her childhood, see Moi 26–30.

15. Beauvoir uses pseudonyms for some characters in *Memoirs of a Dutiful Daughter.* Zaza's family name, given by Beauvoir as "Mabille," is Lacoin.

16. On Beauvoir's repeated attempts to tell Zaza's story, see Angelfors 64–66 and Beauvoir, *Prime of Life* 121–23 and 269.

17. In fact Simone has several earlier, briefer introductions to the dark girl/blond rival plot, first when as a child she sees a film, *Le Roi de Camargue* (1921; dir. André Hugon), in which the hero is engaged to "a sweet blonde heroine, a simple peasant girl" whom he deserts for a "lovely dark gipsy" (*MDD* 53, 54), and later when, reading *Little Women,* she discovers "the news of Laurie's marriage to Jo's young sister, Amy, who was blonde, vain, and stupid. . . . The man I loved and by whom I thought I was loved had betrayed me for a little goose of a girl" (104–5).

18. On the complex ways in which this reference "act[s] as a break upon the engine of heterosexual romance" see Cohen 157–58.

19. On George Eliot's trajectory from anonymity to revelation of her identity to the creation of "George Eliot," see Bodenheimer ch. 5.

20. For an overview and discussion of Beauvoir's representations of lesbianism, see Simons. Melanie Hawthorne places Beauvoir's own same-sex attachments in the context of her pedagogical persona (*Contingent Loves* 55–83). For Beauvoir's own representations, see *Letters to Sartre;* for her categorical denial of engaging in lesbian relationships, see Schwarzer 112.

21. A. Hughes argues that Sartre replaces Zaza as "a partner in a mirror-relationship" who takes on the status of the phallic mother (129).

22. In Beauvoir's French, Zaza does not "seem" to gaze reproachfully at Simone, but simply does so: "elle me regardait avec reproche [she was looking at me reproachfully]" (503; my translation).

23. Beauvoir "published essays, organized and directed the Comité pour Djamila Boupacha, and was the co-author, with Halimi, of a book that sought to expose the young woman's torture while condemning the general brutalities of the colonial situation" (Caputi 120). See also Beauvoir and Halimi, introduction and app. A.

24. For a less sympathetic discussion of Beauvoir's relationship to a national and racial other, see Staedtler-Djédji, who concludes that "the descriptions of Simone de Beauvoir in *La Force des Choses I* reflect a certain resentment in the face of the reality of Africa, but also a total absence of intercultural communication" (215; my translation).

25. On the publication travails and history of *Nervous Conditions,* see Zwicker 3–8.

26. See S. Gallagher and Willey and Treiber for discussions of the novel's rapid absorption into pedagogical canons in the United States. For examples of criticism that combines feminist and postcolonialist emphases, see, e.g., Zwicker, Andrade, Willey, and Androne, all in Willey and Treiber; see also Young, ch. 4. See Mule; and Andrade for readings of *Nervous Conditions* as within the conventions of the Bildungsroman. See Primorac on Zimbabwean fiction and its contexts, esp. 104–17 for her reading of *Nervous Conditions.*

27. For an analysis of the balance of power in the literary field of metropole/center and imperialist/postcolonial configurations, see Pascale Casanova, *The World Republic of Letters,* trans. M. B. DeBevoise (Cambridge: Harvard UP 2004). For overviews of the development of postcolonial literature, see Elleke Boehmer, *Colonial and Postcolonial Literature: Migrant Metaphors,* 2nd ed. (New York: Oxford UP, 2005); and Bill Ashcroft, Gareth Griffiths, and Helen Tiffin, *The Empire Writes Back: Theory and Practice in Postcolonial Literatures,* 2nd ed. (New York: Routledge, 2002).

28. The Southern Rhodesia Literature Bureau was created in 1954 for the publication of literature in two languages, Shona and Ndebele. According to Simon Gikandi in the *Encyclopedia of African Literature,* "Predominantly mission-trained potential writers

attended Literature Bureau new and aspiring writers' workshops, where they learned the 'dos' and 'don'ts' of writing literature in the political context of colonialism. . . . The rules established at these workshops led to the crystallization of a literary tradition that most Zimbabwean writers have had to reckon with. In addition, the resultant literature grew under the watchful eyes of publications officers whose job was to ensure that writers did not publish politically subversive works" (Gikandi 495).

29. In *The Three Golliwogs,* for example, the eponymous blackface dolls are named Gollie, Wollie, and Nigger. Blyton remained mainstream well into the twentieth century. In one review of a study of Blyton, two contemporary literary scholars remember reading Blyton in Angola (then Portuguese West Africa) and Zimbabwe (then Rhodesia) (Olson 294–95); another remembers receiving a copy of *The Three Golliwogs* as "a presentation copy from an English Sunday School for perfect attendance" (Olson 296). I read Blyton's girls' school series in England in the 1970s.

30. A *New York Times* article from 1899 on "attar of roses" recalls the days of "the grandmothers, or possibly even the great-grandmothers," when "the slender little bottle of attar of roses flourished in all its glory," and explains that "Bulgaria is the chief country from which comes the attar . . . while a very considerable amount is also made in Germany" ("Story of Attar of Roses" 6).

CHAPTER THREE

1. See Barzilai 81–83 for a discussion of the differences between Winnicot and Lacan in regard to the concept of mirroring.

2. For a different account of the motive and effects of Gaskell's biography, see D'Albertis ch. 1.

3. Sharon Connor, in an essay on "loneness" in Brontë's letters, provides a succinct summary. In the period from 1829–1855 covered by Brontë's published letters, "There was a particular emphasis on the problem of so called 'excess women,' those half a million or more extra single women 'discovered' by the 1851 census, who were supposedly doomed never to marry. . . . Many articles and essays in the press during this period were asking questions such as 'What shall we do with our old maids?' and discussing the perceived problem of middle-class women who would never be able to find a husband" (91). Connor also discusses the letter to Nussey and distinguishes between "single" and "lonely" (94–95).

4. See also Berlant and Warner for a foundational argument about the destruction of intimacy, particularly queer intimacies, under the ideology of "heterormativity," in which "intimate life" becomes "the endlessly cited elsewhere of political public discourse, a promised haven that distracts citizens from the unequal conditions of their political and economic lives, consoles them for the damaged humanity of mass society, and shames them for any divergence between their lives and the intimate sphere that is alleged to be simple personhood" (553).

5. For an analysis of the distinction between Arnold's and Brontë's representations of isolation, see Gilbert and Gubar 401–2. They suggest that "While male poets like Arnold express their desire to experience an inner and more valid self, Brontë describes the pain of women who are restricted to just this private realm. Instead of seeking and celebrating the buried self, these women feel victimized by it; they long, instead, for actualization in the world" (402). See also Loeffelholz 97; and Jacobus 41.

6. On the normative direction of Shirley's conclusion, see Bodenheimer; and Gilbert and Gubar. See Wilt for arguments for a more radical interpretation of the novel's conclusion.

7. See, e.g., the review by G. H. Lewes of *Shirley* (Allott 160–70).

8. See also Ferguson, "Memory" 169 and Simmons 75 for a summary of Kincaid's references to *Jane Eyre.*

9. Kincaid's statement that "it said that it was truly an African novel" presumably refers to the novel's blurbs, since *Nervous Conditions* itself, as discussed in the previous chapter, makes copious reference to Tambu's own familiarity with English literature. Different printings of the novel sport different back and front covers and copy. One Seal Press edition (c. 1988, published 2002) has a blurb from *The African Times* that calls the novel "Another example of a bold new national literature . . . one which bears no mimicry of European forms and experience"; a later Seal Press edition (2004) does not include this blurb.

10. Oddly, Shockley considers Kincaid and her protagonist as "African American" subjects (see 46 and passim), although Kincaid and her protagonist are both, in fact, West Indian, raised under an English colonial regime, and come to the United States only as young adults. See Yost for another analysis of Lucy's relationship to Villette.

11. See *A Small Place* (1988), Kincaid's polemical account of the contemporary situation of Antigua, as a former colony largely dependent on a tourist economy.

12. See Viswanathan, particularly the Introduction, for an influential analysis of colonialist pedagogy as hegemonic, although one focused on India. For a discussion of the effects of colonialist pedagogy specifically on women, see Katrak ch. 3.

13. The mother-daughter relationships, and particularly the implication of the mother in the transmission of colonialist ideologies, in Kincaid's work have been frequently discussed by critics. On this relationship in Lucy, see Bouson ch. 4; and Ferguson, *Where the Land Meets the Body* 123–28.

14. Dangarembga plans to continue Tambu's narrative in a third volume; see Rooney 62.

15. On Kincaid as an angry writer, see Ferguson, Land 95–96. For examples of U.S. reviews of *A Small Place* that discuss Kincaid's anger, see Kakatuni, 16; and Nicholson, "The Exile's Bitter Return" x14.

CHAPTER FOUR

1. On the connection among closetedness, coming out, knowledge, and recognition, see Sedgwick, *Epistemology* 3–4 and 67–90.

2. The definitions are, respectively, *OED*, "queer," adj., def. 1a; def. 1, "Special Uses," "queer theory" (n.). Despite the homonymial, punning possibilities, "queer" and "query" do not, according to *OED*, share etymological roots.

3. For a thorough discussion of the "versioning" of Woolf as an iconic cultural figure of the female intellectual, see Silver.

4. See, for example, Gay. The S. Ellis introduction provides a useful summary of debates over Woolf's relationship to the Victorian period.

5. See "George Gissing" (*CE* 1: 297–301) and "Notes on D. H. Lawrence" (352–55).

6. Woolf's Modernist *oeuvre* canonically begins with *Jacob's Room* (1922), her third

novel. This emphasis can be justified by Woolf's own estimate of *Jacob's Room* as the work in which she "[has] found out how to begin (at 40) to say something in my own voice" (qtd. in Froula 63). But Woolf made a similar assertion earlier, while writing *The Voyage Out:* "I should say that my great change [in working on successive drafts of the novel] was in the way of courage, or conceit; and that I had given up adventuring after other people's forms" (qtd. in Froula 22).

7. On the readerly persona of Woolf's literary criticism, see also Dusinberre; Cuddy-Keane; and Caughie ch. 6.

8. For another analysis of Woolf's allusiveness, see Dusinberre.

9. Helen Ambrose explicitly rejects angelic domesticity in her mentorship of Rachel: "Nor did she encourage those habits of unselfishness and amiability founded upon insincerity which are put at so high a value in mixed households of men and women" (*VO* 137).

10. Although Potter's and Daldry's films and Cunningham's novel have all been received as queer texts, they have also all been controversial in that role. For a discussion of the reception of and an analysis of the representation of queer sexuality in *Orlando*, see Silver 225–34.

11. For a discussion of the internal and external pressures of Victorian sexual ideology on Woolf's representations of lesbian sexuality, see Cramer Introduction.

12. Moore, like De Salvo, reads *The Voyage Out* in terms of Woolf's imputed psychological state while writing it, as "the novel in which Woolf is least able to transform her own material, and Rachel Vinrace is her most unsuccessful creator figure" (82).

13. Moments in which Helen experiences or expresses contentment with her heterosexual role abound, often in contradistinction to the dissatisfaction of less adaptable characters. For example, St. John Hirst, represented as more actively dissatisfied with heterosexual norms (and particularly with women), remarks with some frustration as he watches Helen work at her embroidery:

> "You're absolutely happy". . . .
>
> "Yes?" Helen enquired, sticking in her needle.
>
> "Marriage, I suppose," said St. John.
>
> "Yes," said Helen, gently drawing her needle out.
>
> "Children?" St. John enquired.
>
> "Yes," said Helen, sticking her needle in again. "I don't know why I'm happy," she suddenly laughed, looking him full in the face. (*VO* 233)

While we can register Helen's elusiveness here—she is at once the Trojan seductress (Hirst calls her "the most beautiful woman I've ever seen") and Penelope, shielding her evasion of unwanted suitors behind her needlework—we have no reason to doubt her stated contentment. At the hotel dance, as well, she exhibits frank sensual pleasure—"She seemed to fade into Hewet, and they both dissolved in the crowd" (170). Helen is often elusive and not always admirable; but she is also often admired and sometimes even rudely direct. It seems to me precisely part of the "complex, multilayered style" to which Cramer refers that the reader cannot pin the narrative to any one attitude toward Helen Ambrose (or to Clarissa Dalloway or Mrs. Ramsay) nor fix Helen herself in any single attitude or identity—and this lack of fixity can itself be counted as *part of* Woolf's effort to "begin to describe my own sex" (*Diaries* 3: 3), rather than as an effect of the repression of such an effort. See Froula 38–56 for a consideration *inter alia* of Helen as a "wife, mother, friend (especially of men), and complaisant mentor" to Rachel (46). For a discussion of Helen as the "Great Mother" see Moore.

14. For another reading of queer silence in the novel, in this case surrounding the character of Miss Allen, see Hunn.

15. Hirst is conventionally read as based on Lytton Strachey; see, e.g., Lee 210 and 252–54. Lee describes *The Voyage Out* as "euphemistic but clear about St. John's homosexuality" (210), but I think the degree to which this meaning is "clear" might depend upon the reader.

16. Woolf sniffs, for example, that *Ulysses* (which the Hogarth Press declined to publish) exhibits "the conscious and calculated indecency of a desperate man who feels that in order to breathe he must break the windows. At moments, when the window is broken, he is magnificent. But what a waste of energy! And, after all, how dull indecency is, when it is not the overflowing of a super-abundant energy or savagery, but the determined and public-spirited act of a man who needs fresh air!" ("Character in Fiction" 434). On Woolf's desire to "[tell] the truth about [her] own experiences as a body and speak the truth about [her] passions" ("Professions" 240) see Cramer introduction, 118; on her resistance to polemic, again in the context of a writer (Lawrence) particularly concerned with sexuality, see Cuddy-Keane 33. For Woolf herself as a polemicist, see J. Marcus, *Art and Ardor* chs. 5 and 6.

17. Important for any comparison of Hall and Woolf is the strong argument made by Jane Marcus for Woolf's intertextual awareness of, inspiration by, and allusive inclusion of *The Well* in *A Room of One's Own* (J. Marcus, "Sapphistory" 164–79).

18. See Barnes 91–99 for her complete discussion of the operation of sympathetic identification in *Uncle Tom's Cabin.*

19. The conditions that, in the antebellum United States in the 1850s, made *Uncle Tom's Cabin* an electrifying public document—the union of a broadly popular genre (the sentimental novel), a mainstream religious form (Evangelical Protestantism), and a pressing public cause (abolitionism)—did not obtain in Edwardian and Georgian England. And Hall even before the publication of *The Well* was hardly as persuasive a public mouthpiece as Stowe. Her persona and history—daughter of parents who separated when she was young; wealthy; Catholic; more-or-less publicly partnered with a woman separated from her husband—connoted decadence rather than respectability.

20. The publication of a several biographies of Hall, including the most sympathetic and thorough, Sally Cline's *Radclyffe Hall: A Woman Called John,* makes it possible for interested readers to have those responses not only to Stephen but also to Hall herself, given her anti-Semitic and proto-fascist inclinations (see Cline 336–37 and 360–61) and the predatory and manipulative elements of her relationship, in her last years, with Evgenia Souline (see Cline pt. 5).

21. Sir Philip dies when a tree that he is cutting down falls on him (115), echoing D. H. Lawrence's strikingly homophobic novella "The Fox" (1923), in which a falling tree kills the more butch of two women, freeing her feminine partner to marry the man who wielded the axe. (On Hall's interest in Lawrence, see Cline 269–70.)

22. On technologies of sexuality, see Foucault, particularly 116–20. On the medicalization of lesbianism, see Chauncey; on the "construction of homosexuality" by sexology, see Weeks. For a summary of some assertions of the negative impact of sexology on women's same-sex interactions in particular, and also the possibilities for resistance, see Doan, "Sexology's Intervention" 199, 211.

23. Epstein, who cites Laqueur's account of the historical development of these forms (29–30), argues that "the case report . . . produces a context around groupings of symptoms and signs and findings and articulates these data into a narrative whose goal is to move toward explanation, therapy, and resolution" (75).

24. Storr discusses another case in *Psychopathia*—that of Ilma S.—in similar terms: "Even as Krafft-Ebing records his power over Ilma, he records her resistance too. The intensity of his treatment of her is, at least in part, a response to the intensity of her refusal [to be "cured"]. . . . Indeed all of the case histories in *Psychopathia Sexualis* reveal their subjects to be not just material, unruly or otherwise, for Krafft-Ebing's categories, but complex sites of negotiation" (23). Some of the case histories, however, reveal this complexity more clearly than others. I am not the first reader to take Sandor as the most appropriate object for Stephen's identification: see, e.g., Prosser 158; and O'Rourke 3. But against such certainty, see Storr: "Hall does not actually tell us which chapter Stephen is reading. Even that section of chapter 4 which pertains particularly to homosexuality or 'inversion' is full of diverse possibilities" (12).

25. The identification is particularly apt to the extent that Stephen can be understood to have taken the place of the brother whom she was supposed to be.

26. For a discussion of the biblical narrative of Ruth and Naomi in *Oranges Are Not the Only Fruit,* see Cosslett 16–20.

27. As Sally Munt notes with justified skepticism, "It is lesbian folklore that Radclyffe Hall's life with Una Troubridge"—one of the "two women" to whom Rule refers—"was a happy one. Perhaps we tell ourselves this in order to mitigate the pain of her fictional protagonist" (206). The more complex reality, including the inauspicious beginning of the relationship with Troubridge, while Hall was living with another woman, and the unhappy *ménage à trois* of their last years together, is detailed in Cline's sympathetic biography (91–126, 311–78) and in Souhami's startlingly hostile one (79–99, 288–416).

28. See Roof, particularly chap. 4, for another discussion of the "heteronarrative" domination of fictional conventions. The arguments of both Abraham and Roof have the effect of elevating historical (for Abraham) and experimental Modernist (for Abraham and Roof) narratives over those of the domestic novel tradition that Hall belongs to. For a defense of the romance plot in lesbian narrative, see Juhasz.

29. On relations between Woolf and Winterson see also Booth.

30. Artistic manifestos date as a writer's interests and practice change; however, the editorial content of Winterson's website, jeanettewinterson.com, remains consistent with the positions taken in *Art Objects.*

31. Winterson aligns herself with one of Matthew Arnold's ideological descendants, Harold Bloom, on the necessity of art (*AO* 5–6).

32. Winterson herself observes, "I can find little to cheer me between the publications of *Four Quartets* (1944) and Angela Carter's *The Magic Toyshop* (1967)" (*AO* 41; also cited by Pykett 60*n*12). This notable lacuna in her self-construction has not prevented critics from analyzing her as a postmodern author; see, e.g., Doan, "Jeanette Winterson's Sexing the Postmodern."

33. Thomas Hardy, *Jude the Obscure;* (1894–95); D. H. Lawrence, *Sons and Lovers* (1913) and *The Rainbow* (1915); Philip Larkin, *Jill* (1946); Frederic Raphael, *The Glittering Prizes* (1977).

34. Thanks to Elizabeth Young for pointing out the structural parallel between anagram and identification.

35. The train journey echoes Doris Lessing's short story "England vs. England," whose protagonist, the son of a Yorkshire miner, undergoes a brief nervous breakdown on a train back to Oxford from a visit home. Lessing's story in turn pays homage to D. H. Lawrence in its protagonist's background and its titular echo of Lawrence's collection of short stories, *England, My England* (1922). On connections between *Oranges* and Lawrence's fiction, see Onega 20–21; see *AO* 69–70 for Winterson on Lawrence.

36. See, however, Bailey for a discussion of the role of the fairytales in Jeanette's "narrative reconstruction" of her identity; Cosslett on Winterson's use of the Bible, Mallory, and *Jane Eyre;* and DeLong's Irigarayan analysis of Winterson's figure of Tetrahedron. See also Onega ch. 1.

37. See Woolf, *Roger Fry* 33.

WORKS CITED

Abel, Elizabeth, Marianne Hirsch, and Elizabeth Langland, eds. *The Voyage In: Fictions of Female Development.* Hanover, NH: UP of New England, 1983.

Ablow, Rachel. *The Marriage of Minds: Reading Sympathy in the Victorian Marriage Plot.* Stanford, CA: Stanford UP, 2007.

Abraham, Julie. *Are Girls Necessary? Lesbian Writing and Modern Histories.* New York: Routledge, 1996.

Alberghene, Janice, and Beverly Lyon Clark. *Little Women and the Feminist Imagination: Criticism, Controversy, Personal Essays.* New York: Garland, 1999.

Alcott, Louisa May. *Little Women.* Ed. and intro. Elaine Showalter. New York: Penguin, 1989.

Allegra, Donna. "Between the Sheets: My Sex Life in Literature." *Lesbian Erotics.* Ed Karla Jay. New York: New York UP, 1995. 71–81.

Allott, Miriam, ed. *The Brontes: The Critical Heritage.* New York: Routledge, 1995.

Althusser, Louis. "Ideology and Ideological State Apparatuses (Notes toward an Investigation)." *Lenin and Philosophy, and Other Essays.* Trans. Ben Brewster. New York: Monthly Review Press, 1972. 127–86.

Andrade, Susan. "Tradition, Modernity, and the Family as Nation: Reading the Chimurenga Struggle into and out of *Nervous Conditions.*" Willey and Treiber. 25–59.

Androne, Mary Jane. "Tsitsi Dangarembga's *Nervous Conditions:* An African Woman's Revisionist Narrative." Willey and Treiber. 271–80.

Angelfors, Christina. "Memoires d'une jeune fille rangée: Autobiographie ou fiction?" *Simone de Beauvoir Studies* 14 (1998–1999): 64–71.

Appiah, K. Anthony. "Cosmopolitan Reading." *Cosmopolitan Geographies: New Locations in Literature and Culture.* Ed. Vinay Dharwadker. New York: Routledge, 2001. 197–227.

———. Introduction. *Nervous Conditions.* By Tsitsi Dangarembga. Emeryville, CA: Seal Press, 2004.

Armstrong, Nancy. *Desire and Domestic Fiction: A Political History of the Novel.* New York: Oxford UP, 1987.

Austen, Jane. *Pride and Prejudice.* Ed. James Kinsley. New York: Oxford UP, 1998.

Badia, Janet, and Jennifer Phegley, eds. *Reading Women: Literary Figures and Cultural Icons from the Victorian Age to the Present.* Toronto: U of Toronto P, 2005.

Badowska, Eva. "Genius Loci: The 'Place' of Identification in Psychoanalysis." *Psychoanalytic Review* 95.6 (December 2008): 947–72.

Bailey, Peggy Dunn. "Writing 'Herstory': Narrative Reconstruction in Jeanette Winterson's *Oranges Are Not the Only Fruit.*" *Philological Review* 32.2 (Fall 2006): 61–78.

Bakhtin, M. M. *The Dialogic Imagination: Four Essays.* Ed. Michael Holquist. Trans. Caryl Emerson and Michael Holquist. Austin: U of Texas P, 1981.

Balibar, Etienne, and Pierre Macherey. "On Literature as an Ideological Form." *Untying the Text: A Post-Structuralist Reader.* Ed. and intro. Robert Young. Boston: Routledge and Kegan Paul, 1981. 79–99.

Barnes, Elizabeth. *States of Sympathy: Seduction and Democracy in the American Novel.* New York: Columbia UP, 1997.

Barrett, Eileen, and Patricia Cramer, eds. *Virginia Woolf: Lesbian Readings.* New York: New York UP, 1997.

Barzilai, Shuli. *Lacan and the Matter of Origins.* Stanford, CA: Stanford UP, 1999.

Beauvoir, Simone de. *All Said and Done, 1962–1972.* Trans. Patrick O'Brian. Intro. Toril Moi. 1974. New York: Paragon House, 1993.

———. *Force of Circumstance.* Trans. Richard Howard. 2 vols. New York: Putnam, 1965.

———. *Letters to Sartre.* Trans. and ed. Quintin Hoare. New York: Arcade, 1992.

———. *Memoires d'une jeune fille rangée.* Paris: Editions Gallimard, 1958.

———. *Memoirs of a Dutiful Daughter.* Trans. James Kirkup. New York: Harper and Row, 1959.

———. *The Prime of Life.* Trans. Peter Green. New York: Lancer Books, 1960.

———. *The Second Sex.* Trans. and ed. H. M. Parshley. New York: Vintage, 1974.

Beauvoir, Simone de, and Gisèle Halimi. *Djamila Boupacha: The Story of the Torture of a Young Algerian Girl Which Shocked Liberal French Opinion.* Trans. Peter Green. London: Andre Deutsch; Weidenfeld and Nicholson, 1962.

Beer, Gillian. *Virginia Woolf: The Common Ground.* Ann Arbor: U of Michigan P, 1996.

Berlant, Lauren, and Michael Warner. "Sex in Public." *Critical Inquiry* 24.2 (Winter 1998): 547–66.

Bernstein, Susan. "Promiscuous Reading: The Problem of Identification and Anne Frank's Diary." *Witnessing the Disaster: Essays on Representation and the Holocaust.* Ed. Michael Bernard-Donals and Richard Glejzer. Madison: U of Wisconsin P, 2003. 141–61.

Birbalsingh, Frank, ed. *Frontiers of Caribbean Literature in English.* New York: St. Martin's Press, 1996.

Bland, Lucy. "Trial by Sexology?: Maud Allan, *Salome,* and the 'Cult of the Clitoris' Case." Bland and Doan 183–98.

Bland, Lucy, and Laura Doan, eds. *Sexology in Culture: Labelling Bodies and Desires.* Chicago: U of Chicago P, 1998.

Bodenheimer, Rosemarie. *The Real Life of Mary Ann Evans: George Eliot, Her Letters and Fiction.* Ithaca, NY: Cornell UP, 1994.

Boes, Tobias. Introduction to "On the Nature of the *Bildungsroman.*" *PMLA* 142.2 (March 2009): 647–49.

Booth, Alison. "The Scent of a Narrative: Rank Discourse in *Flush* and *Written on the Body*." *Narrative* 8, 1 (2000): 3–22.

Borch-Jacobsen, Mikkel. *The Freudian Subject*. Trans. Catherine Porter. Stanford, CA: Stanford UP, 1988.

Bouson, J. Brooks. *Jamaica Kincaid: Writing Memory, Writing Back to the Mother*. Albany: SUNY Press, 2005.

Brantlinger, Patrick. *The Reading Lesson: The Threat of Mass Literacy in Nineteenth Century British Fiction*. Bloomington: Indiana UP, 1998.

Brecht, Bertolt. "Alienation Effects in Chinese Acting." *Brecht on Theater: The Development of an Aesthetic*. Ed. and trans. John Willett. New York: Hill and Wang, 1964.

Brontë, Charlotte. *Jane Eyre*. Ed. and intro. Margaret Smith. Oxford: Oxford UP, 1993.

———. *Selected Letters of Charlotte Brontë*. Ed. Margaret Smith. Oxford: Oxford UP, 2007.

———. *Shirley*. Ed. Andrew Hook and Judith Hook. New York: Penguin, 1974.

———. *Villette*. Ed. Margaret Smith and Herbert Rosengarten. Intro. Margaret Smith. New York: Oxford UP, 1984.

Brontë, Emily. *Wuthering Heights*. Ed. Ian Jack. Intro Patsy Stoneman. New York: Oxford, 1995

Brooks, Peter. *Psychoanalysis and Storytelling*. Cambridge, MA: Blackwell, 1994.

Butler, Judith. *Bodies That Matter: On the Discursive Limits of "Sex."* New York: Routledge, 1993.

———. *Gender Trouble: Feminism and the Subversion of Identity*. New York: Routledge, 1990.

Caputi, Mary. "Beauvoir and the Case of Djamila Boupacha." Marso and Moynagh. 109–126.

Carlisle, Janice. "The Mirror in *The Mill on the Floss:* Toward a Reading of Autobiography as Discourse." *Studies in the Literary Imagination* 23.2 (Fall 1990): 177–96.

———. *The Sense of an Audience: Dickens, Thackeray, and George Eliot at Mid-Century*. Athens, GA: University of Georgia Press, 1981.

Carroll, David, ed. *George Eliot: The Critical Heritage*. New York: Barnes and Noble, 1971.

Castle, Geoffrey. *Reading the Modernist Bildungsroman*. Gainesville: UP of Florida, 2006.

Castle, Terry. *The Apparitional Lesbian: Female Homosexuality and Modern Culture*. New York: Columbia UP, 1993.

Caughie, Pamela. *Virginia Woolf and Postmodernism: Literature in Quest and Question of Itself*. Urbana: U of Illinois P, 1991.

Chambers, Ross. *Story and Situation: Narrative Seduction and the Power of Fiction*. Minneapolis: U of Minnesota P, 1984.

Chauncey, George Jr. "From Sexual Inversion to Homosexuality: Medicine and the Changing Conception of Female Deviance." *Salmagundi* 58–59 (Fall 1982–Winter 1983): 114–46.

Cheng, Anne Anlin. *The Melancholy of Race*. Oxford: Oxford UP, 2001

Clark-Beattie, Rosemary. "Fables of Rebellion: Anti-Catholicism and the Structure of *Villette*." *ELH* 53.4 (Winter 1986): 821–47.

Cline, Sally. *A Woman Called John*. Woodstock, NY: Overlook Press, 1998.

Cobb, Michael. "Lonely." *South Atlantic Quarterly* 106.3 (Summer 2007): 445–57.

Cohen, William A. *Sex Scandal: The Private Parts of Victorian Fiction*. Durham, NC: Duke UP, 1996.

Connor, Sharon. "'Loneness' in the Letters of Charlotte Brontë." *Brontë Studies* 33 (July 2008): 91–96.

Cosslett, Tess. *Woman to Woman: Female Friendship in Victorian Fiction*. Atlantic Highlands, NJ: Humanities Press International, 1988.

Cramer, Patricia. Introduction. Barrett and Cramer. 3–9.

Cuddy-Keane, Melba. *Virginia Woolf, the Intellectual, and the Public Sphere*. New York: Cambridge UP, 2003.

Dangarembga, Tsitsi. *The Book of Not*. Oxford: Ayebia Clarke, 2006.

———. *Nervous Conditions*. 1988. Emeryville, CA: Seal Press, 2004.

Daugherty, Beth Riegel. "'You see you kind of belong to us, and what you do matters enormously': Letters from Readers to Virginia Woolf." 137 letters transcribed and annotated by Beth Riegel Daugherty. *Woolf Studies Annual* 12 (2006).

Dean, Tim. *Unlimited Intimacy: Reflections on the Subculture of Barebacking*. Chicago: U of Chicago P, 2009.

DeLong, Anne. "The Cat's Cradle: Multiple Discursive Threads in Jeanette Winterson's *Oranges Are Not the Only Fruit*." *Lit: Literature Interpretation Theory* 17.3–4 (2006): 263–75.

DeSalvo, Louise, ed. *Melymbrosia: an Early Version of the Voyage Out*. New York: New York Public Library, 1982.

Dickens, Charles. *David Copperfield*. Ed. Jeremy Tambling. New York: Penguin, 1997.

———. *Great Expectations*. Ed. Charlotte Mitchell, intro David Trotter. New York: Penguin, 2003.

Doan, Laura. "'Acts of Female Indecency': Sexology's Intervention in Legislating Lesbianism." Bland and Doan 199–213.

———. "Jeanette Winterson's Sexing the Postmodern." *The Lesbian Postmodern*. Ed. Laura Doan. New York: Columbia UP. 137–55.

Doan, Laura, and Jay Prosser, ed. *Palatable Poison: Critical Perspectives on the Well of Loneliness*. New York: Columbia UP, 2001.

DuPlessis, Rachel Blau. *Writing beyond the Ending: Narrative Strategies of Twentieth-Century Women Writers*. Bloomington: Indiana UP, 1985.

Dusinberre, Juliet. *Virgina Woolf's Renaissance: Woman Reader or Common Reader?* Iowa City: U of Iowa P, 1997

Eagleton, Terry. *Literary Theory: An Introduction*. 2nd ed. Minneapolis: U of Minnesota P, 1996.

Eliot, George. *Adam Bede*. Ed. and Intro. Valentine Cunningham. New York: Oxford U P, 1996.

———. *Middlemarch*. Ed. and intro. David Carroll. New York: Oxford UP, 1986.

———. *The Mill on the Floss*. Ed. Gordon S. Haight. New York: Oxford UP, 1998.

———. *Romola*. Ed. and Intro. Andrew Sanders. New York: Penguin, 1980.

———. *Selected Essays, Poems, and Other Writings*. Ed. A. S. Byatt and Nicholas Warren. New York: Penguin, 1990.

Ellis, Lorna. *Appearing to Diminish: Female Development and the British Bildungsroman, 1750–1850*. Cranbury, NJ: Associated UP, 1999.

Ellis, Steve. *Virginia Woolf and the Victorians*. New York: Cambridge UP, 2007.

Epstein, Julia. *Altered Conditions: Disease, Medicine, and Storytelling*. New York: Routledge, 1995.

Evans, Dylan. *An Introductory Dictionary of Lacanian Psychoanalysis*. New York: Routledge, 1996.

Fallaize, Elizabeth. Introduction. *Simone de Beauvoir: A Critical Reader.* Ed. Elizabeth Fallaize. New York: Routledge, 1998. 1–12.

Fanon, Frantz. *Black Skin, White Masks.* Trans. Charles Lamm Markmann. New York: Grove Weidenfeld, 1991.

Ferguson, Moira. *Jamaica Kincaid: Where the Land Meets the Body.* Charlottesville: UP of Virginia, 1994.

———. "A Lot of Memory: An Interview with Jamaica Kincaid." *Kenyon Review* 16.1 (Winter 1994): 163–88.

Flint, Kate. *The Woman Reader, 1837–1914.* New York: Oxford UP, 1993.

Flynn, Elizabeth, and Patrocinio Schweickart, eds. *Gender and Reading: Essays on Readers, Texts, and Contexts.* Baltimore: Johns Hopkins UP, 1986.

Foucault, Michel. *The History of Sexuality: An Introduction.* Vol. 1. Trans. Robert Hurley. New York: Vintage Books, 1990.

Fraiman, Susan. *Unbecoming Women: British Women Writers and the Novel of Development.* New York: Columbia UP, 1993

Freud, Sigmund. "Creative Writers and Daydreaming." *On Freud's "Creative Writers and Day-Dreaming."* Ed. Ethel Spector Person et al. New Haven, CT: Yale UP, 1995.

———. *Dora: An Analysis of a Case of Hysteria.* Ed. and intro Philip Rieff. New York: Collier, 1963.

———. *The Ego and the Id.* 1923. Trans. and ed. James Strachey. New York: W. W. Norton, 1960.

———. *Group Psychology and the Analysis of the Ego.* 1921. *The Standard Edition of the Complete Psychological Works of Sigmund Freud.* Trans. and ed. James Strachey. Vol. 18. New York: Liveright, 1967. 65–143.

———. "The Psychogenesis of a Case of Homosexuality in a Woman." Trans. Barbara Low and R. Gabler. *Sexuality and the Psychology of Love.* Ed. and intro. Philip Rieff. New York: Collier, 1963. 153–54.

Friedman, Susan Stanford. "Spatialization, Narrative Theory, and Virginia Woolf's *The Voyage Out.*" Kathy Mezei, ed. *Ambiguous Discourse: Feminist Narratology and British Women Writers.* Chapel Hill: U of North Carolina P, 1996.

———. "Virginia Woolf's Pedagogical Scenes of Reading: *The Voyage Out, The Common Reader,* and Her "'Common Readers.'" *Modern Fiction Studies* 38.1 (Spring 1992): 101–25.

Froula, Christine. *Virginia Woolf and the Bloomsbury Avant-Garde: War, Civilization, Modernity.* New York: Columbia UP, 2005

Fuderer, Laura Sue. *The Female Bildungsroman in English: An Annotated Bibliography of Criticism.* New York: MLA, 1990.

Fuss, Diana. *Identification Papers.* New York: Routledge, 1995.

Gagnier, Regenia. *Subjectivities: A History of Self-Representation in Britain, 1832–1920.* New York: Oxford University Press, 1991.

Gallagher, Catherine. "George Eliot: Immanent Victorian." *Representations* 90 (Spring 2005): 61–74.

———. *Nobody's Story: The Vanishing Acts of Women Writers in the Marketplace, 1670–1820.* Berkeley: U of California P, 1994.

Gallagher, Susan Van Zanten. "Contingencies and Intersections: The Formation of Pedagogical Canons." *Pedagogy: Critical Approaches to Teaching Literature, Language, Composition, and Culture* 1.1 (Winter 2001): 53–67.

Garner, Dwight. Interview with Jamaica Kincaid. *Salon.com.* 8 November 1995.

Gay, Jane de. *Virginia Woolf's Novels and the Literary Past.* Edinburgh: Edinburgh UP, 2006.

George, Rosemary Marangoly, and Helen Scott. "An Interview with Tsitsi Dangarembga." *Novel* (Spring 1993): 309–19.

Gibson, Walker. "Authors, Speakers, Readers, and Mock Readers." Tompkins 1–6.

Gikandi, Simon, ed. *Encyclopedia of African Literature.* New York: Routledge, 2003.

Gilbert, Sandra. "*Jane Eyre* and the Secrets of Furious Lovemaking." *Novel: A Forum on Fiction* 31.3 (Summer 1998). 351-372

Gilbert, Sandra, and Susan Gubar. *The Madwoman in the Attic: The Woman Writer and the Nineteenth-Century Literary Imagination.* New Haven, CT: Yale UP, 1979.

Gilroy, Paul. *Postcolonial Melancholia.* New York: Columbia UP, 2005.

Gordon, Lyndall. *Charlotte Brontë: A Passionate Life.* New York: Norton, 1994.

Gray, Beryl. "'Animated Nature': *The Mill on the Floss.*" *George Eliot and Europe.* Ed. John Rignall. Aldershot, England: Scolar, 1997. 138–55.

Grosz, Elizabeth. "The Hetero and the Homo: The Sexual Ethics of Luce Irigaray." *Engaging with Irigaray: Feminist Philosophy and Modern European Thought.* Ed. Carolyn Burke, Naomi Schor, and Margaret Whitford. New York: Columbia UP, 2004. 335–50.

Hager, Kelly. *Dickens and the Rise of Divorce: The Failed-Marriage Plot and the Novel Tradition.* Burlington, VT: Ashgate, 2010.

Haight, Gordon. *George Eliot: A Biography.* 1968. New York: Penguin, 1985.

Halberstam, Judith. *In a Queer Time and Place: Transgender Bodies, Subcultural Lives.* New York: New York UP, 2005.

———."The Politics of Negativity in Recent Queer Theory." *PMLA* 121.3 (May 2006): 823–25.

Hardy, Thomas. *Tess of the D'Urbervilles.* Ed. Tim Dolin. New York: Penguin, 1998.

Hawthorne, Melanie. "Leçon de Philo/Lesson in Love: Simone de Beauvoir's Intellectual Passion and the Mobilization of Desire." Melanie C. Hawthorne, ed. and intro., *Contingent Loves: Simone de Beauvoir and Sexuality.* Charlotte: U of Virginia P, 2000. 55–83.

Hazlitt, William. "On the English Novelists." *The Complete Works of William Hazlitt in Twenty-One Volumes.* Ed. P. P. Howe. London: J. M. Dent, 1930–34. 21 vols. Vol. 6: 106–32.

Heller, Janet. *Coleridge, Lamb, Hazlitt, and the Reader of Drama.* Columbia: U of Missouri P, 1990.

Hirsch, Marianne. "The Novel of Formation as Genre: Between Great Expectations and Lost Illusions." *Genre* 12 (Fall 1979): 293–311.

Holcomb, Gary. "Travels of a Transnational Slut: Sexual Migration in Kincaid's *Lucy.*" *Critique* 44.3 (Spring 2003): 295–312.

Homans, Margaret. *Bearing the Word: Language and Female Experience in Nineteenth-Century Women's Writing.* Chicago: U of Chicago P, 1986.

———. "Dinah's Blush, Maggie's Arm: Class, Gender, and Sexuality in George Eliot's Early Novels." *Victorian Studies* 36.2 (Winter 1993): 155–78.

Hughes, Alex. "Murdering the Mother in *Memoirs of a Dutiful Daughter.*" *Simone de Beauvoir: A Critical Reader.* Ed. Elizabeth Fallaize. New York: Routledge, 1998. 120–31.

Hughes, John. "The Affective World of Charlotte Brontë's *Villette.*" *SEL* 40.4 (Autumn 2000): 711–26.

Hunn, Deborah. "'This Curious Silent Unrepresented Life': Representation and Lesbian Sexuality in Woolf's *The Voyage Out.*" *LiNQ* 20.2 (1993): 53–67.

Iser, Wolfgang. *The Act of Reading: A Theory of Aesthetic Response.* Baltimore: Johns Hopkins UP, 1978.

Jacobus, Mary. "The Buried Letter: *Villette.*" *Reading Woman: Essays in Feminist Criticism.* New York: Columbia UP, 1986.

Jaffe, Audrey. *Scenes of Sympathy: Identity and Representation in Victorian Fiction.* Ithaca, NY: Cornell UP, 2000.

James, Henry. *The Portrait of a Lady.* Ed. and intro. Nicola Bradbury. New York: Oxford UP, 1995.

Juhasz, Suzanne. "Lesbian Romance Fiction and the Plotting of Desire: Narrative Theory, Lesbian Identity, and Reading Practice." *Tulsa Studies in Women's Literature* 17.1 (Spring 1998): 65–82.

Kakatuni, Michiko. "Portrait of Antigua, Warts and All." *New York Times,* 16 July 1988: 16.

Katrak, Ketu. *Politics of the Female Body: Postcolonial Women Writers of the Third World.* New Brunswick, NJ: Rutgers UP, 2006.

Keen, Suzanne. *Empathy and the Novel.* New York: Oxford UP, 2007.

Kennedy, Rosanne. "Mortgaged Futures: Trauma, Subjectivity, and the Legacies of Colonialism in Tsitsi Dangarembga's *The Book of Not.*" *Studies in the Novel* 40, 1 and 2 (Spring and Summer 2008). 86–107.

Kent, Kathryn. *Making Girls into Women: American Women's Writing and the Rise of Lesbian Identity.* Durham, NC: Duke UP, 2003.

Kincaid, Jamaica. *Annie John.* New York: Penguin (Plume/NAL), 1983.

———. *Lucy.* New York: Plume/Penguin, 1990.

———. *A Small Place.* New York: Penguin, 1988.

Klein, Melanie. "Love, Guilt, and Reparation." 1937. *The Writings of Melanie Klein.* Vol. 1. Intro R. E. Money-Kyrle. New York: Free Press, 1975. 306–43.

Krafft-Ebing, R. von. *Psychopathia Sexualis: A Medico-Forensic Study.* Intro. Ernest van den Haag. Trans. Harry E.Wedeck. 1st unexpurgated English ed. NewYork: Putnam, 1965.

Kucich, John. *Repression in Victorian Fiction: Charlotte Brontë, George Eliot, and Charles Dickens.* Berkeley: U of California P, 1987.

Lacan, Jacques. *Les complexes familiaux dans la formation de l'individu: Essai d'analyse d'une fonction en psychologie.* Navarin, 1984.

———. "The Mirror Stage as Formative of the *I* Function as Revealed in Psychoanalytic Experience." *Ecrits: A Selection.* Trans. Bruce Fink. New York: Norton, 2002. 1–9.

Lane, Christopher. "Charlotte Brontë on the Pleasure of Hating." *ELH* 69 (2002): 199–222.

Lanser, Susan. *Fictions of Authority: Women Writers and Narrative Voice.* Ithaca, NY: Cornell UP, 1992.

LaPlanche, J., and J.-B. Pontalis. "Identification." *The Language of Psycho-analysis.* Trans. Donald Nicholson-Smith. French ed., 1967. New York: Norton, 1973. 205–9.

Laqueur, Thomas W. "Bodies, Details, and the Humanitarian Narrative." *The New Cultural History.* Ed. Lynn Hunt. Berkeley: U of California P, 1989: 176–204.

Lawrence, D. H. *Sons and Lovers.* Ed. and intro. Helen Baron and Carl Baron. New York: Penguin, 1992.

Layton, Lynne. *Who's That Girl? Who's That Boy? Clinical Practice Meets Postmodern Gender Theory.* 2nd expanded ed. New York: Routledge, 2004.

Lee, Hermione. *Virginia Woolf.* New York: A. A. Knopf, 1997.

Lilienfeld, Jane. "'The Gift of a China Ink-Pot': Violet Dickinson, Virginia Woolf, Elizabeth Gaskell, Charlotte Brontë, and the Love of Women in Writing." Barrett and Cramer 37–56.

Loeffelholz, Mary. *Dickinson and the Boundaries of Feminist Theory.* Chicago: U of Illinois P, 1991.

Love, Heather. *Feeling Backward: Loss and the Politics of Queer History.* Cambridge, MA: Harvard UP, 2007.

———. "Modernism at Night." Introduction to Cluster on Queer Modernism. *PMLA* 124,3 (May 2009). 744–48

———. "'Spoiled Identity': Stephen Gordon's Loneliness and the Difficulties of Queer History." *GLQ* 7.4 (2001): 487–519.

Marcus, Jane. *Art and Ardor: Reading Like a Woman.* Columbus: Ohio State UP, 1988.

———. "Thinking Back Through Our Mothers." Marcus, Jane, ed. *New Feminist Essays on Virginia Woolf.* Lincoln: U of Nebraska P, 1981. 1–30.

———. "Sapphistory: The Woolf and the Well." *Lesbian Texts and Contexts: Radical Revisions.* Ed. Karla Jay and Joanne Glasgow. New York: New York UP, 1990. 164–79. Rpt., in abridged form, from *Virginia Woolf and the Languages of Patriarchy.* Bloomington: Indiana UP, 1987.

Marcus, Sharon. "Anne Frank and Hannah Arendt, Universalism and Pathos." *Cosmopolitan Geographies: New Locations in Literature and Culture.* Ed. Vinay Dharwadker. New York: Routledge, 2001. 89–131.

———. *Between Women: Friendship, Desire, and Marriage in Victorian England.* Princeton, NJ: Princeton University Press, 2007.

Marso, Lori Jo, and Patricia Moynagh, eds. *Simone de Beauvoir's Political Thinking.* Urbana: U of Illinois P, 2006.

McCaw, Neil. *George Eliot and Victorian Historiography: Imagining the National Past.* New York: St. Martin's Press, 2000.

McLaughlin, Juliet. "*The Mill on the Floss:* Fiction or Autobiography?" *Cahiers victoriens et édouardiens* 25 (1988): 127–39.

McNaron, Toni. "A Lesbian Reading Virginia Woolf." In Barrett and Cramer, eds. 10–20.

Miller, Nancy K. *Subject to Change: Reading Feminist Writing.* New York: Columbia UP, 1988.

Millett, Kate. *Sexual Politics.* New York: Avon, 1969.

Mitchell, Stephen. *Relational Concepts in Psychoanalysis: An Integration.* Cambridge, MA: Harvard UP, 1988.

Moers, Ellen. *Literary Women.* New York: Anchor, 1977.

Moi, Toril. *Simone de Beauvoir: The Making of an Intellectual Woman.* New York: Blackwell, 1994.

Moore, Madeline. "Some Female Versions of the Pastoral: *The Voyage Out* and Matriarchal Mythologies." *New Feminist Essays on Virginia Woolf.* Ed. Jane Marcus. Lindoln, NE: U of Nebraska P, 1981. 82–104.

Moretti, Franco. *The Way of the World: The Bildungsroman in European Culture.* London: Verso, 1987.

Morrison, Jago. "'Who Cares about Gender at a Time Like This?' Love, Sex and the Problem of Jeanette Winterson." *Journal of Gender Studies* 15.2 (July 2006): 169–80.

Mule, Katwiwa. "Blurred Genres, Blended Memories: Engendering Dissidence in Nawal el Saadawi's *Memoirs of a Woman Doctor* and Tsitsi Dangarembga's *Nervous Conditions.*" *Meridians: feminism, race, transnationalism* 6, 2 (2006): 93–116.

Muñoz, José. *Disidentifications: Queers of Color and the Performance of Politics.* Minneapolis: U of Minnesota P, 1999.

Munt, Sally. "The Well of Shame." Doan and Prosser 199-215.

Nicholson, David. "The Exile's Bitter Return." *Washington Post,* 3 July 1988: x14.

Olson, Marilyn. Rev. of *Enid Blyton and the Mystery of Children's Literature,* by David Rudd. *The Lion and the Unicorn* 27.2 (April 2003): 293–97.

Onega, Susana. *Jeanette Winterson.* Manchester: Manchester UP, 2006.

O'Rourke, Rebecca. *Reflecting on the Well of Loneliness.* New York: Routledge, 1989.

Peterson, Carla L. *The Determined Reader: Gender and Culture from Napoleon to Victoria.* New Brunswick, NJ: Rutgers UP, 1987.

Phelan, James. "Present Tense Narration, Mimesis, the Narrative Norm, and the Positioning of the Reader in *Waiting for the Barbarians.*" *Understanding Narrative.* Ed. James Phelan and Peter Rabinowitz. Columbus: Ohio State UP, 1994. 222–45.

Portuges, Catherine. "Attachment and Separation in *Memoirs of a Dutiful Daughter.*" *Yale French Studies* 72 (1986): 107–18.

Primorac, Ranka. *The Place of Tears: The Novel and Politics in Modern Zimbabwe.* London: Tauris, 2006.

Prince, Gerald. "Introduction to the Study of the Narratee." Tompkins 7–25.

Prosser, Jay. *Second Skins: The Body Narratives of Transsexuality.* New York: Columbia UP, 1998.

Pykett, Lyn. "A New Way with Words? Jeanette Winterson's Postmodernism." *"I'm Telling You Stories": Jeanette Winterson and the Politics of Reading.* Ed. Helena Grice and Tim Woods. Amsterdam: Rodopi, 1998. 53–60.

Rabinowitz, Peter. *Before Reading: Narrative Conventions and the Politics of Interpretation.* Ithaca, NY: Cornell UP, 1987.

Radway, Janice. *Reading the Romance: Women, Patriarchy, and Popular Culture.* Rev. ed. U of North Carolina P, 1991.

Ramel, Annie. "Bras, ravages, et barrages dans *The Mill on the Floss.*" *Cahiers victoriens et édouardiens* 59.25 (2004): 307–21.

Rigby, Elizabeth. "*Vanity Fair*—and *Jane Eyre.*" *Quarterly Review* 84.167 (December 1848): 153–85.

Roof, Judith. *Come as You Are: Sexuality and Narrative.* New York: Columbia UP, 1996.

Rooney, Caroline. "Interview with Tsitsi Dangarembga." *Wasafiri: The Transnational Journal of International Writing* 51 (Summer 2007): 57–62.

Ruehl, Sonja. "Inverts and Experts: Radclyffe Hall and the Lesbian Identity." *Feminist Criticism and Social Change: Sex, Class, and Race in Literature.* Ed. Judith Newton and Deborah Rosenfelt. New York: Methuen, 1985. 165–80.

Sanders, Julie. *Adaptation and Appropriation.* New York: Routledge, 2006.

Sanders, Valerie. *The Brother-Sister Culture in Nineteenth-Century Literature from Austen to Woolf.* New York: Palgrave, 2002.

Schlack, Beverly. *Continuing Presences: Virginia Woolf's Use of Literary Allusion.* University Park: Pennsylvania State UP, 1979.

Schwartz, Lynne Sharon. *Leaving Brooklyn.* Boston: Houghton Mifflin, 1989.

———. *Ruined by Reading: A Life in Books.* Boston: Beacon Press, 1996.

Schweickart, Patrocinio. "Reading Ourselves: Toward a Feminist Theory of Reading." In Flynn and Schweickart, eds. 31–62.

Sedgwick, Eve Kosofsky. *Between Men: English Literature and Male Homosocial Desire.* New York: Columbia UP, 1985.

———.*Epistemology of the Closet.* Berkeley: U of California P, 1990.

———. "Melanie Klein and the Difference Affect Makes." *South Atlantic Quarterly* 106.3 (Summer 2007): 625–42.

———. *Tendencies.* Durham, NC: Duke UP, 1993.

Shaw, Harry E. *Narrating Reality: Austen, Scott, Eliot.* Ithaca, NY: Cornell UP, 1999.

Shockley, Evie. "The Horrors of Homelessness: Gothic Doubling in Kincaid's *Lucy* and Brontë's *Villette.*" *Jamaica Kincaid and Caribbean Double Crossings.* Ed. Linda Lang-Peralta. Newark: U of Delaware P, 2006. 45–62.

Showalter, Elaine. "The Greening of Sister George." *Nineteenth-Century Fiction* 35.3 (1980): 292–311.

Sicherman, Barbara. "Reading *Little Women*: The Many Lives of a Text." *U.S. History as Women's History: New Feminist Essays.* Ed. Linda K. Kerber, Alice Kessler-Harris, and Kathryn Kish Sklar. Chapel Hill: U of North Carolina P, 1995. 245–66.

Silver, Brenda. *Virginia Woolf Icon.* Chicago: U of Chicago P, 1999.

Simons, Margaret A. "Lesbian Connections: Simone de Beauvoir and Feminism." *Signs: Journal of Women in Culture and Society* 18.1 (1992): 136–61.

Sinfield, Alan. "Lesbian and Gay Taxonomies." *Critical Inquiry* 29 (Autumn 2002): 120–38.

Slaughter, Joseph. *Human Rights, Inc.: The World Novel, Narrative Form, and International Law.* New York: Fordham UP, 2007

Smith, Adam. *The Theory of Moral Sentiments.* Ed. D. D. Raphael and A. L. MacFie. Oxford: Clarendon Press, 1976.

Smith, Ian. "Misusing Intertexts: Jamaica Kincaid and Colonialism's 'absent things.'" *Callaloo* 25,3 (Summer 2002). 801–20.

Smith, Patricia Juliana. "The Things People Don't Say: Lesbian Panic in *The Voyage Out.*" In Barrett and Cramer, eds. 128–45.

Souhami, Diana. *The Trials of Radclyffe Hall.* New York: Doubleday, 1999.

Spivak, Gayatri. "Three Women's Texts and a Critique of Imperialism." *Feminisms: An Anthology of Literary Theory and Criticism.* Ed. Robyn Warhol and Diane Price Herndl. New Brunswick, NJ: Rutgers UP, 1991. 896–912. Rpt. from *Critical Inquiry* 12 (Autumn 1985): 243–61.

Sproles, Karyn. *Desiring Women: The Partnership of Virgina Woolf and Vita Sackville-West.* Toronto: U of Toronto P, 2006.

Staedtler-Djédji, Katharina. "Jean-Paul Sartre, Simone de Beauvoir, et l'Afrique." Echanges franco-allemandes sur l'Afrique. Ed. János Riesz and Hélène d'Almeida-Topor. Bayreuth: U Bayreuth, 1994. 197–216.

Staël, Germaine de. *Corinne, or Italy.* Trans. Avriel H. Goldberger. New Brunswick, NJ: Rutgers UP, 1987.

Stephen, Leslie. *George Eliot.* 1902. New York: Cambridge UP, 2010.

Stewart, Garrett. *Dear Reader: The Conscripted Audience in Nineteenth-Century British Fiction.* Baltimore: Johns Hopkins UP, 1996.

Stimpson, Catharine. "Reading for Love: Canons, Paracanons, and Whistling Jo March." *New Literary History* 21.4 (Autumn 1990): 957–76.

Stockton, Kathryn Bond. *Beautiful Bottom, Beautiful Shame: Where "Black" Meets "Queer."* Durham: Duke UP, 2006.

Stoneman, Patsy. *Brontë Transformations: The Cultural Dissemination* of Jane Eyre *and* Wuthering Heights. New York: Prentice Hall/Wheatsheaf, 1996.

Storr, Merl. "Transformations: Subjects, Categories and Cures in Krafft-Ebing's Sexology." Bland and Doan 11–26.

"The Story of Attar of Roses." *New York Times,* 9 September 1899: 6.

Stowe, Harriet Beecher. *Uncle Tom's Cabin.* Ed. Jean Fagin Yellin. New York: Oxford UP, 1998.

Sutton, Imogen, dir. *Daughters of de Beauvoir.* Filmmakers Library, 1999.

Tidd, Ursula. "The Self-Other Relation in Beauvoir's Ethics and Autobiography." *Hypatia* 14.4 (Fall 1999): 163–74.

Tompkins, Jane, ed. *Reader-Response Criticism: From Formalism to Poststructuralism.* Baltimore: Johns Hopkins UP, 1980.

Viswanathan, Gauri. *Masks of Conquest: Literary Study and British Rule in India.* New York: Columbia UP, 1989.

Vorda, Allan. "An Interview with Jamaica Kincaid." *Mississippi Review* 20.1–2 (1991): 7–26.

Warhol, Robyn. *Having a Good Cry: Effeminate Feelings and Pop-Culture Forms.* Columbus: Ohio State UP, 2003.

Weeks, Jeffrey. *Sex, Politics, and Society: The Regulation of Sexuality Since 1800.* New York: Longman, 1981.

Wilde, Oscar. *The Importance of Being Earnest and other Plays: Lady Windermere's Fan; Salome; A Woman of no Importance; an Ideal Husband; The Importance of Being Earnest.* New York: Oxford UP, 2008. 247–307.

Wilkinson, Jane, ed. *Talking with African Writers.* Portsmouth, NH: Heinemann, 1992.

Willey, Ann. "Modernity, Alienation, and Development: *Nervous Conditions* and the Female Paradigm." Willey and Treiber 61–82.

Willey, Ann, and Jeanette Treiber, eds. *Emerging Perspectives on Tsitsi Dangarembga: Negotiating the Postcolonial.* Trenton, NJ: Africa World Press, 2002.

Williams, Raymond. *Culture and Society, 1780–1950.* New York: Harper & Row, 1958.

Wilt, Judith. "*Shirley:* Reflections on Marrying Moores." *Victorian Literature and Culture* 30.1 (March 2002): 1–17.

Winterson, Jeanette. *Art Objects.* New York: Vintage, 1997.

———. *Oranges Are Not the Only Fruit.* New York: Grove Press, 1985.

Woolf, Virginia. "Character in Fiction." *The Essays of Virginia Woolf.* Vol. 3. Ed Andrew McNeillie. San Diego: Harcourt Brace Jovanovich, 1988.

———. *Collected Essays.* Ed. Leonard Woolf. 4 vols. London: Hogarth, 1966.

———. *The Death of the Moth and Other Essays.* New York: Harcourt, Brace, 1942.

———. *The Diaries of Virginia Woolf.* Vol. 3, *1925–1930.* Ed. Anne Olivier Bell, asst. Andrew McNeillie. New York: Harcourt Brace, 1980.

———. *The Letters of Virginia Woolf.* Vol. 3, *1923–1928.* Ed. Nigel Nicolson and Joanne Trautmann. New York: Harvest/HBJ, 1977.

———. "Modern Fiction." *The Essays of Virginia Woolf.* Vol. 3. Ed Andrew McNeillie. San Diego: Harcourt Brace Jovanovich, 1988.

———. *Moments of Being.* Ed. and intro. Jeanne Schulkind. New York: Harcourt Brace Jovanovich, 1976.

———. *Roger Fry: A Biography.* New York: Harcourt, Brace, 1940.

———. *A Room of One's Own.* New York: Harcourt Brace Jovanovich, 1929.

———. *To the Lighthouse.* New York: Harcourt, Brace, 1955.

———. *The Voyage Out.* Ed. Lorna Sage. New York: Oxford UP, 2001.

Yost, David. "A Tale of Three Lucys: Wordsworth and Brontë in Kincaid's Antiguan *Villette.*" *MELUS* 31.2 (Summer 2006): 141–56.

Young, Hershini Bhana. *Haunting Capital: Memory, Text, and the Black Diasporic Body.* Hanover, NH: Dartmouth College Press (UP of New England), 2006.

Zwicker, Heather. "The Nervous Collusions of Nation and Gender: Tsitsi Dangarembga's Challenge to Fanon." Willey and Treiber 3–23.

INDEX

THEORY AND INTERPRETATION OF NARRATIVE

James Phelan, Peter J. Rabinowitz, and Robyn Warhol, Series Editors

Because the series editors believe that the most significant work in narrative studies today contributes both to our knowledge of specific narratives and to our understanding of narrative in general, studies in the series typically offer interpretations of individual narratives and address significant theoretical issues underlying those interpretations. The series does not privilege one critical perspective but is open to work from any strong theoretical position.

Narrative Theory: Core Concepts and Critical Debates
DAVID HERMAN, JAMES PHELAN AND PETER J. RABINOWITZ, BRIAN RICHARDSON, AND ROBYN WARHOL

After Testimony: The Ethics and Aesthetics of Holocaust Narrative for the Future
EDITED BY JAKOB LOTHE, SUSAN RUBIN SULEIMAN, AND JAMES PHELAN

The Vitality of Allegory: Figural Narrative in Modern and Contemporary Fiction
GARY JOHNSON

Narrative Middles: Navigating the Nineteenth-Century British Novel
EDITED BY CAROLINE LEVINE AND MARIO ORTIZ-ROBLES

Fact, Fiction, and Form: Selected Essays
RALPH W. RADER. EDITED BY JAMES PHELAN AND DAVID H. RICHTER

The Real, the True, and the Told: Postmodern Historical Narrative and the Ethics of Representation
ERIC L. BERLATSKY

Franz Kafka: Narration, Rhetoric, and Reading
EDITED BY JAKOB LOTHE, BEATRICE SANDBERG, AND RONALD SPEIRS

Social Minds in the Novel
ALAN PALMER

Narrative Structures and the Language of the Self
MATTHEW CLARK

Imagining Minds: The Neuro-Aesthetics of Austen, Eliot, and Hardy
KAY YOUNG

Postclassical Narratology: Approaches and Analyses
EDITED BY JAN ALBER AND MONIKA FLUDERNIK

Techniques for Living: Fiction and Theory in the Work of Christine Brooke-Rose
KAREN R. LAWRENCE

Towards the Ethics of Form in Fiction: Narratives of Cultural Remission
LEONA TOKER

Tabloid, Inc.: Crimes, Newspapers, Narratives
V. PENELOPE PELIZZON AND NANCY M. WEST

Narrative Means, Lyric Ends: Temporality in the Nineteenth-Century British Long Poem
MONIQUE R. MORGAN

Joseph Conrad: Voice, Sequence, History, Genre
EDITED BY JAKOB LOTHE, JEREMY HAWTHORN, AND JAMES PHELAN

Understanding Nationalism: On Narrative, Cognitive Science, and Identity
PATRICK COLM HOGAN

The Rhetoric of Fictionality: Narrative Theory and the Idea of Fiction
RICHARD WALSH

Experiencing Fiction: Judgments, Progressions, and the Rhetorical Theory of Narrative
JAMES PHELAN

Unnatural Voices: Extreme Narration in Modern and Contemporary Fiction
BRIAN RICHARDSON

Narrative Causalities
EMMA KAFALENOS

Why We Read Fiction: Theory of Mind and the Novel
LISA ZUNSHINE

I Know That You Know That I Know: Narrating Subjects from Moll Flanders *to* Marnie
GEORGE BUTTE

Bloodscripts: Writing the Violent Subject
ELANA GOMEL

Surprised by Shame: Dostoevsky's Liars and Narrative Exposure
DEBORAH A. MARTINSEN

Having a Good Cry: Effeminate Feelings and Pop-Culture Forms
ROBYN R. WARHOL

Politics, Persuasion, and Pragmatism: A Rhetoric of Feminist Utopian Fiction
ELLEN PEEL

Telling Tales: Gender and Narrative Form in Victorian Literature and Culture
ELIZABETH LANGLAND

Narrative Dynamics: Essays on Time, Plot, Closure, and Frames
EDITED BY BRIAN RICHARDSON

Breaking the Frame: Metalepsis and the Construction of the Subject
DEBRA MALINA

Invisible Author: Last Essays
CHRISTINE BROOKE-ROSE

Ordinary Pleasures: Couples, Conversation, and Comedy
KAY YOUNG

Narratologies: New Perspectives on Narrative Analysis
EDITED BY DAVID HERMAN

Before Reading: Narrative Conventions and the Politics of Interpretation
PETER J. RABINOWITZ

Matters of Fact: Reading Nonfiction over the Edge
DANIEL W. LEHMAN

The Progress of Romance: Literary Historiography and the Gothic Novel
DAVID H. RICHTER

A Glance Beyond Doubt: Narration, Representation, Subjectivity
SHLOMITH RIMMON-KENAN

Narrative as Rhetoric: Technique, Audiences, Ethics, Ideology
JAMES PHELAN

Misreading Jane Eyre: *A Postformalist Paradigm*
JEROME BEATY

Psychological Politics of the American Dream: The Commodification of Subjectivity in Twentieth-Century American Literature
LOIS TYSON

Understanding Narrative
EDITED BY JAMES PHELAN AND PETER J. RABINOWITZ

Framing Anna Karenina: *Tolstoy, the Woman Question, and the Victorian Novel*
AMY MANDELKER

Gendered Interventions: Narrative Discourse in the Victorian Novel
ROBYN R. WARHOL

Reading People, Reading Plots: Character, Progression, and the Interpretation of Narrative
JAMES PHELAN

www.ingramcontent.com/pod-product-compliance
Lightning Source LLC
LaVergne TN
LVHW091047080826
845145LV00002B/657

* 9 7 8 0 8 1 4 2 5 6 3 9 8 *